THE NEW SOCIAL I

How the politicians g

Geoff Payne

The little book of cheese

P

First published in Great Britain in 2017 by

Policy Press
University of Bristol
1-9 Old Park Hill
Bristol
BS2 8BB
UK
t: +44 (0)117 954 5940
pp-info@bristol.ac.uk
www.policypress.co.uk

North America office:
Policy Press
c/o The University of Chicago Press
1427 East 60th Street
Chicago, IL 60637, USA
t: +1 773 702 7700
f: +1 773-702-9756
sales@press.uchicago.edu
www.press.uchicago.edu

British Library Cataloguing in Publication Data
A catalogue record for this book is available from the British Library

Library of Congress Cataloging-in-Publication Data
A catalog record for this book has been requested

ISBN 978-1-4473-1065-5 paperback
ISBN 978-1-4473-1066-2 hardcover
ISBN 978-1-4473-1069-3 ePub
ISBN 978-1-4473-1070-9 Mobi
ISBN 978-1-4473-1067-9 ePdf

Cover design by Soapbox Design
Front cover image: Judy Payne and Geoff Payne
Printed and bound in Great Britain by CMP, Poole
Policy Press uses environmentally responsible print partners

Contents

List of tables and figures		iv
Acknowledgements		v
Preface: the confusing world of social mobility		vi
one	'There's a lot of it about'	1
two	Log cabins and field marshals' batons	17
three	Politicians rediscover social mobility	29
four	Documenting mobility	47
five	Tracing the origins	63
six	Why low, why now?	73
seven	The pessimism of earlier academic mobility analysis	89
eight	The emergence of a new society	109
nine	The new mobility regime	127
ten	Misconceptions of schooling and meritocracy	139
eleven	Tightening bonds and professional access	149
twelve	Moving on	161
Appendix		175
References		185
Index		219

List of tables and figures

Tables

1.1	Two paradigms of British social mobility	15
7.1	Variations in labour markets	104
8.1	Trends in parent–child class differentials	123
9.1	Male and female social mobility, 2014	131
9.2	Self-recruitment levels and class size	133
11.1	Qualifications and approximate earnings for occupations, September 2015	152
12.1	British elites	162
A.1	An illustrative mobility table	175
A.2	ONS-SeC analytical categories	179
A.3	Operational definitions in British mobility studies	180
A.4	The Social Mobility Identification Kit	181

Figures

2.1	Rephrasing older questions	19
3.1	Annual number of social mobility items in UK 'quality press'	42
3.2	*Call You and Yours* interview	44
5.1	Main sources of mis-definitions and research evidence	64
5.2	Mobility as claimed by the Cabinet Office #1	66
5.3	Relative mobility as claimed by the Cabinet Office #2	67
8.1	Occupational transition since the First World War	114
8.2	Recent occupational transition	117
8.3	The gendered class distribution	118
8.4	Gender differences in recent occupational transition	119
8.5	Changes in male origins and destinations 1972–2005	124
10.1	The origin/education/destination triangle	140

Acknowledgements

In writing this book, I am grateful to have been able to reproduce data and short quotations from a variety of sources. These are formally acknowledged in conventional form where they are included; brief quotations and data have only been used to the extent accepted under 'fair dealing' principles. The Commons Licence, which provides access to data from the National Office for Statistics, has been a particularly valuable public asset.

Although in the body of the text I acknowledge several colleagues who have made specific contributions, I can only record my general gratitude to many colleagues, too many to list by name, for their much appreciated exchanges of views about mobility over a number of years. They include those at Aberdeen University involved in the original Scottish Mobility Study; members of the Cambridge Social Stratification Seminar and CREST (Research Centre for the Study of Socio-Cultural Change) at Manchester University; participants in numerous British Sociological Association Annual Conferences and the 2016 'Every One a Winner' Conference funded by York University, and the Sociology Teaching Group at Newcastle University (including my long-suffering students!). They are of course not responsible for what is written here, and I hope they will not be offended if they are not individually acknowledged by name. However, as always, I must record my gratitude to Judy Payne for her patience and common sense in deflating some of my wilder ideas, as well as her work on the cover photograph. Finally, I am grateful for the excellent support of the editorial team at Policy Press.

Preface: the confusing world of social mobility

This book is about the political, economic and moral salience of social mobility in Britain today. The way that, and the extent to which, people move or fail to move from one position in society to another – up or down the social hierarchy, through education and employment – is one of the central processes in contemporary society. It involves issues of inequality in individuals' opportunities to use their talents in our society, the fairness and legitimacy of social and political status quo, and the effective use of the country's most basic resource: its people. Not only are differential mobility opportunities a form of social inequality in themselves, but *belief* in the future prospect of potential improvement – at least for one's children – and thereby in the legitimacy of mobility can make current social inequities easier to bear.

Social mobility is also one of the most misunderstood processes of our time.

This is ironic, because social mobility has been moving up the political agenda since the turn of the century at an astonishing rate, with media coverage increasing literally tenfold in the last decade (see chapter Three). In 2014, a report observed how: 'in recent years government has introduced a number of initiatives to improve social mobility and a Social Mobility and Child Poverty Commission (SMCPC) has been created to monitor progress in this area right across government policy … a clear indication of broad political support' (Brown 2014, 9).

Immediately before this book went to production, the European Union (EU) referendum and its result blew regular political issues away. But all five of the Conservative leadership candidates except for Andrea Leadsom invoked social mobility in their campaign launch speeches (Fox 2016; Gove 2016; Johnson 2016; May 2016a); May's inaugural speech as Prime Minister highlighted pledges to improve opportunities for everybody to go as far their talents could take them (May 2016b). However, because of its complex nature, understanding social mobility and its social significance has challenged public commentators and non-specialist academics alike.

The result has been too much loose talk about 'needing more mobility' without clarity about what mobility means or what its consequences might be. Although in common parlance mobility is generally seen as a comparison across generations – between a person's family background and his or her adult career achievement – there has been a perhaps inevitable lack of precision in the definitions implicit in public debate. Defining mobility has even been a challenge to highly trained academic specialists in mobility analysis. But to discuss it properly, and to understand what is going on, requires a more exact specification of mobility and how it is to be measured (which can be found in the Appendix of this book) and an upfront honesty about one's moral and political stance. I am happy to make my own position clear: with regards to the specific *kinds* of mobility outlined in this book, I believe we need a more mobile and open society in which there is greater equality of outcome and compassion for those who remain anchored to the bottom of society.

Of course, the term 'mobility' is convenient shorthand, and will be used as such in what follows. Unless otherwise qualified, the meaning here will imply amounts of *movements (and lack of movements) by individuals up and down the social scale, calculated over two generations and usually across seven 'classes'*. The main implications of this definition will be explored in the next chapter. The aim will be to reduce some of the collective confusion by taking a fresh look at mobility in a way that makes sense to a wide readership (rather than a standard introductory text aimed solely at mobility analysts or social science undergraduates, although it can of course be used by them).

The next chapter will also present evidence from a number of high quality sociological surveys using comparable and widely accepted methods of analysis and stretching back to 1949. This work covers people – particularly men – in the labour force and compares their own current social/occupational positions with those of their parents. In the technical jargon, this is the amount of 'absolute intergenerational social mobility' (in England and Wales, where the level of mobility is a little higher than in Scotland and Northern Ireland). However – to enter the first of what will be a number of caveats – while it is true that absolute mobility rates have been higher than commonly assumed, many of the movements have been 'short-range'; that is, to new destinations that are different from the original background but not hugely so and not from one end of the social scale to the other.

Nor do the actual conditions of Britain's high mobility rates (most of us have been socially mobile; see chapter One) mean that everybody has an equal *chance* of getting on in life. It still matters who one's parents are. There are substantially unequal prospects of 'relative social mobility', in the differing chances of groups being mobile. The book can therefore be seen as loosely consisting of four parts. After the introductory chapters, which identify core issues and provide a context for current mobility discourse, the second section (chapters

Three to Six) documents the remarkable rise of social mobility in public awareness during this century and shows how political discussion has systematically and seriously misconstrued mobility. The third part of the book (chapters Seven and Eight) acknowledges that even mainstream mobility analysis has not always come up with reliable alternatives; however, it necessarily leaves several areas of the research literature underexplored – or even untouched – and there is no pretence that the whole of the very extensive field of contemporary mobility analysis can be included. The later chapters (Nine to Twelve) develop an alternative view, concentrating on mobility's connections with, and consequences for, wider social conditions. The intention is to review how much social mobility there actually is (despite what many public figures have assumed, the real levels are actually quite high), how it is perceived (both in social science accounts and by the public), why it is politically significant and what has been missing from more traditional perspectives.

The common thread running through all social mobility discussion is that movement takes place between groups in society that are differentially advantaged or disadvantaged, harder or easier to access and membership of which is deemed desirable or undesirable. Explanations for these group differences, the scale of social inequalities, their significance or legitimacy and the reasons for movements differ, but there is basic agreement that mobility takes place up and down a social hierarchy. Much of the dialogue about mobility's winners and losers in Britain has either explicitly used the term 'social class' or has class differences implicit in its discussion. I hope that potential readers who are uncomfortable with thinking about Britain as consisting of social classes will not be put off by this. In mobility studies, 'class' often carries little ideological baggage; it means only a category of persons that share discernibly similar material circumstances. Furthermore, reliable evidence about mobility can only come from proper research; given that this has predominantly been expressed in units of class movement, the terms of current debate are constrained unless we rely purely on rhetoric and opinion.

This use of classes to measure mobility need not prevent this book presenting a fresh account of social mobility – one that is new in several respects. It is the first full account of the dramatic rise in popular interest in mobility, directly confronting both the 'new' version of mobility created by its recent political bowdlerisation and the common-sense view that it engendered. Building instead on the previous generation of mainstream studies in social science, the alternative new social mobility presented here is based on up-to-date sociological research *evidence* to challenges politicians' persistent misrepresentations of opportunity and inequality. On the other hand, this book also seeks to challenge several assumptions on which some of this academic research has been based. By placing mobility in a context of wider social change, the ultimate intentions are to begin to refocus on a fuller range of dimensions of mobility and life chances and to assess more accurately their causes and consequences as social processes.

Trying to change perspectives, opinions and factoids that are well established in the minds of politicians, pressure groups, the press, academics and the public is a major challenge. It means starting from first principles, unpacking the core ideas of social mobility and offering readers an accessible way of deepening their understanding of what is actually quite a complex subject. Academic experts from more traditional schools of mobility analysis may be frustrated by the pace and style of this approach, but it is hoped that they too will find something useful in the alternative perspective offered here. In particular, the case made for a return to consideration of the labour market invites further reflection.

Addressing actual levels of mobility (often referred to in the literature as 'absolute intergenerational mobility') and their significance for contemporary society involves a double task: trying to reclaim mobility from politicians' misrepresentations, and wrestling a more accessible account from academic research reports without relying on specialist statistical analysis. Given the underlying complexity of social mobility, this is no small task – but it is worth attempting, because sorting out implicit meanings and respecting the evidence are doubly important when, as now, issues of national social policy depend on how much mobility we *think* there is. It may be morally satisfying to contemplate a utopian world of complete mobility or absolute fairness, but the real issue is what can actually be accomplished, starting not with a clean slate but here and now. This means identifying the causes of mobility and immobility and being aware of why various groups see mobility in the ways they do.

But social mobility – and its evil twin, social immobility – also matters for each of us in a more personal way. Through our accumulated life experiences, it becomes a major component of each person's individual sense of identity. Whether seen as a society-wide process, setting life chances, or in more immediate terms of ourselves and our own children, mobility matters, so it matters that we get it right.

ONE

'There's a lot of it about'

Almost every political figure in Britain believes 'we need more social mobility' and wants social policies to achieve it. Suppose they are right, and that 'mobility rates are low and falling' (they are not right, but just suppose they were): what would happen if their policies worked?

First, more people would have the 'requirements' (qualifications, aspiration, cultural capital) to compete for the stock of 'good' jobs. These good jobs are presently filled by other people, who would have to be displaced – made downwardly mobile – to make room for the potential newcomers. If some of the present incumbent families did cling on to their advantages (because they also have the requirements to occupy the good jobs, and are doing them well), would some of those newly qualified with the requirements then not be upwardly mobile and so become doubly disillusioned by their lack of achievement? Even if there were to be some increase in upward mobility, what would happen to those who, despite new policies, did not acquire the requirements and remained trapped in 'poor' jobs, immobile at the bottom of the heap?

'Ah!' say the politicians, 'but the number of highly skilled jobs is increasing, so making greater room at the top'. There is some truth in this, but the increase would have to neatly match the inflow of the newly qualified. And it would have to be a very large increase. Previous studies indicate that an expanded number of new good jobs gets shared out more or less equally between the children of families already holding good jobs and those from families who had less good jobs.

What our politicians really want is greater *upward* mobility. They want less immobility among those who start at the bottom of the social heap and fairer access to managerial, professional and elite positions at the top. But what they have failed to grasp is that 'more social mobility', by both definition and practical outcome, also means greater *downward* mobility. You can't have one without the other. If we are to understand 'mobility', we need to look at the whole picture. Indeed, when we look at the research evidence – which the politicians, their civil servants, the 'think tanks' (that is, lobbyists) and the media have been slow to do – we find that:

- mobility rates are high;
- rates of upward mobility show little sign of falling;
- downward mobility is increasing;
- there are nevertheless considerable inequalities in who gets to be mobile; there are 'pockets' of low mobility.

And all this before we take account of differences in gender, ethnicity, region and other broad social issues that interact with mobility – such as the impact of further innovation in digital technologies on employment, inequalities of wealth and taxation, an alienated electorate and urban unrest, an aging population, migration and globalisation. If the material and social differences between social classes grows wider, movement between them becomes harder.

While the politicians have got it wrong by obsessing about the single dimension of upward mobility, academic mobility analysts have also missed the boat. Most have concentrated too narrowly on the detailed comparative chances of mobility between various groups and not spent enough energy considering the social *causes* and political *consequences* of real people being mobile. It is time for a New Social Mobility.

None of this is to say that more social mobility is completely undesirable, that the policies aimed at increasing it are bad ones – in themselves, independent of mobility and within the limitations in their scope – or that it does not matter that the chances of achieving good jobs are grossly and unfairly distorted in favour of already advantaged families. Mobility matters not simply as an economic or political issue, but also as a moral one. Furthermore, it matters because the personal experience of being mobile or immobile – in this or that part of the social hierarchy – shapes our social identities and how we feel about ourselves and our social destinies. These subjective and qualitative responses have received too little attention from British sociologists.

To call for more consideration of the personal experience of being mobile is not, however, to adopt an *individualist* explanation of mobility. Although our political masters have been concerned with social policies, their underlying model is that, by equalising opportunity, individuals will be better able to compete. In other words, that achieving upward mobility (or retaining social advantage) ultimately depends on *individual ability*. This does not take into account the way social structures have an impact on not only who gets the mobility 'requirements', but also how organisations actually function to provide jobs and to determine who gets them. Not every one of us can be a winner. We are all caught up in a world of constraining social forces and pre-existing social processes. Thus a policy of improving and widening access to education (inherently desirable aims) cannot guarantee good jobs for all. Education is a necessary, but not sufficient, requirement for most occupational upward mobility. Social class differences remain in place. If we focus only on the upwardly mobile – and even if we do succeed in helping some of those previously immobile – we give too little attention to those who will still be left behind. To understand mobility, we must include *all* forms of mobility. The first question to ask must therefore be: how much mobility is there in contemporary Britain?

How much mobility is there?

A preliminary answer to the basic question of how much social mobility there is in Britain is that *about three quarters of today's adult population are no longer in the social class in which they grew up.* And while we are dealing with basic issues, contrary to what most politicians would have us believe, rates of social mobility have *not* been steadily decreasing since the 1970s (when reliable UK records first began). Of course, like all measurements, these two statements depend on definitions; rates of mobility are determined by what exactly mobility is taken to mean and how it is counted, which will require further discussion later on (see also the 'mobility test' in the Appendix).

For the moment, these two basic statements about mobility levels can be fleshed out by summarising evidence from a series of reputable research studies. The Nuffield Mobility Study, which counted movements between seven social classes in a large sample survey of men in England and Wales in 1972, found 71.6% had been mobile (Goldthorpe 1987, Table 2.2). A further study (Goldthorpe and Jackson 2007) found that, of participants born in 1958, 72% of males and 76% of females had experienced mobility by the age of 33 – the same levels as the slightly younger people (aged 30) in a comparable cohort born in 1970. In 2011, Li and Devine analysed data from the British Household Panel Survey (BHPS) for 1991 and the General Household Survey (GHS) for 2005, finding male mobility at 77.5% and 77.6% and female mobility at 78.2% and 78.4% respectively. The authors noted that, although some of the component movements in female mobility were a little different, their main findings:

are basically similar to Goldthorpe and Jackson's finding from their analysis of the NCDS [National Child Development Study of children born in 1958] and BCS [British Cohort Study of children born in 1970] ... They are in line, however, with Goldthorpe and Mill's (2008, Figure 5) subsequent work on intergenerational class mobility. (Li and Devine 2011, sections 4.2 and 4.4)

More recently, Bukodi et al (2015) compared four cohorts – born in 1946, 1958, 1970 and 1980–84 – early in their careers; reporting between 77% and 80% mobility and that this rate 'has been fairly stable throughout the later twentieth century for men and women alike' (95). Laurison and Friedman (2015) produced a similar figure – 78.7% – by using data from the 2014 Labour Force Survey for men and women in the narrower age range of 25–59.

While minor variations in mobility rates between datasets over a period of several decades are to be expected due to sampling error and small variations in operational definitions, these various findings demonstrate high levels of agreement. They go a long way towards meeting the conventional scientific test of reproducibility (Academy of Medical Sciences 2015). All these figures are not only closely aligned, but also show that rates of mobility have *not* been systematically declining since the early 1970s, contrary to the popular consensus. It may even be true that mobility has *increased* slightly; the jury is still out on this, not least because detailed comparisons between studies encounter technical difficulties (see Appendix). In addition, mobility rates do not change by large amounts, or very quickly, so that we often find ourselves arguing about very small percentage differences.

It therefore needs to be made clear from the outset that being mobile means, as indicated in the preface, 'the extent to which people move – or fail to move – from one position in society to another, up *or down* the social hierarchy'. In common parlance, the phrase 'social mobility' is often taken to mean only *upward* mobility, but this is a classic example of casual misuse of an originally precise definition. The factual figure of three quarters of us being mobile includes both those who now occupy a better position than their parents *and those who now occupy a worse position*. In round figures, for every four or five people who are upwardly mobile, three are downwardly mobile and two or three are immobile. Although there is no complete agreement about trends, there are indications that any more recent increase in total mobility is mainly due an increase in downward mobility, for reasons to be explained later.

While a lot of the technical detail can be safely left to in the Appendix, it makes sense to sort out a few points at this early stage because they are necessary for a full understanding of how Britain's mobility regime has often been misinterpreted. Readers wishing to cut to the chase can skip even these technicalities and move to chapter Two, provided they are willing to trust the author's later assertions about types and levels of class and occupational mobility. Other readers versed in mobility analysis will in any case be familiar with most of the arguments. However, without appreciating what lies behind the way in which mobility is measured and conceptualised, it is hard to fully follow contemporary debates.

Categories and classes

Although social mobility rates can be calculated using correlation coefficients and similar statistical techniques that measure the closeness of association between parents' and their offspring's classes, levels of mobility are conventionally computed from 'mobility tables' that cross-tabulate family origins with social destinations. For seven classes or occupational groupings of origin and seven classes of destination, this produces a 7×7 table with 49 possible combinations. The amount of upward mobility, for instance, is assessed by adding together the people in all the combinations in which the destination class ranks higher than the origin. An example and further discussion of this can be found in the Appendix.

It follows that the way the mobility table is set up – that is, with seven categories and 49 combinations – determines the levels of mobility found. Of course, this in turn assumes that mobility can be discussed in terms of social classes, which not all readers may welcome. (Another indicator, not used here, is to compare incomes. The limitations of income will be elaborated in chapter Seven; for the moment, we shall follow the standard sociological method of comparing classes, using mobility tables).

While it is common practice to measure mobility using seven classes, if fewer than seven occupational classes are used, as sometimes becomes necessary due to the limitations of the available data, fewer moves would be recorded. If classes are drawn very broadly, they hide more *internal* variation. Larger categories contain movements that would have crossed boundaries if more subdivisions had been retained, so less absolute mobility is recorded as appearing to take place.

Using *six* classes, Paterson and Iannelli (2007) report slightly lower mobility (but they also exclude workers who are very early on in their careers), while a six-category study including older and some retired people found 65% of men and 75% of women had been mobile (Heath and Payne 1999). Using an extension of the same dataset, Payne and Robert's (2002) consolidation of these six classes into three larger ones reduced male mobility to around 53%. Using five classes, a more recent analysis of the Longitudinal Study Census data by Buscha and Sturgis (2014) found about 70% mobility, while a paper presented by Min Zhang at the British Sociological Association's 2015 Annual Conference, again using five classes, reported 65% mobility for men and 64% for women in data from the British Household Panel Study (1991–2014).

Although they will not be used here, two important alternatives used in mobility analysis are worth noting. The Cambridge Social Grading Scale (CAMSIS) operationalises hierarchical differences as a continuous scale rather than a small number of clusters (Lambert and Prandy 2012). Continuous scales ease the problem of where to draw class boundaries and facilitate more sophisticated statistical analysis. Work using CAMSIS tends to reveal greater mobility than fixed classes (for example, Lambert et al 2007). Second, Weedon and Grusky (2005; 2012) argue that more social inequality can be explained by using 80 or more 'micro-classes' instead of a small number of relatively big classes. Although Weedon and Grusky offer a compelling argument for greater precision, technical problems mean their contribution has as yet had little impact on UK mobility research (but see Gayle and Lambert 2011).

As with all mobility data, these levels of movement among the working age population show what has *already* been achieved. 'Destinations' are usually those at the time the data were gathered, but origins come earlier: from the point when the sample informants were in their mid-teens. In other words, the 'three quarters' figure from even the most recent studies includes some people aged, say, 60, educated in the 1960s and entering employment in the very different economic circumstances of the early 1970s. This prompts the questions of whether today's younger workers, who are living under an austerity regime early in their working lives, share the same mobility prospects as those from earlier decades – and what should be done *now* with a view to improving the prospects of future generations. Thus the 'austerity' policies adopted by the Conservative-led Coalition government of 2010–15 and the Conservative government elected in 2015, which critics on the Left argue are designed to shrink the State in order to reduce taxation for the better off, are likely to depress future mobility in two ways. If the State is smaller and provides fewer functions like education, healthcare and social work, the workforce of highly skilled professionals will be reduced (functions outsourced to commercial undertakings almost inevitably employ fewer people with lower levels of expertise, while other parts of what was previously supplied by the State have to be provided in an amateur way by family and friends). If there are fewer professional jobs, the opportunities for upward mobility will be fewer – although conversely, downward mobility is likely to increase, because the children of the professional class will find it harder to find employment at the same level as their parents.

But these policies have an impact on mobility in a second, more powerful way. Cuts in funding have reduced Sure Start centres, youth opportunity schemes, grants for further education and public libraries. Former industrial cities (mainly in the North of England) with high proportions of working-class residents had their budgets sharply cut: Newcastle upon Tyne, for example, lost £40 million of its annual income (ChronicleLive 2015). Together with increased rates of VAT, the disadvantages of the lower classes were increased. Being poor is a bigger disadvantage when household budgets now have to pay for services the State previously provided for free (Grusky 2015). Meanwhile, taxation cuts that benefit the relatively wealthy – such as reductions in income and inheritance tax – have added to the advantages of the higher social classes, further differentiating them from the rest of society.

These Conservative government policies increase the difference or 'distance' between the classes so that future opportunities for movement between them are likely to be reduced. Mobility between classes is easier if the classes are not too different from each other. Movement is also easier between adjacent classes ('short-range mobility') than between those at either end of the class structure. Increasing underlying social inequalities stretches the social distance between top and bottom.

Mobility within a (class) hierarchy

This chapter's opening remarks regarding mobility refer specifically to the proportion of the *recent labour force* who have experienced *intergenerational 'absolute' mobility*, up or down, across *seven occupational classes* in *England and Wales*. It is 'intergenerational' because it compares two successive generations. 'Absolute' social mobility is the total number of people who have directly experienced mobility. It treats the movement between any two classes initially as equally significant, whether the moves are between adjacent classes or across the whole hierarchy. To be more precise, mobility is here being calculated by counting each case in which a person at school leaving age had an origin in one grouping out of seven (defined by parental Office for National Statistics Socio-economic Classification ('NS-SeC') category – see Appendix – or a very similar class schema) and is now in another grouping (defined by their own NS-SeC situation as a working-age adult).

However, high rates of intergenerational absolute mobility do not mean that every group has an *equal chance* of upward mobility. The chances of entering or staying in the top social grouping or falling into or exiting from the most disadvantaged sectors of society are very different. We shall later require an alternative measurement to explore these *relative* chances (for some time this latter 'relative mobility' has diverted the attention of many sociologists doing mobility analysis away from absolute mobility).

Movements take place between 'social locations', which are usually regarded as forming a hierarchy, although the nature of this hierarchy is open to dispute. Choosing the dimension in which mobility is regarded as happening has practical, political and moral implications. Most academic research on British social mobility has measured mobility as movement between locations in one of two social spaces: income or social class. Income mobility, introduced by economists, is a relatively late innovation in the UK research; sociologists had mainly used the 'class mobility' indicator before that, sometimes in a strict post-Marxist sense but more often in a looser sense of hierarchies of 'social standing' or prestige in the community (for example, Glass 1954, 10, 31). Although income appears to deal with the one specific dimension of money whereas social class is a more complicated and diffuse concept, both money and class stand as indicators of a host of associated life chances and relationships and have limitations as measurements (see chapter Seven).

As observed in the Preface, some readers may feel uncomfortable treating mobility as movements between social classes because they believe that 'class is dead' – if indeed it was ever an appropriate way of framing British society. Such scepticism should not prevent them from engaging with the underlying arguments about mobility, as the following brief discussion of class as an operational measurement will help to demonstrate. There are sound reasons for using class as an indicator of mobility despite its limitations and the availability of alternative versions of how to think about class (Crompton 2008; Savage et al 2015) – not least that class is part of public culture.

For example, YouGov survey data show that considerable majorities of people agree that many people are disadvantaged because of their background, and have to work much harder than others of equal basic talent to overcome the obstacles they face (55% agree vs. 22% disagree). (Baumberg 2014, quoting Bamfield and Horton 2009, 24)

The 2013 British Social Attitudes Survey reported that more than two thirds of respondents felt that class background affected people's opportunities a great deal or quite a lot – a figure that has been reported in successive surveys since the early 1980s. The publication in April 2013 of the Great British Class Survey saw an immediate avalanche of nearly 5 million online participants using the BBC's Class Calculator (Savage 2013) amid blanket media coverage. If nothing else, this reflects the way in which many British people show an interest in class differences and perceive their society as structured in class terms, albeit in an imprecisely articulated manner.

This is not to claim that members of the British public are interested in social class in a political or Marxist sense or that all share the same definition of what class means, but rather that there is a widespread awareness of social inequalities. Thus whereas individuals may be reluctant to identify themselves as belonging to a specific class unless prompted (Savage et al 2001; Payne and Grew 2005), many are quite willing to talk about the social and economic inequalities between groups of people that exist in Britain. These kinds of social inequalities can be loosely subsumed under the heading of 'social class' (Bottero 2005).

A second and pragmatic reason for adopting a class framework is that when previous studies have addressed 'class mobility' their findings are expressed in this format, which constrains subsequent reuse of their data. However, while many mobility analysts do indeed subscribe to social theories that draw directly on debates about social class, or see the groupings they discuss as real social classes or at least an imperfect representation of them (see Goldthorpe 1987; Lee and Turner 1996), others have used the term class simply as a convenient shorthand for patterns of advantage and disadvantage that help to describe how people fall into various categories. Rather than being based on a Marxist perspective, such intercategory differences may take the form of differences in 'social status' or 'occupational skill levels'. One result is that the way research studies have referred to classes has created a space for confusion between *social class* in *sensu strict* and descriptive categories of people sharing social standing or skills.

In this second, categorical sense, 'class' describes groups of individuals sharing situations of social advantage or disadvantage, thus differentiating them from other groupings within a hierarchy. Words like 'category', 'group', 'sector' or 'band' might do equally well. For instance, working-class students going into Higher Education are normally categorised not by class but as coming from 'disadvantaged backgrounds', 'low participation neighbourhoods' and 'under-represented', 'poorer' or 'low income background' (for example, BIS 2014, 6, 17, 27, 15 and 39; see Coulson et al 2017). Of course, a more explicit use of 'social class' offers not just a *description* of structural differences but also an *explanation* of why these differences exist and how they are interconnected.

Thus, following Max Weber's (1920/1968) classic line of reasoning, making a living requires either possessing capital to live on (and to generate more capital and/or employ others) or, for those without material capital resources, engaging in paid employment to make a livelihood. Individuals without capital have a variety of skills to sell in the socially determined labour market, which further differentiates their class positions. The results of hiring themselves out for employment appropriate to their occupational skills are specific working conditions, material rewards and a range of ways of life and life chances 'outside the factory gates'. These in turn give rise to status groups, whose members mark themselves off from others even in the same social class position by customs, dress, speech and so on, and which may in turn form the basis for political activity (Scott 2013). Thus occupations are a good marker of the various market and employment situations generated by the needs of material production and human survival. Mobility between 'occupational classes' or status groups can be added to the framework of explanatory mechanisms of why people lead the lives they do.

This framework can – and often does – have political connotations. Those in similar class or status positions may combine in political movements. More conventional Marxist versions of social class point to the opposition of class interests and the potential for a radicalised working class to challenge the distributions of capital and control of production under capitalism. But that is not a necessary outcome of recognising the hierarchy of occupational characteristics, with or without its original causes. Nobody interested in the distribution of 'life chances' – who gets what – should be deterred from engaging with mobility just because a lot of mobility analysis has been couched in terms of class. Embracing a commitment to any of the varieties of class theory is not a condition for talking about mobility between 'classes'.

The consequences of mobility for winners *and losers*

Even without being committed to a class perspective, there is widespread recognition that societies are hierarchically structured with unequal distributions of advantage and disadvantage. It follows that, while mobility offers a description of how the members of a society come to occupy their positions, it does not explain why those positions exist; it therefore feeds only indirectly into the question of 'who gets what'. In other words, mobility does not encompass all aspects of social inequality, and therefore cannot provide a solution to inequality per se. It can only help to explain how shares of inequality are shuffled within the pack.

However, because a prerequisite of the notion of mobility is that there are differential positions between which it is in principle possible to be mobile, mobility also involves explanations of *why* some people are mobile and/or occupy desirable positions whereas others do not. It is almost inevitable that the words that label the concept 'social mobility' have semiotically framed it as *movement*. Chapters Ten and Eleven discuss justifications made for upward mobility, and its benefits for those who win in the mobility race, which range from personal 'ability' to random chance and social processes that determine outcomes independent of individual agency. But less attention has been given to the way immobile losers are labelled and experience their lack of success. A similar point can be made about those who are downwardly mobile: a category largely ignored in public debate.

Mobility is not one-size-fits-all. However, not everybody has the same capacity to contribute to the way we think collectively about mobility. Compared with a typical shop assistant or labourer (let alone marginalised people like the unemployed), other groups in society – such as articulate, educated managers and professionals or politicians and media columnists – are better able to promote their own visions of mobility. Everybody pushes for the kind of mobility that expresses their own experiences and best serves their own interests, but not everybody carries the same clout in shaping public perceptions.

Explanations that feature 'ability' or 'merit' – as in the idea of meritocracy (see chapter Ten) – or equality of *opportunity* have a less obvious downside. If success goes to those with ability, then by definition those without success must lack ability and so *deserve their disadvantaged fate*. They are lesser human beings, whose lack of aspiration or performance marks them as inferior. In the words of Michael Young (2001) – who coined the word 'meritocracy' – in contemporary Britain, 'it is hard indeed in a society that makes so much of merit to be judged as having none. No underclass has ever been left as morally naked as that'. Paradoxically, the higher the rate of upward mobility the worse it becomes for those who are left behind or fall down the social ranks. Mobility can actually increase the hidden hurts of inequality.

To treat mobility as a solution to all social ills is therefore illusory. Arguments in favour of equality of *opportunity* (even if that utopian state could realistically be achieved) will not produce an equal society. As David Cameron (2015) inadvertently demonstrated in his criticism of Labour policies for not rewarding 'aspiration', Conservatives hold a 'belief in equality of opportunity, as opposed to equality of outcome ... not everyone ending up with the same exam results, the same salary, the same house'. In other words, it is morally right that losers in the mobility stakes are punished by the stigma of school failure, lower incomes and inferior accommodation.

We thus encounter a second paradox. Those politicians who have advocated well-meaning, sensible policy reforms (better early life healthcare, reforms to schooling, more diversity in university intakes or more open recruitment to the professions – see chapter Four) genuinely wish to reduce social inequality. The results of their good intentions may *perhaps* ultimately be higher upward mobility rates – but that neither reduces the underlying inequalities nor makes it any easier to be a loser in the mobility game. The 70% or 80% mobility rates identified at the start of this chapter are not an unalloyed joy.

While dichotomising everybody into 'winners' or 'losers' is simplistic, it remains true that the personal *experience* of changing one's social class also involves challenges in terms of sense of identity and social relationships. Much of the discussion in this book is concerned with mobility on a large-scale national level; however, in this sociopolitical context mobility is also something more concrete and personal, consisting of individual and family experiences of life. Academic mobility research and party-political ideological disputations can easily lose sight of the human stories behind the bare statistics.

Writing nearly a century ago, Sorokin (1927) illustrated the complexity of life experience and the ways mobility happens to people – including upward mobility through marriage and downward mobility through geographical migration or political revolution (he had himself emigrated to the US after his involvement in the Russian Revolution). Bell's (1953) *Crime as an American Way of Life* showed how gambling, liquor rackets and prostitution provided less conventional and legitimate opportunities for new livelihoods (see also Cayton and Drake 1945; O'Kane 1992). Routes to mobility extend beyond inheritance of occupational or positions of political power. Indeed, if the broader definition of social class used in the Great British Class Survey were used, mobility would also cover cultural issues such as taste, consumption patterns and material assets.

Mainstream post-war mobility studies have instead focused narrowly on class mobility based on occupational groupings, although recently interest has returned to the detailed ways in which people experience mobility and its consequences in their lives (for example, Lawler and Payne 2017). Reducing mobility to numbers can obscure the effects mobility has on individual lives and how people are caught up in the processes determining mobility outcomes. Reay and colleagues, for example, explored how very specific knowledge and understandings of the school system constrain parental aspirations (Reay 1998). Miles et al (2011) discovered variations in the career narratives used by men to explain their individual lives; being mobile does not mean the same to everybody experiencing it. Giazitzoglu (2014) found that upwardly mobile young men struggle to find a new cultural identity. Friedman (2014; 2015) argues that mobility extends beyond occupation into wider cultural experience and that its significance for emotional life and family relationships should be taken into account.

These contributions represent another New Social Mobility: a substantial alternative perspective to mainstream concerns regarding calculating national mobility rates in terms of occupation or income. This fresh way of seeing mobility is likely to continue to make important contributions as well as to implement a wider range of methods in selecting and exploring topics and thus drawing in more scholars.

On the other hand, despite the attractions of more subtle qualitative approaches the perspective adopted here is instead that of large-scale, absolute mobility between social classes. This is a fruitful way of understanding political and policy processes in contemporary society because it engages directly with earlier research and is important for showing mobility outcomes in a political arena that operates at a national level. In particular, in turning to the more political aspects of mobility – in terms of both recent party politics and wider questions of political stability and social order – this approach provides a solid foundation for the analysis and criticism of how a false political consensus came to emerge among members of the British political class.

The political rediscovery of social mobility

Whereas academic mobility analysts have argued among themselves over subtle differences in measurement methods and theories of social class, recent years have seen political leaders of all parties showing less hesitance in expressing their own opinions about amounts of social mobility. In the words of the 2010–15 Conservative–Liberal Democrat Coalition government's policy statement, *Opening Doors, Breaking Barriers: A Strategy for Social Mobility* (Cabinet Office, 2011), social mobility is highly significant because it is the politically sensitive 'degree to which the patterns of advantage and disadvantage in one generation are passed onto the next' (2011, 11). Party leaders, ministers and shadow ministers have increasingly invoked the need for greater social mobility in their speeches. All three major Westminster parties have published official documents, including Labour's White Paper (and their equivalent to the Coalition government's Policy Statement) *New Opportunities: Fair Chances for the Future* (Labour Government, 2009) and the Liberal Democrats' *Report of the Liberal Democrats' Independent Commission on Social Mobility* (Narey, 2009). These documents, supported by the report of the National Equality Panel led by Harriet Harman and produced by a team of leading academics at the LSE Centre for Analysis of Social Exclusion (Hill et al 2010), asserted that British intergenerational mobility rates were low as a result of structural inequalities.

An All-Party Parliamentary Group on Social Mobility was established in 2011, while the Social Mobility and Child Poverty Commission (SMCPC), first proposed by the previous Labour Government, was set up in 2012 to report each year on the annual progress of mobility policies. Their common theme was a growing consensus that mobility is important and that current rates are apparently too low and should be raised.

While sharing the view that mobility is indeed important, the political consensus of low mobility flies in the face of the evidence presented at the start of this chapter.

Politicians have not only juggled the mobility evidence from research studies and invented their own sweeping definitions of what mobility means (as we shall see in chapters Three and Four), but have also turned mobility on its head to justify other party-political and policy aims. This tampering with the facts has resulted in assumptions – widely shared across parties, but nevertheless incorrect – that 'mobility' rates are low and have been shrinking systematically over the last 50 or 60 years or have radically collapsed under the opposition's previous government (for example, Cameron 2015). Not surprisingly, much of the consequent media coverage of social mobility has also been misleading, often little more than rehashes of press releases from government and think tank lobbyists (understanding national rates of mobility involves *numbers* – not the greatest strength of British journalism (Payne 2011)).

The upshot of all this is that two distinctive views – or 'paradigms' – of social mobility have developed, which shape perceptions, policy formation and interpretation of evidence. These are summarised in Table 1.1.

Table 1.1: Two paradigms of British social mobility

View of politicians, media and public	View of sociological analysts
Britain's mobility rates are lower than comparable countries	Focus on measuring large-scale, national levels of mobility rates
British social mobility rates are low	Data collected through social surveys
Mobility rates have been falling for a long time	Data analysed using relatively sophisticated quantitative methods
Mobility rates continue to fall	Measured over two generations
This creates an 'underclass' of immobile people at the bottom of the heap	Based on a seven- or eightfold (or collapsed) classification of social classes
Low mobility is an inefficient use of human resources	Occupations used as indicator of class
Mobility is therefore important and requires social policy interventions	Focus on mobility *chances*, not actual counts of *mobile people*
Our opponents' policies have failed	Addresses *'social class' mobility*
'We need more social mobility'	Motivated by *moral concerns* about social inequality

Of course, these two paradigms do not cover every politician's views or all sociological research. However, as summarising lists they indicate how the two approaches are not mirror images of each other: each paradigm has its own internal logic and 'feel'. The dominant view of the politicians, the media and the public (on the left of Table 1.1) consists of assertions leading to a simple (indeed, simplistic) conclusion: 'we need more social mobility'. The dominant view of sociological analysts (on the right of Table 1.1) – still influenced by the 'classic' study carried out by sociologists at the London School of Economics in the 1950s (Glass 1954) – is more technical and concerned with what and how research is done. However, as we shall see in chapter Seven, the experts have not always got it right either.

These two paradigms also illustrate the problem with which this chapter started. There clearly is a great deal of mobility taking place, but this does not satisfy our political leaders. If 70% or 80% is not enough, it presumably follows that this mobility must actually be the *wrong* kind of mobility (for example, too much downward mobility and not enough upward mobility?).

To be fair, mobility is a complex phenomenon, involving specific operational definitions that significantly affect one's conclusions. It is easy to obfuscate the debate by talking at cross purposes or using oversimplified versions of technical terms. It is for this reason that this chapter has taken the time to clarify some assumptions and terminology underlying the phenomenon. Ideas about mobility have also been inherited from a variety of earlier writings, which condition how mobility is seen and how it is adapted to contemporary circumstances. It may be thought that mobility is a neutral statement of movements and that research into mobility consists of findings equally of use to rival political parties; however, when it is combined with other philosophical positions, mobility is subject to sharply divergent political slants. To understand how mobility has been misused in recent British politics, it helps first to look at this background.

TWO

Log cabins and field marshals' batons

The domestic problems facing modern politicians – the decay of the two-party system, calls for the breakup of Britain and deepening apprehension about a disaffected 'underclass', not least that part made up of alienated young Muslims – are symptoms of a political order less secure than at any time since the Second World War. While it would be ridiculous to attribute the entire blame for support for anti-establishment political parties or urban riots to a lack of upward social mobility, perceptions of blockages to mobility, as part of a wider disappointment of prospects for improving social and material conditions, have become an important part of a toxic mix in which discontent festers.

What matters is not that upward mobility is a realistic likelihood but that people believe it to be. If mobility were happening in a loosely meritocratic way, it could be seen as 'fair'. The hope of upward mobility – if not for oneself, then for one's children – makes mobility a potent source of political legitimacy. Mobility plays a significant role in social discontent when it is seen as either unlikely or based on unequal opportunities. It is therefore a political issue; not only in the narrow sense of parties, manifestos and elections, but also in how people believe societies should function. The contemporary electoral challenge of nationalist parties is only the latest version of the difficulty all ruling classes have in persuading those they rule to accept the legitimacy of the status quo.

Mobility therefore needs to be not only clearly defined and measured, but also understood in a wider framework of social thought: contemporary ideas about mobility have roots in earlier conceptualisations of the political process. The evolution of ideas about mobility extends from questions in classical Greek philosophy about the role of rulers, through the Enlightenment and attempts to account for the emergence of a more secular, post-agricultural society, into early fascism and on to US foreign policy. This inheritance has influenced the work of mobility analysts and the ways in which their findings have trickled out to be consumed in new forms in the public consciousness.

Mobility in political philosophy and history

Changes in membership of hierarchical political groups were debated long before the term 'social mobility' was first introduced in the mid 1920s (Random House Dictionary 2011). Some of Plato's and Aristotle's questions about rulers can be rephrased as debates about mobility and immobility. At the start of the 20th century, these classical ideas stimulated the work of others, who in turn influenced the seminal first national mobility study (see Glass's discussion of the 'middle classes': 1954, 3–5). When the Italian economists Mosca (1896) and Pareto (1902) were developing their proto-Fascist ideas that all societies consisted of two groups, the rulers and the ruled, they required explanations both for the continuity of elites (what could be called elite social *immobility*) and that the groups constituting the elite changed over time (that is, *upward and downward mobility*). While Mosca (1896) believed elites ruled because they are 'superior persons', he attributed this not to genetics but to their *cultural* superiority – an idea since popularised by Bourdieu (1984) – and their coordinated capacity to maintain a coherent system of beliefs and values to which the masses adhere.

Like accounts of social changes earlier in the 19th century, Mosca (1896) saw the emerging commercial upper-middle class, rather than the old landed gentry of the upper class, as the key; this new elite was taking power in industrialised societies. Pareto (1902) introduced the idea of a 'circulation of elites' – a limited kind of social mobility *within* the upper reaches of society – to explain how elite groups change over time due to political processes and their styles of governance. Figure 2.1 rephrases older formulations of questions in social mobility terminology.

The interaction between mobility analysis and the ideas of Mosca (1896), Pareto (1902) and Michels (1911) has largely gone unacknowledged, less because these writers do not explicitly use the term 'social mobility' than because of their association with Italian Fascism. The sociological classic *Social Mobility in Britain* (Glass 1954) was initially unconcerned with social class per se, starting out instead as an investigation of the backgrounds of senior civil servants: the elite 'mandarins' who effectively ran the country and obstructed the introduction of the democratically elected post-war Labour government's reform policies.

Figure 2.1: Rephrasing older questions

Older formulation	Mobility formulation
What are the qualities of rulers and why might their excellence benefit those who are ruled, so that their rule could be justified?	Why do some people remain immobile in advantageous positions? Does their expertise make this arrangement socially 'efficient'?
How is this made legitimate and acceptable to society as a whole?	What are the cultural justifications for this that make us accept the elites' immobility, inherent in their social advantage and others' disadvantage?
How can the composition of elite groups change?	What processes of social mobility bring about change in group membership?

'Traditional' and 'modern' societies: the politics of immobility

Around the time of the publication of *Social Mobility in Britain* a parallel linkage between older ideas and new mobility analysis was gaining popularity, particularly in the US. Foundation ideas from the Enlightenment evolved into new accounts of the contemporary emergence of a post-agricultural social order in which individuals (or, at least, middle-class men) were becoming free from traditional constraints imposed by the landowning aristocracy and their clergy. These changes became reframed as stages of human development, or types of society characterised by distinctive forms of economic production. In this 'old mobility' perspective, conventional accounts thus contrasted the relative openness of 20th-century North America, and even other Western societies, with traditional societies in the early stages of economic development – such as Ancient China, medieval Europe or 19th-century India, where no mobility opportunities existed.

In such traditional societies, each person's status was 'ascribed': defined by one's birth. In the Indian caste system, for example, the four *varnas* (castes) of Brahmin, Kshatriya, Vaishya and Shudra were separate hierarchical groupings, which allowed no movement between them. Neither was movement allowed between these four varnas and the Untouchables: the fifth and lowest group of all, with whom even close proximity was a source of religious pollution.

The unity of Hinduism as a cultural and social system is paradoxically maintained by its traditional inflexible subdivisions in mundane practice. In Gandhi's words in the early 1920s:

> interdrinking, interdining, intermarrying, I hold, are not
> essential for the promotion of the spirit of democracy …
> the hereditary principle is an eternal principle. To change it
> is to create disorder. I have no use for a Brahmin if I cannot
> call him a Brahmin for my life. It will be chaos if every day
> a Brahmin is to be changed into a Shudra and a Shudra
> is to be changed into a Brahmin. … (Ghandi, quoted in
> Anderson 2012, 10)

For Ghandi, the rigidity of caste was 'the best remedy against heartless competition and social disintegration born of avarice and greed' (Anderson 2012, 10) – a rigidity redressed by Hindu religious beliefs in reincarnation and the transmigration of souls.

In societies like these, successive generations of peasants were recruited from their parents while elite castes or clans inherited positions of power and wealth. There was an emphasis on blood ties (akin to the pedigree breeding rules of the Kennel Club or the monarchy in modern Britain), with land and elite titles handed down through families. Life was organised around family units and patronage. The purpose of marriage was to create new kinship and material links with influential and rich families – not for the individual, but for the collective benefits of associating one's kinship group with a new patron or another powerful family.

In these closed societies, rigid social rules not only shaped broad life experiences but also governed everyday life. The landowners were the lawgivers and enforcers, protecting the boundaries of rank and demanding deference and obedience in every interaction with lesser mortals. As Charles Tilly (1998, 2–4) pointed out, phrases like 'looking up to' somebody, 'haughty' and 'looking down one's nose' all originate in the stunted physical growth resulting from malnutrition among the common people, as well as the fact that only the gentry rode on horseback.

Religious dogma legitimated this hierarchy, both within and between religions: in the English high-church version of Christianity, this became 'the rich man in his castle, the poor man at his gate' the Jew in his ghetto, the woman in her kitchen. There was little room for change or movement. Most avenues were blocked off, not only preventing the poor from inheriting the earth but also limiting the capacity of the elite to modify their own customs and conventions.

Access to many social positions was closed. Those at the top of society were superior beings; a different species from those of less fortunate birth, who could never metamorphose from lesser mortals into true aristocrats. Rigidity extended to the middle ranks of society: under the medieval guild system, the sons of master craftsmen took precedence over other apprenticeship candidates and the acquisition of craft skills was jealously guarded to protect privileged master craftsmen positions. There was, however still a limited scope for individuals to achieve positions of administrative power or replace existing rulers. A minority of exceptionally gifted people in the arts, the Church and the rulers' household administrations and their mistresses were able at least briefly to change their stations in life (although see Kaelble 1985; van Leeuwen and Maas 2010).

Traditional societies (to use the conventional label) evolved slowly, remaining largely agrarian, using simple technologies and consequently offering few specialist occupations. Following each country's industrial revolution, societies in later stages of economic development became modern (or indeed, post-modern), largely due their increasing dependence on complex technologies and their multiplicity of occupational and social roles. Economic activity transferred from agricultural ('primary') production to manufacturing ('secondary') and subsequently 'tertiary' services.

This appeared to create substantial mobility opportunities, an idea first systematically formulated by Paul Hatt and Nelson Foote in a contribution to an American Economics Society conference and subsequently published in the *American Economic Review* in May 1953. Their paper, 'Social Mobility and Economic Advancement' (authored as 'Foote and Hatt' after the latter's death prior to publication)

> not only refined Clark's "tertiary" category (setting forth quaternary and quinary sectors) but linked these sector changes to patterns of social mobility....Hatt and Foote singled out as the most important development the trend toward professionalization of work. (Bell 1973, 35)

When new occupational functions come into being, and particularly before they become routinised into formal occupations with standardised entry qualifications, they cannot by definition be directly inherited. There has to be a first cohort of computer programmers, airline pilots, conference organisers, personal trainers, PR spokespersons and so on, especially when there is an extensive and relatively rapid growth of this type of work. It is less clear which class will supply the new recruits. Some degree of intergenerational mobility is likely, because there are no occupational forebears from whom they could be recruited.

Technical functions, such as computer programming, also require education and expertise to perform them effectively. Advocates of the old mobility's distinction between traditional and modern societies, such as Blau and Duncan (1967), argued that filling occupations could no longer be based on birth or patronage because that would result in ineffectual people getting jobs despite lacking requisite skills. A modern economy requires efficiency. Universalistic standards of achievement like educational qualifications would replace the particularistic and ascribed character of job aspirants (Parsons 1951). How well jobs are done matters more than who the occupants or their families are. Useful though this insight was, it seriously overestimated the requirement for economic efficiency and the power of market forces to stimulate mobility. Functional efficiency and universalistic values do not adequately explain why, for example, in the United States during much of the last century women and people of colour have worked in different kinds of employment from white men.

An alternative perspective in occupational recruitment, especially when a vacant post produces an oversupply of applicants with similar formal occupational qualifications and skills (currently a common occurrence), is that selection is based on other criteria. Recruiters choose candidates who would best 'fit in with our way of doing things' or have 'good all-round CVs': common euphemisms for the preferred social class background, gender, ethnicity and possession of cultural capital.

Despite this, the device of a dichotomy of types of society and (later) fixed stages survived, notably in a basic orientation to mobility analysis in North American sociology. Whereas at a very general level the notion has plausibility, a more detailed level of analysis shows that, in practice, societies are at different phases of changing from traditional to modern and there is more than one route through this transition (Germani 1980; Wucherpfennig and Deutsch 2009). While contrasting the two idealised models of modern and traditional types of society offers us a general historical perspective and calls attention to distinctive tendencies in society today, the social processes of change, transformation and industrialisation are too complex and irregular to be contained in this way. The dichotomy used in the old mobility is not the most fruitful way of thinking about which contemporary nation states are more open or closed.

Multistage economic development and modernisation

Alongside the model of a dichotomy, an alternative version based on a fixed number of economic stages became politically influential. This split economic development into three stages at first and later into five or more. In the former, the transition was from economies based on primary agricultural production to ones in which manufacturing (secondary) industries dominated and subsequently into societies in which provision and consumption of services in the tertiary sector was the main economic activity. This thesis, set out by Fisher (1935) and Clark (1940) and subsequently elaborated on by Kuznets (1958) and Fuchs (1968), came to be seen as 'the most important and best documented demographic/economic shift ever in every country in the world' (Cohen and Zysmen 1987, 13). In the words of a report to the US Congress (1985, 43),

> The move from an industrial society toward a 'postindustrial' service economy has been one of the greatest changes to affect the developed world since the Industrial Revolution. The progression of an economy ... from agriculture to manufacturing to services is a *natural* change. (emphasis added)

This idea of 'stages' owed a lot to classical economics, which started with the 18th-century French school of Physiocrats, who saw services as consumption rather than as production or investment and whose work later influenced Adam Smith and subsequent economists. Although this was essentially an economic model – much of the literature defines this 'best documented' shift as proportions of gross domestic product (GDP) rather than persons employed – its significance for mobility was that the occupational requirements of different industries produced, destroyed and recreated the jobs (and classes) on which mobility was based.

Between 1950 and the early 1970s, sociologists and political scientists such as Lerner (1958); Lipset (1959); Feldman (1960); Kerr et al (1960); Rostow (1960); Hoselitz and Moore (1963), Moore (1963; 1965) and Levy (1966) presented variations on the theme that all societies evolved in the same way through very similar stages of economic and social development. This modernisation school of development theorists fed the Fisher–Clark thesis into political policy. As Browning and Singelmann (1978, 485) later objected in their more detailed analysis, the modernisation interpretation meant that the 'Fisher–Clark formulation is more than a classification scheme; it is also a model of development'.

Noting that traditional – predominantly agrarian – societies tended to have low rates of mobility, and fearful of the spread of communist and nationalist movements in Asia and Latin America, the modernisers argued for the promotion of higher rates of mobility as part of more 'open' societies. Accelerating movement through economic stages would mobilise the talented from among the peasant classes, reducing the risk of their participation in revolution and contributing to the creation of new, economically efficient, stable, plural democracies. By encouraging industrialisation (and with it, greater occupational specialisation and hence social mobility) the North American model of democratic pluralism could be exported to 'underdeveloped' countries in order to prevent the growth of communism in what were still predominantly traditional societies. Upward mobility would act as a safety valve, reducing the attraction of radical reforms such as communism.

While the modernisers' writing recognised some of the interconnected economic, political and social forces involved – and had an influence well beyond their time, not least in US foreign policy – their underlying argument of how to move from the traditional 'undemocratic' to (the North American view of) the 'democratic modern' was based on a simplification of social change and the role of social mobility therein. As Aron observed, this was at heart an attempt at camouflaging capitalism as democracy (Payne 1987a).

The modernisation school is a good illustration of how easily mobility can be linked to notions of *more* social mobility and incorporated into wider and often abstract ideological discourses. There is nothing new or parochial in the idea that mobility is political, even if US foreign policy is on a somewhat grander scale than British domestic concerns with the Scottish Independence referendum or urban unrest: two issues associated with blocked upward mobility. In legitimating the status quo with its promise of opportunity and meritocratic fairness and by calming the discontent of individuals whose aspirations are blocked, mobility is a potentially powerful weapon in the hands of a ruling elite.

The opportunity myth and the safety valve

By 2017, after more than 225 years, only 44 US citizens have been sworn in as US President. Although not every North American citizen has actually been able to make the symbolic journey 'from log cabin to the White House', this popular phrase – used by Presidents

Lincoln (1861–65) and Garfield (March–September1881) – has been in common currency since the 19th century. The similar bon mot, 'every soldier carries a Marshal's baton in his pack', is universally attributed (although undated) to Napoleon Bonaparte – but there were only a limited number of marshals in the Grande Armée. Whatever opportunities may have been available to the French did not extend to the Indian Army under British imperial rule, when native Indian soldiers were not allowed to become officers, let alone military leaders. Notional *opportunities* may serve political ends but are not the same as *outcomes*. Myths do not have to be literally true or even plausible once examined by experts. In modern society, all social positions are supposedly open to be 'achieved' by anybody, even if at the time of writing we have yet to see a female field marshal or an openly gay US President.

Mosca's (1896) identification of a coherent system of beliefs and values to which the masses could adhere is key to understanding how mobility can work to justify the status quo. Differences in outcome and associated rewards become warranted by the apparently 'deserved' greater achievement of the upwardly mobile and the lesser achievement of the downwardly mobile or immobile, as Lipset and Bendix (1959) have argued. This works both in terms of how we think about society in general and our individual lives. Provided that mobility is *believed* to be taking place and that the selection of individuals for movement up and down the whole of the social scale is based on some *presumed* principle of apparent fairness, social mobility legitimates the political and social order. In the classic sense of a 'myth', mobility does not have to be literally true in order for it explain and justify the status quo.

Supposed opportunities for upward mobility not only legitimate the political order; where they do genuinely exist, they may also weaken the capacity of disadvantaged groups to bring about change in the system of disadvantage. Michael Young's *The Rise of the Meritocracy* (1958) warned about the loss of potential political leadership within the working class. As he later lamented: 'They have been deprived by educational selection of many of those who would have been their natural leaders, the able spokesmen and spokeswomen from the working class who continued to identify with the class from which they came' (Young 2001). This echoes one of the few direct references to social mobility in Marx's writing. In an aside in *Capital*, he observed that 'the more a ruling class is able to assimilate the prominent minds of a ruled class, the more stable and dangerous becomes its rule' (1894: 587).

Here, the emphasis is placed on those individuals with supposedly exceptional talents. By bleeding off these people, potential leaders are lost from the working class, retarding the proletarian revolution. These most able people are allowed to join the ruling class, with whom they then side, reinforcing the rulers' capacity to rule. As Sorokin (1927, 533) put it, 'a mobile society offer[s] a great chance for the majority of leaders and ambitious people to rise. Instead of becoming leaders of a revolution they are turned into protectors of social order'. Sorokin, drawing on Marx, misses the development of a more complex alternative story in India. If talented members of the lower orders are given an advantaged but still essentially subordinate position, acceptance of the rule of an elite need not necessarily follow from increased upward mobility into the rank of lieutenant. Under the Raj, there was an explicit policy of developing a new class of educated native Indians to run the country on behalf of the British: 'a class of persons, Indian by blood and colour, but English in taste, in opinions, in morals and in intellect' (Lord Macaulay 1835, quoted in Anderson 2012, 5). This new, upwardly mobile class would in turn raise the Indian masses to be more eager consumers of English manufactured goods.

However, the new class did not stay subservient to their colonial masters forever. Indeed, Lord Macaulay may have foreseen some of the unwelcome potential for this to happen: 'Do we think that we can give them knowledge without awakening ambition? Or do we mean to awaken ambition and to provide it with no legitimate vent?' (Macaulay 1833, quoted in Anderson 2012, 5). He seems – somewhat optimistically – to have favoured an element of greater national self-government, provided it still involved India being a consumer market for English goods. But a century later the descendants and inheritors of Macaulay's new Indian professional and intellectual class joined Hindu nationalists in the Congress Party clamouring for full independence. The 'prominent minds' and the 'ambitious people' had not become fully integrated into the ruling class and their belief system; nor had they become the 'protectors' of the status quo.

Despite this counter-example, those on the Left have a history of nervousness about mobility because of its supposed potential to de-radicalise the working class. In the 1887 North American edition of *The Condition of the Working Class in England,* Engels identified 'the ownership of cheap land, and the influx of immigration' as an alternative outlet for social discontent in North America; he used the analogy of a 'safety valve': a device that prevents the internal pressure in a steam engine from becoming too great. Although Marx did not cope well with mobility in the class system (Harris 1939), many post-Marxists have seen mobility as providing a mechanism for reducing the supposed revolutionary potential of the working class by offering a partial alternative – not solely for the potential leaders or exceptional individuals – to permanent entrapment in disadvantaged circumstances. In addition, high rates of mobility undermine the very notion of rigidly separated and oppositional social classes (see Payne 1987a, 34–40).

However, taking account of mobility does not mean an automatic commitment to any given political position. It can be combined with a variety of 'interests' (that is, ideological standpoints), as Goldthorpe convincingly argues (1987, 1–36). He points out that among early socialists, Sombart worried that actual upward mobility was preventing proletarian class formation and undermining the burgeoning labour movement. Michels (1911 [1962]) was more concerned with the way in which, despite mobility opportunities actually being limited, *aspiration* for mobility reinforced basic psychological tendencies towards individualism. In contrast, Tawney saw the importance of demonstrating the *limitations* on mobility as a way of challenging classical liberalism.

Goldthorpe (1987) contrasts these standpoints with the rather different interpretations of later contributors. Blau and Duncan (1967) were more concerned with rational decision-making as the core characteristic of modern society. They saw mobility as simply a product of the division of labour in a technologically advanced world based on status attainment – the individual achievement of positions in the occupational hierarchy through educational qualifications and quality of work performance. However, their contemporary, Lipset (1959) – while arguing that high rates of upward mobility had contributed to the security of the liberal-democratic political regimes he espoused – saw mobility as also involving psychological and social penalties, which could lead to status inconsistency, political disaffection, extremism and social disorder. Together with elements mined from Marx's writing, the complexity of these various contributions offers a defence against the potential criticism that mobility research is automatically antagonistic to Marxist theories of social class. Nonetheless, despite Lipset's anxieties, most centre-Right commentators have been more at ease with the idea of a mobile society than the Left; the latter, particularly in European sociology, were reluctant to embrace mobility analysis.

Social mobility accordingly found a mainly welcome home in the USA, where it largely avoided questions of social class and was seen to support the 'American way of life' and US foreign policy. The fairly short entry for 'social mobility' in Wikipedia (2016) – normally an unreliable source – indicates this legitimacy of mobility analysis. Since 2004, this entry contrasted low amounts of mobility in older traditional societies with the open opportunities of contemporary

America. Only relatively late in its sequence of over 400 edited modifications did it mention the indisputable facts that ethnic groups in the USA experience different mobility outcomes, that by definition many millions of US citizens cannot be upwardly mobile into the tiny number of the most senior positions in society and that the economic system in which American mobility takes place has the technical name of 'capitalism'. The accuracy of these minor clarifications did not prevent these entries being wiped on several occasions and replaced with even briefer statements; such as 'Communism', 'Communists!' and 'Commies!'. Social mobility is a political issue.

THREE

Politicians rediscover social mobility

Initially social mobility was not an important *policy* topic for the British political class, whatever their personal beliefs and experiences. Towards the end of the 20th century this began to change. Previous public figures had occasionally cast an eye towards mobility, but a new generation of politicians gradually came to recognise that there might be votes to be won by calling for 'more' social mobility.

The result in Britain has been that:

> in recent years social mobility has become a topic of central political concern. The importance of increasing mobility has been a recurrent theme in speeches by government ministers ... attracting much attention under the remit of the Equalities Review (Phillips 2006) and in the Treasury and elsewhere the possibility has been seriously considered of establishing official 'social mobility targets'. (Goldthorpe and Jackson, 2007, 525–6)

This recognition of increased political interest was not something new, having been first identified at the British Sociological Association's Annual Conference two years earlier (Payne 2005). However, relatively little evidence was then available to substantiate the case, and there is even less in the later Goldthorpe and Jackson article. The contention that interest has widened 'far beyond the usual academic circles' (Goldthorpe and Jackson 2007, 526) relies – with relatively brief discussion – on evidence from only four speeches, all by leading members of New Labour: Tony Blair, Ruth Kelly and David Miliband in 2005 and Jim Murphy in 2006. As this chapter shows, a more systematic coverage and analysis of political speeches over a more representative period suggest that politicians' interest in social mobility is even more extensive, if also somewhat more complicated, than Goldthorpe and Jackson imply. They pay insufficient attention to the way the meanings attributed to the term 'social mobility' have been inconsistent, and miss the crucial point that it is not just a consensus among the political and chattering classes about mobility, but rather a *pessimistic consensus* that mobility rates are variously low, falling, and/or worse than in the 1970s. While the first stages in the renewed concern over upward mobility can be traced to the 1997 election of New Labour, there has been a steady increase in invocations of mobility not just among ministers but also from opposition parties, reaching well beyond the four speeches identified by Goldthorpe and Jackson (2007).

This wider but still superficial politicised interpretation has resulted in one crucial misrepresentation. In so far as there is a crisis of low mobility, what matters is where it applies. It is not *general* low mobility but rather the concentration of low flows in pockets, both at the *top* and at the very *bottom* of society. Much of the call for greater mobility has really been aimed at the latter group, albeit disguised as a more general problem of mobility. This is not entirely a moral concern with disadvantaged people. An anxiety about a potentially excluded and disruptive underclass of 'immobiles' has been a powerful (if often implicit) motive in arguments in favour of greater mobility, while on another level dissatisfaction with mobility rates may actually stand as proxy for a wider social disenchantment. The call for a general increase in mobility also targets the 'squeezed' middle-class voters worried about threats to the relative affluence they and their children enjoy.

Early and long-term political concerns with social mobility

Politicians' concern for social mobility is not just recent. For many years they simply took a casual interest in social mobility, asserting high or low rates as suited their views on other ideological matters. Mobility occupied an intellectual terrain contested by reformers and social thinkers, rather than party politicians, in which exchanges between academics and social commentators formed a two-way process. However, the first major mobility survey – the 1949 Social Mobility of Britain Study – was directly sponsored by the Ministry of Labour under Atlee (Glass and Hall 1954: 80, 85), while its London School of Economics (LSE) research team's interest in educational opportunity and mobility was echoed in Crosland's *The Future of Socialism* (1956).

Mobility was not, however, exclusively an issue for the Labour Party in the post-war years. The Conservative Party was also concerned with the need for equal opportunities – at least on its more liberal, one-nation, meritocratic wing – and saw the necessity for expanding the skilled workforce by drawing from the lower classes. Butler's White Paper, laying the groundwork for the 1944 Education Act, sought to 'ensure a fuller measure of education and opportunity for young people and provide means for all of developing the various talents with which they are endowed and so enriching the inheritance of the country of which they are citizens' (Board of Education 1943, para 1).

This often repeated theme can also be found in the 1959 Conservative Manifesto, which called for 'a massive enlargement of educational opportunity', and in Alec Douglas-Home's 'Introduction' to the Conservative Manifesto for the 1964 General Election (Conservative Party 1964, para 4). A somewhat less optimistic version can be found in Sir Keith Joseph's promotion of the idea of 'cycles of transmitted deprivation' in the 1970s (Welshman 2007), a phrase that continued in circulation among all parties (Clegg 2008b; Blunkett 2008). The Conservatives' emphasis on educational opportunity has frequently been linked to moral statements about individual freedom and economic prosperity in a similar manner to the later rhetoric of New Labour.

Conservative support for social mobility was not purely rhetorical. Edward Heath was the son of a carpenter, and as Peter Saunders reminds us:

> Margaret Thatcher was, after all, the daughter of a Grantham grocer and John Major's father worked in a circus ... In one of his first speeches after assuming the premiership, John Major made clear his commitment to the principle that any individual should be able to achieve success in life provided only that they have the necessary talent and that they are prepared to work hard. (Saunders 1996, 1–2)

In contrast, the Labour Cabinet of 2009 contained a dozen connections between siblings, partners and ancestors who were political leaders (Saunders 2010, 142). However, Saunders' more recent *Social Mobility Delusions* (2012) has less to say about the new crop of Conservative leaders. Twenty-three out of 29 ministers in the first Coalition Cabinet *each* possessed assets and investments estimated to be worth more than £1 million (Owen, 2010). Saunders does not mention David Cameron (multimillionaire; family background of baronets, stockbrokers and royal courtiers; educated in Eton and Oxford) or George ('Gideon') Osborne (multimillionaire; family background of baronets and the Osborne and Little wallpaper company; educated in St Paul's and Oxford), whose arrival was less obviously marked by calls for greater equality of opportunity. As one commentator on the Right of the party put it, only partly in jest, 'the main purpose on earth of the Conservative party was, and still should be, to keep Britain's ancient and well-proven social and political hierarchy in power – give or take a few necessary upward mobility adjustments' (Worsthorne 2010).

Labour's rediscovery of social mobility as a political issue

The Labour Party led in giving renewed prominence to social mobility as a policy priority in the 1990s. This new interest can be traced to New Labour's move to the centre-Right and the party's search for symbols of non-socialist legitimation that would not frighten the horses or the middle classes. Tony Blair's accession marks a turning point for Labour's renewed concern with social mobility (Blair 1996). His 'personal message' in the 1997 Labour Party Manifesto told electors: 'I want a country where people get on, do well, make a success of their lives. ... But these life-chances should be for all the people' (Labour Party 1997). Blair and his ministers soon repeated this message about 'getting on' and opportunity 'for all the people' in various permutations (Payne 2012a, 2012b). In speeches and subsequent party manifestos, Blair called for 'real upward social mobility' (Blair 2001a) and 'opportunity for all' (Labour Party 2001) and promised to 'make the spread of greater social mobility between the classes the cornerstone' of his third term (Blair 2004). The 2005 Labour Party Manifesto used red banner headlines to proclaim that 'in our third term we will build new ladders of social mobility' (Labour Party 2005, 19).

However, the first signs of a cooling of party commitment started to appear by 2015; manifestos now referred only to 'opportunity for all', which 'must belong to everyone not just a few' in a 'future for all our young people' (Labour Party 2015). A slightly more Left-of-centre call for reducing 'inequality' replaced the catchphrase 'social mobility' (Labour Party 2015, Foreword, 12, 67). Yet just one day after the result of General Election this was followed by leaders of the old-guard New Labour faction and candidates for the Labour leadership invoking 'aspiration' as a key theme in future Labour policies. Although not explicitly deploying the term social mobility, Tony Blair (2015) in *The Guardian* objected that '"Hard-working families" don't just want us to celebrate their hard work; they want to know that by hard work and effort they can do well, rise up, achieve'. Tristram Hunt called for more 'hope for those who aspire to climb life's ladder', as he and Mandelson, Johnson, Ummuna and Kendall did the rounds of the weekend political programmes (Wintour 2015a; 2015b). Of course, 'aspiration' was code for political manoeuvring to hold the party in the Right-of-centre ground previously occupied by New Labour, but mobility was restored to the agenda in the process.

Similarly, the specific references to social mobility in earlier Labour statements had initially been overshadowed by Blair's prioritisation of 'education, education, education'; a catchphrase first used in his Party

Conference Leader's Address in 1996 and subsequently recycled in campaign launches in successive General Elections (for example, Blair 1997; 2001b; 2005). However, the calls for improved education were linked to utilising British talents and increasing opportunities for those from less advantaged backgrounds: 'opportunity for all through realising the talent of all' (Blair 2001b). Improving education could appeal to Labour's working-class supporters and to the educated middle classes, thus meeting the need to legitimate New Labour.

There are two messages here. First is general advocacy of mobility as inherently desirable and therefore that there should be 'a lot of it', regardless of present levels. But second, his call for 'greater social mobility' and 'new ladders' begins to hint at the idea that UK social mobility is in some way actually too low. When ministers picked up the mobility theme, they repeated both ideas of more mobility and low mobility. *The Guardian,* as a 'newspaper of record', demonstrates what politicians of all parties were saying in public. Shadowing Blair's lead, Labour education ministers made a general case in favour of mobility, justifying Further Education (FE) and Higher Education (HE) reforms and changes in secondary education because they would 'improve people's prospects and, therefore, social mobility' (Rammell 2006). The purpose of school reforms was to: 'promote social mobility'. In the words of Lord Adonis (2006) (recently echoed by Conservative Schools Minister, Nick Gibb (2016)) 'academies should be engines of social mobility'. Adonis (2008) later said 'I am proud to be a meritocrat. Increasing social mobility and social justice through education has always been my goal, indeed my passion' (Adonis 2008). Speeches by Ruth Kelly (2005; 2006a; 2006b; 2007) and Alan Johnson (2007) further exemplify this education theme.

The link with education has continued. At the 2014 Labour Party Conference, Shadow Education Minister Tristram Hunt (2014) identified 'great teaching' as 'the surest route to social mobility', while Shadow Women and Equalities Minister Gloria de Piero (2014) praised schemes that gave 'bright students without connections that foot-in-the-door opportunity'. In Parliament, Labour MPs Lucy Powel, Kate Green, Graham Jones and David Winnick asked about social mobility and educational opportunity during Oral Questions to the Deputy Prime Minister (Hansard 2014). More recently, Frank Field (2016) queried whether mobility might be 'the great home issue that could be central to representing voters' hopes'.

The mobility message has not been restricted to education. Employment, unemployment and welfare have also been drawn into the debate by a succession of Labour politicians of the time. These include

David Lammy (2007), Stephen Timms (2008) and Department of Work and Pensions (DWP) ministers John Hutton (2006; 2007)and James Purnell (2007; 2008). In the DWP version of the message, mobility was not only about fairness but much more about social *efficiency*: it is sound policy for the nation to utilise all talents, to encourage everybody into paid employment and to reduce welfare payments.

Only one or two voices, such as those of David Blunkett or James Purnell, did not wholeheartedly endorse the idea that mobility had been shrinking and an expansion would solve all our problems. Purnell's version of 'the principle of a fair chance' (2007) accepted that 'an open society means that some people will do better than others, indeed that those who put in more effort deserve to do better' (2008). But for most commentators the main theme has been the need for more upward mobility, combined with either explicit or implicit claims that mobility rates are low and/or falling.

These politicians' comments might be read as indicating that the mobility message was exclusively associated with the Blairite faction in the Labour Party. To some extent this is true; for example, in 2006 Stephen Byers linked mobility prospects to his attack on Gordon Brown's public finance policies (Byers 2006), while in a similar critique of Brown's position Alan Milburn (2006) expressed concern about accommodating rising expectations with current rates of social mobility.

However, it was not only the Blairites who embraced social mobility. As early as 2004, Gordon Brown had urged intervention because 'social mobility had slowed – in some respects, gone into reverse' in the two decades before 1997 (Brown 2004). Mobility was also portrayed as a moral issue (BBC 2008b; Brown 2008a, quoted in Yandell 2009). In late June 2008, in a speech to the Specialist Schools and Academies Trust, the then Prime Minister announced that a White Paper would be published by the end of the year 'to bring together all the proposals for greater social mobility in our country' (Brown 2008b). This appeared under the title *New Opportunities: Fair Chances for the Future* (TSO 2009). In the long run-up to the 2010 General Election, Brown could be heard aspiring to 'a new meritocracy, a new wave of upward social mobility' (Brown 2008b). This emphasis on educational performance, which has been so much a feature of Labour rhetoric for 20 years, reflects the values of a public sector elite rather than the party's traditional manual working class supporter base (Dench 2006).

Brown's successor as Leader (*probably* not a multimillionaire; political refugee family background; educated at Haverstock Comprehensive, Oxford and LSE) in turn championed the cause of social mobility as the basis for challenging the Coalition government's cuts to the education budget (Miliband 2010). Under his new centralist leadership, Miliband made effects on social mobility one of the three 'touchstones' for evaluating every new policy issue (Stratton 2011). Earlier on, when Miliband was a a minister in the Brown administration, he said that social mobility:

> is measuring the chances that from one generation to the next children have a chance of rising from the place where they are, and the parents they are born to, to a higher level of *income* or a higher *education* level. (2008, emphasis added)

Here, he was in effect asking us to measure social mobility rates by comparing current income levels or educational qualification levels – rather than social class position – to those conditions a generation ago.

The tradition of new leaders appealing explicitly for more mobility was broken by Jeremy Corbyn on his election, who in his early speeches talked more about inequality per se. Nonetheless, to reduce the discussion of social mobility to the level of ideology and internal party power struggles in the Labour Party would be to miss the point. For a start, Milburn's address to the Institute for Public Policy Research in November 2004 together with David Blunkett's (2008) later pamphlet *The Inclusive Society?* represented a more extensive and considered reflection. The former is worth quoting at length:

> We still crave a Britain in which people can go as far they have the talents to go, where prosperity and opportunity are widely shared. Doing so means getting social mobility moving again in Britain. ... Britain's problem in the 21st century will not be too much mobility, but too little. There is a glass ceiling on opportunity in this country. We've raised it – but we haven't yet broken it. Social mobility – by which I mean the ability of children to advance up the ladder relative to their parents – is nowhere near as advanced as it ought to be ... the result of declining mobility is entrenched inequality; the persistence of disadvantage across the generations. ... A slowing down of social mobility is not just an issue for those at the very bottom of the social order. It matters to what Bill Clinton famously called the 'forgotten middle class'. ... This is why social mobility matters. When it is present it provides a fair set of easily understood rules – social incentives – that earn rights through responsibilities, and earn advancement

through effort. When it is absent incentives for individual progress are weakened, rules are transgressed and fairness is undermined. It is then that decent people say what's the point? Poverty of aspiration then kicks in, and worse, social resentment festers and grows. That is why social mobility should be our cause on the centre-left. (Milburn 2004)

Although these quotations from Milburn tend to link the idea of mobility, as part of a fair society legitimating the political order, to the often-repeated theme that mobility is too low and falling, Milburn is expressing a more fundamental concern, and one not limited to short-term Labour goals.

Social mobility: the other parties' rediscoveries

In July 2005, the then Shadow Education Spokesman, David Cameron, objected that 'the failure to increase social mobility has been one of biggest educational failures of the last decade' (Cameron 2005). Three years later, as Party Leader, he called for measures aimed at 'unblocking social mobility' (Cameron 2008). Ian Duncan Smith (2006), one of several former leaders of the Conservative Party, complained of 'now finding that many people are trapped without any mobility at all', while Ed Vaizey, Shadow Minister for Culture, deplored 'a Britain where social mobility has actually diminished over the last five decades' (2006). When he was Shadow Minister for Children, Schools and Families, Michael Gove (2008) believed that 'schools should be engines of social mobility ... but that just isn't happening in Britain'. George Osborne's (2008) 'blueprint for fairness' blamed Labour policies for the fact that 'social mobility is falling'. Graham Stuart (2007), Chair of the Commons Education Committee from 2010–15, complained that 'the gap in opportunities between the rich and poor in Britain was found to be widening' in mobility research. Lesser lights, such as the Chairman of the Tottenham Conservatives, claimed 'upward social mobility for working class children is now lower and slower that it was before World War II' (Hinchcliffe 2006).

Other brief examples of this strand of Conservative rhetoric include John Redwood (2011) arguing for improved urban education; Damian Hinds (2012), Conservative Chair of the All-Party Parliamentary Group on Social Mobility, complaining that mobility 'is relatively low in Britain, and has been for quite a long time'; Adam Afriyie's (2013) claim that 'social mobility is in our own hands', and former Party Co-Chairman Grant Shapps' (2013) assertion the same year that Britain could no longer tolerate the lack of social mobility and consequently needed more small businesses. There was widespread media coverage of the lament from former Prime Minister Sir John Major about 'the collapse of social mobility' in a speech at the South Norfolk Conservative Association's annual dinner:

> In every single sphere of British influence, the upper echelons of power in 2013 are held overwhelmingly by the privately educated or the affluent middle class. To me from my background, I find that truly shocking. (in Hope 2013)

This was echoed by Michael Gove (in Parker and Warrell 2014), whose statement was endorsed (with respect to schooling) by George Osborne (2014a).

Presentation of the Coalition Government's public expenditure decisions and policy campaigns were almost routinely given a political spin as remedies for the supposed low rates of social mobility. This was evident in, for example, George Osborne's 2014 Autumn Statement (Osborne 2014b, 1.153); calls for action on low incomes (PSE 2014) and health programmes like the Healthy Child Programme (2009); the Tobacco Control Plan (2011) and the Health and Social Care Act 2012, all of which included justifications on the grounds that their measures should enhance rates of social mobility (see Deputy Prime Minister's Office 2014, 1.5 and 2.2).

The call continues, sometimes admittedly with a characteristically Conservative interpretation, such as Junior Justice Minister Dominic Raab's (2015) claim that 'jobs, cutting taxes, better education ... are the foundations of the opportunity society that will make our society fairer'. At the October 2015 Conservative Party Conference, David Cameron highlighted:

> the brick wall of blocked opportunity. ... another big social problem we need to fix. In politicians' speak: a 'lack of social mobility'. In normal language: people unable to rise from the bottom to the top, or even from the middle to the top, because of their background. Listen to this: Britain has the lowest social mobility in the developed world. (Cameron 2015)

Although he went on to qualify that what he meant by mobility was opportunity not outcome, Tory concerns with 'aspiration' fit neatly with the idea that chances of movement need to be increased – at least for some.

The following month the Green Paper, *Fulfilling our Potential: Teaching Excellence, Social Mobility and Student Choice* (BIS 2015) was published. Despite having social mobility in its title, the text included the term barely a dozen times. The stated aim may have been that 'widening participation in higher education … will help to drive social mobility' (BIS 2015, 35), but there was no clarification of either what 'driving' social mobility actually means or exactly how increasing diversity in higher education recruitment will change social mobility. For instance, would the extra working-class boys who might become students be able to create jobs in the higher classes into which they could move upon graduating, or would they displace their currently more mobile female counterparts with little net effect?

Naturally, Conservative rhetoric extended to other matters too. Cameron's 2015 speech headlined national security; migration; the European Union (EU); the economy; housing, poverty and extremism. Cameron's 2015 government made a little less show of making more mobility a specific goal, these illustrations indicating a continuing Tory focus on mobility as a factor in other social issues as indicated by the rhetoric of Theresa May's inaugural speech as Prime Minister (May 2016).

Among the smaller parties, Nick Clegg (multimillionaire; family background of bankers and Russian aristocrats; educated at Westminster School and Cambridge), leader of the Right-of-centre 'Orange Book' Liberals who took over the Liberal Democratic Party, used his leadership acceptance speech to call for a country 'where social mobility becomes a reality once again, so that no-one is condemned by the circumstances of their birth' (Clegg 2007). In an echo of New Labour's search for legitimacy symbols, mobility has since loomed large in Clegg's priorities. In January 2008 he set up an 'entirely independent' 'Commission on Social Mobility, to be chaired by Martin Narey, Chief Executive of Barnardo's and the Chair of the End Child Poverty Coalition … [to] investigate the reasons for Britain's apparently low levels of social mobility' (Liberal Democrats 2008). A YouTube video clip of Nick Clegg identifying 'the lack of social mobility in the UK … [as] one of the greatest challenges that we now face' has since been incorporated into numerous blogs (Clegg 2008a). His further assertion that 'Britain has a social mobility crisis', made during a speech at the Institute for Public Policy Research, was made available as a downloadable audio recording (Clegg 2008b).

Clegg has since repeated his message in a variety of speeches and newspaper articles (Clegg 2008c; 2008d). But like both Labour and the Conservatives, the Liberal Democrats' 2015 manifesto made less explicit reference to social mobility. Instead, and to a greater extent than the other two parties, it called for 'opportunity' and 'access', decrying disadvantage passed down through generations: 'Too many people have their chances in life determined by who their parents are, rather than by their own efforts and abilities' (Liberal Democrats 2015, 54).

Perhaps unsurprisingly, the other smaller parties also have had less to say about social mobility. As a party primarily concerned with separating the Scottish people from the rest of the UK, the Scottish National Party (SNP) has not spent a great deal of energy addressing social mobility; its 2007 manifesto mentioned it only once, burying it in a list of key targets to be reported annually including crime; health; education; the environment; opportunity; life expectancy, business startups and economic activity (SNP 2007: 16). A later policy claim on HE fees saw mobility singled out by Alex Salmond (personal wealth details not readily available; family background civil servants; educated at Linlithgow Academy and St Andrews; career in Scottish Office and banking). During an SNP Conference in Glasgow, Salmond invoked a nostalgic past of high levels of mobility: 'out of educational access came social mobility as we reached all the talents of a nation to change the world for the better – we can do so again' (Black 2011). In response to a Social Mobility and Child Poverty Commission (SMCPC) report in 2012, Plaid Cymru (2013) also identified access to education as a mobility issue, contrasting English levels of poverty with those in Wales in what appears to be one of its few public comments on mobility.

A similar brief reflection on education and poor comparative performance can be found in the UK Independence Party (UKIP), whose English nationalists have relatively little to say beyond Nigel Farage's (millionaire; family background City of London stockbrokers; educated at Dulwich College; former City commodity trader) complaint in 2014 that the 'lack of social mobility in Britain is quite shaming' (Swinford 2014). The solution advocated is to have 'a grammar school in every town' and compulsory 're-introduction of selection, setting, streaming', according to UKIP spokesperson Paul Nuttall (2014). The party's relatively new existence may partly account for its limited commentary on mobility, but all three nationalist parties have seen the solution to low mobility as removing the yoke of the English elite.

The Green Party has also linked social mobility to the increase in HE fees (2010a), but views the fees issue as only one of several mobility-related problems. For example, their 2005 manifesto lamented the 'lack of social mobility' and connected an expansion of opportunities to the need for childcare (Green Party 2005, 11–12). This theme of a lack of mobility has since been repeated in claims that 'mobility has declined in Britain in recent years' (2010b, 7) and that Britain has 'one of the lowest rates in the world' (2013) and the Green Party has called for policies to reduce social inequalities and high wage differentials. Although the author must admit to not having monitored the policy statements of the smaller parties as systematically as the three larger ones, it seems that the Greens show a more sophisticated and active interest in mobility policy than the nationalists. With its strong regional structure, local Green Party activists have blogged extensively on the need to tackle low rates of social mobility in order to address a variety of social problems.

In addition, these specific party political concerns have also been reflected and amplified by new national pressure groups aiming primarily to improve schooling and increase access to HE and the top professions. These include the Sutton Trust (set up in 1997), the Social Mobility Foundation (set up in 2005) and the Toolkit programme sponsored by Professions For Good, a collaborative body of ten finance, engineering and law professions (set up in 2009). Among other pressure groups in the education system, special pro-mobility programmes have been promoted by million+ (set up in 1997); University Alliance (set up in 2006); Future First (set up in 2008); the Bridge Group (set up in 2010); the Progression Trust (set up in 2011), National Association of Head Teachers (NAHT) (set up in 2012) and Association of School and College Leaders (ASCL) (set up in 2014). Every university has its own 'widening diversity' programme, and organisations as disparate as the Trades Union Congress (TUC) (2010, 2014) and the 'big four' accountancy firms have also entered the field (Coleman 2014).

Examples from an even longer (but here incomplete) list of business campaigns supporting and/or marketing social mobility and careers advice are Big Choice Group Ltd (set up in 1999), Careers England (set up in 2003) and the Brokerage City Link (set up in 2004). In the third sector there are specialist charities like Bridge Builders (set up in 2007), upRising (set up in 2008) and upReach (set up in 2012), as well as activities from umbrella group organisations such as the Royal Society of Arts (set up in 2010) and the National Council of Voluntary Organisations (NCVO) (set up in 2011) and social policy think tanks such as the Institute of Economic Affairs and Civitas (see Saunders 1996; 2010), CentreForum (set up in 2013) and the Demos Centre for London (set up in 2011). As this list of bodies hints, many of the new mobility 'experts' climbed aboard the mobility wagon from their prior interests in education, childcare, early-life health problems or professional recruitment, finding it easy to tack these onto the cause of 'more mobility'.

The range and sheer volume of this 'mobility industry' has not previously been recognised (see, for example, Loveday's (2014) otherwise interesting account). Drawn together like this, the scale of these activities is remarkable. Laid end to end, they would reach from here to Utopia. What is more – as indicated by the dates when these specialist bodies were established or when the more general organisations joined the debate – this is an essentially 21st-century phenomenon.

The media and mobility

At the same time, media coverage of social mobility has increased literally tenfold; unlike many other political topics, treatment of what politicians have said about social mobility has been fairly balanced. There is little sign of Britain's right-wing press attempting to ridicule Labour statements and mobility policies and official reports – such as SMCPC's annual reports (SMCPC 2014; 2015c) or Labour's White Paper – have received prominent coverage, accurately reflecting the growing consensus about supposedly low levels of mobility.

Indeed, we can use extent of coverage as another indicator of how mobility has moved up the public agenda.

If relative frequency of reporting is taken as the indicator of importance, the LexisNexis Butterworth newspapers archive gives a reasonable estimate of annual frequency of press media reports dealing with social mobility. In 2014, a review of previous coverage in the 'quality' press (*The Guardian, The Independent, The Observer* and *The Sunday Times – The Times* no longer being available on LexisNexis and *The Telegraph* having progressively ceased to be a serious newspaper) consisting mainly of political speeches, press releases and columnists' commentaries confirmed that social mobility has achieved a greater importance in political circles. The results in Figure 3.1 show a sharp increase in awareness of mobility among the 'quality' media (if the definition of 'quality' is less restricted than the one used here, the results would be even more marked).

Figure 3.1: Annual number of social mobility items in UK 'quality press'

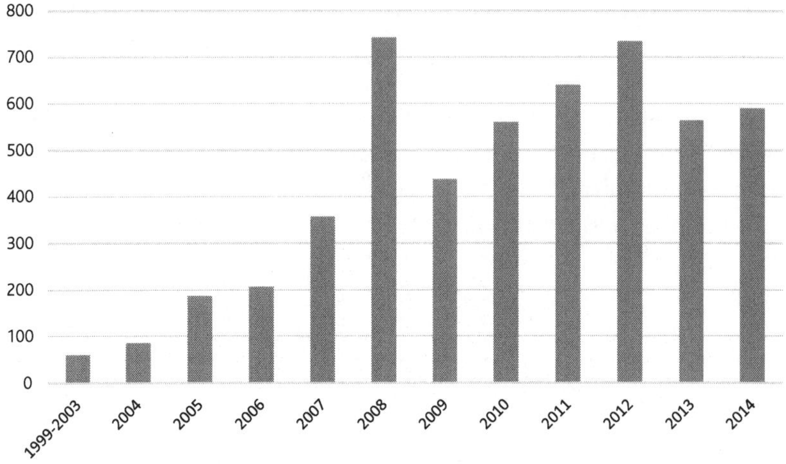

Source: calculated from LexisNexis Butterworth Archive (see text).

Between 1999 and 2003, these four British 'broadsheets' carried an average combined total of about 60 social mobility stories per annum; in other words, any one of the newspapers might typically carry a news story once a month if there were a uniform frequency throughout the year. Of course, papers in fact run more stories around the publication dates of reports or statements when press releases are provided. The combined coverage increased to a peak of 741 in 2008, equivalent to each newspaper running over 150 stories per annum – more than ten times the coverage found from 1999–2003. The author's analysis of data from the LexisNexis Butterworth database in 2014 found that annual combined coverage since 2008 has fluctuated between a low of 437 in 2009 and a high of 734 in 2012, with a mean of just under 600 reports per annum.

Not all of the media coverage has been news reporting. The parties' statements and press releases were also fodder for commentators. As a minimum, we can reasonably conclude that social mobility has become increasingly common in the 'Westminster Village' chatter during the last decade, even if it is not unique in this respect. Such visibility is at least consistent with mobility receiving a higher policy priority. Thus contributors to *The Guardian* (and other broadsheets, the columns of which the author has not monitored with the same devotion) have taken up the politicians' theme of low mobility as a social problem, including 'serious' columnists Polly Toynbee (2005; 2008), Nick Cohen (2006), Barbara Ellen (2006) Jenni Russell (2008) and Zoe Williams (2012). Peter Yorke, author of the *Sloane Ranger Handbook*, lamented the declining rate of real social mobility in this country (quoted in Adonis, 2008). Writing in the *New Statesman*, Peter Wilby (2008) has been one of the few voices (excluding unofficial blogs) to doubt this media consensus of low mobility.

The media's early acceptance of the idea that mobility rates were low continued under the Coalition government. On the publication of the *Mobility Strategy*, Hélène Mulholland and Allegra Stratton (2011) reported Clegg's intention to 'make Britain a fairer and more socially mobile place', while Michael White, blogging for *The Guardian*, commented on 'the need for greater social mobility' (White, 2011). However, a new negativity was beginning to appear, perhaps associated with the unpopularity of the Lib Dem leader; White notes that mobility 'is always upwards, never downwards', while a few days later Suzanne Moore's (2011) critical column was headed 'Speak to us peasants, posh boys, for we know all about social mobility'. An editorial in *The Guardian* (O'Hara and Shepherd, 2011) observed that 'Nick Clegg's plan to make internships transparent is all very well, but for the government's real priorities, follow the money'. In *The Daily Telegraph*, Matthew d'Ancona (2011) was surprised that the Conservatives had tolerated Clegg's enthusiasms, while *The Independent*'s John Rentoul (2011) blogged that 'social mobility is now a meaningless phrase' and should be banned.

In the parallel universe of social media, mobility also gained in popularity. Googling the general term 'social mobility' in 2014 produced in excess of 10 million hits, a quarter of them about UK social mobility. To take an example of how political speeches can be taken up, the author's Bing search for 'Clegg condemns social mobility myth' found a single speech made by Nick Clegg on 21 May 2012 had within one month been reproduced in its entirety on 83 separate sites. In addition to these 83 cases, many more hits used variations of the same words. Increased media and internet attention has, of course, been fuelled by their symbiotic relationship with the new pressure groups campaigning for more diverse entry into HE and professional occupations, such as the Sutton Trust. These charities, pressure groups and commercial organisations – almost all conveniently based in London – employ professional communications and PR staff to organise events, place stories and generate research evidence (of varying quality) in order to promote their causes. For example, the internet coverage of the 2012 Clegg speech reported earlier resulted from a Sutton Trust event. Another example of the success of this highly professional communications operation is illustrated by one press release about a piece of Sutton Trust research at LSE, which resulted in nearly 60 linked news stories including from Reuters, *Agence France Presse* and The Press Association, published in *The Sun*, *The Daily Mail*, *The Daily Express* and *The Metro* as well as the 'quality sheets' and regional newspapers (LSE 2008). Saunders reports that, in 2010, the Sutton Trust was mentioned 171 times in the national press (Saunders 2012, 30).

It is important, however, not to exaggerate the extent of the shared view that mobility rates are too low. The combined efforts of the political parties and these other organisations may have produced a degree of superficial consensus in media interpretations of the state of UK social mobility; certainly, all can agree that in order to introduce change something has to be shown to be wrong with the status quo. Social mobility rates must therefore be presented as having become inadequate.

Figure 3.2: *Call You and Yours* interview (BBC Radio 4, July 2008)*

'Interviewer	
(Winifred Robinson):	It's more difficult now to jump up a social class that it was a generation ago.
Minister at the Office of Inequality	
(Barbara Follett):	The fact is that it is more difficult is because probably the barrier's gone up. But I know that many people in my own constituency are mobile within the class structure [overlapping] and .....
WR (interrupting):	But they are not as mobile as they were a generation ago. You may anecdotally know of some people who managed to do it. It isn't as easy as it used to be.
BF:	It's, I don't know about that but I do [overlapping] know....
WR (interrupting):	But there's a whole raft of research, isn't there, that suggests that it was easier 30 years ago than it is, and that inequalities have grown over the last decade.
BF:	But I think a raft of research applied to a smaller group of people and now we've got many more aspirant people moving up....[brief exchange about higher education access] I certainly feel....that people's life-chances now, and a lot of research shows that their life-chances are as good if not better than they were then.'

*transcribed by the author from BBC recording of broadcast.

But this does not mean that there is complete all-party agreement about the underlying evidence or specific policies or that journalists and politicians speak with one voice. The complexity of social mobility means that there is scope for confrontational interviews in which both commentators and politicians play fast and loose with research findings.

An example of the superficial level of the political debate over mobility – as well as the way in which the underlying consensus is an uneasy truce based on a poor reading of the available evidence – is illustrated in Figure 3.2, which shows an exchange from a *Call You and Yours* discussion about new inequality legislation in July 2008 (BBC Radio 4 2008).

Here an interviewer faces a minister and the former pushes the view that mobility has been falling under Labour. Rather than directly confronting the unreliability of that claim and discussing the actual research findings, the Minister shifts into anecdote and individual experience. It would be idealistic to assume that ministers can be fully briefed on the detail of background evidence, but as informed citizens – let alone competent sociologists – we cannot ignore public discourse just because ministers get it wrong and display a somewhat cavalier attitude to research findings. Academics may not set the terms of debate, but politicians and the media cannot be left unchallenged, even when the debate between them is not always carried out in a coherent or consistent way.

This brief review shows that our political leaders, backed by the media, have become much more aware of social mobility as a problem in the last decade or so. A shared shorthand says that 'mobility' must be a good thing and 'we need more of it', even if we are not specific about the form it takes. The parties disagree about what mobility is and why it is important; various emphases on moral concerns with 'fairness', economic efficiency, individual freedom and underclass anxiety differentiate their stances. These differences also emerge in the official documents discussed in the next chapter.

FOUR

Documenting mobility

The growth in coverage of, and interest in, mobility in political speeches has been too marked to be dismissed as mere coincidence. However, it might be argued that this talk does not necessarily translate into a real change of *political priorities*. Mobility did not monopolise politics. The period covered in the previous chapter also saw increased verbal traffic about the importance of getting people into paid employment, about gun and knife street crimes, about the threat of terrorism, urban riots and, of course, the impact on the British economy of the world financial crisis caused by the banking system following its deregulation by the Thatcher and Reagan governments. Despite its undoubted increased prominence, social mobility is not the only key term or policy objective; it has yet to loom quite as large as 'social exclusion' did in the rhetoric of the early days of New Labour. Fashions come and go in politics (and sociology).

For balance, it is worth noting for instance that Toynbee and Walker's (2005, 2011) excellent reviews of the Labour governments' performance devote chapters to changes in health, education, wealth and fairness per se, covering shares of national income; poverty; children and benefits; single parents; unemployment; personal income; pensions, gender differences and minority ethnic groups. Social mobility gets a bare handful of pages out of well over 600 pages of text. Mobility is clearly not the only issue that has become fashionable (or a 'generalised panic', as one article in *The Guardian* described it (Clark 2010)); nor has it displaced these rival concerns. Mobility anxiety also stands as proxy for worries about wider social inequality and disenchantment. The revolution of rising expectations has created a powerful source of political discontent, and it is within this context that the sociopolitical impact of mobility takes place.

Although New Labour was first out of the traps in the race for mobility policies, political speeches since the late 1990s show how deeply mobility has become embedded in political discourse. Nonetheless, arguing the case through exclusive reliance on politicians' ephemeral speeches (which are hard to check) or election manifestos would risk unconscious cherry-picking of examples. To insure against this danger of selectivity and confirmation bias this chapter examines a more comprehensive written record, which fortunately has recently emerged. The publication of substantial policy statements by the UK's three largest political parties has cast the distortion of mobility in the public debate into a more concrete, and consequently independently verifiable, format.

These publications include the Labour Government's White Paper on mobility, *New Opportunities* (TSO 2009); the report of the Liberal Democrats' 'Independent Commission on Social Mobility' (Narey 2009), the Conservatives' two policy papers *Building Skills, Transforming Lives* (Conservative Party 2008a) and *Through the Glass Ceiling* (Conservative Party 2008b) and the Coalition government's *Opening Doors, Breaking Barriers: A Strategy for Social Mobility* (Cabinet Office 2011) and its White Paper *Higher Education: Students at the Heart of the System* (BIS 2011b). In addition there are the annual reports from the Coalition government's SMCPC (2014b; 2015c), the interim report of the All-Party Parliamentary Group on Social Mobility (2012) and background briefing papers such as the Cabinet Office's (2008a) *Getting On, Getting Ahead*, which had considerable influence on these other publications. Examination of these documents shows a similar picture of a distorted consensus. Even a simple content analysis, rather than strict Foucauldian discourse or linguistic analysis, shows that research findings and major arguments are being *omitted* and thereby delegitimised. An alternative 'new social mobility' is being *constructed by* the public discourse.

Before turning to the political parties' documents it is worth briefly noting the slightly atypical statements of the All-Party Parliamentary Group (APPG) on Social Mobility. Although these share the consensus about low mobility, their pronouncements have focused on early life and aspirations. Perhaps because of their members' prior concerns with children and education, the policies advocated by the All-Party Group in their document *Interim Report: 7 Key Truths About Social Mobility* (2012) addressed parenting skills; child readiness for school; quality of teachers; improved participation in out-of-school activities, role models and social/emotional 'skills' (APPG 2012, 10). Their later report, addressing schooling, argues for changes in personal psychology to increase mobility:

> belief in one's ability to achieve, an understanding of the relationship between effort and reward, the patience to pursue long-term goals, the perseverance to stick with the task at hand, and the ability to bounce back from life's inevitable setbacks ... fundamental drive, tenacity and perseverance needed to make the most of opportunities

and to succeed whatever obstacles life puts in your way. Character and Resilience are major factors in social mobility. (APPG 2013, 4, 6)

While ambition, hard work and drive to succeed in school are relevant factors, the APPG is attributing lack of (upward) mobility to *personal failings of character*: if people were encouraged to try harder, they would succeed. This is blaming the victim. It ignores inheritance of capital or talent, class bias in recruitment and a myriad of other mundane social inequalities and disadvantages, as well as whether there is 'room at the top' to absorb the newly motivated, characterful personnel. Others' laudable wishes to raise aspirations to be upwardly mobile (for example, Milburn 2004; Blunkett 2008) run the risk of becoming mistaken attempts to tackle the blockage of systemic social arrangements by changing individual character, as well as stigmatising those who fail.

The devil is in the detail: Labour's White Paper

Political discourse has been built around definitions of mobility that are inaccurate, inconsistent, misleading and at considerable distance from those used in mainstream mobility analysis. A central passage in Labour's 2009 White Paper (TSO 2009) offers an incorrect definition of absolute mobility as 'each successive generation gaining better jobs' (para 1.20), while relative mobility means 'ensuring that everybody has the chance to achieve their potential and gain better jobs, no matter what their background' (para 1.21).

One may sympathise with these sentiments as political or moral goals, but they bear little relationship to how sociologists have defined and measured social mobility since the Second World War, and certainly since the 1972 Nuffield Mobility Study (see Goldthorpe 1987; Payne 1987b).

Thus, contrary to the White Paper's assertion, *absolute social mobility* does not mean 'each successive generation gaining better jobs'. Rather, it is the measurement of the 'proportion of individuals found in a different *class* to that in which they originated, and in the upward and *downward* components of total rates' (Goldthorpe and Mills 2008, 86; emphasis added).

Nor does absolute social mobility mean 'changes in the class structure or average incomes of society as a whole', as the Liberal Democrats Independent Commission on Mobility (Narey 2009, 13) put it. Tellingly, neither the two aforementioned Conservative policy papers (Conservative Party 2008a; 2008b) nor the Coalition government's

Opening Doors, Breaking Barriers (Cabinet Office 2011) provide identifiable formal definitions – an omission that is itself revealing.

Suppose each generation achieved better jobs (whatever 'better' means); who would then do the 'worse' jobs that some parents previously did? Except in the technological fantasies of science fiction, we continue to need people to do the cleaning and labouring, the fetching and carrying, the caring and cooking. If, despite its practical impossibility, each successive generation were able to move up one step, the pattern of allocation would not necessarily alter. The 'social distance' or social inequalities between each occupational group would remain. We would simply all have floated to a higher level on an endlessly rising tide of occupational enhancement without any improvement in *redistribution* of jobs among the population. But we cannot all be middle class. Society cannot consist exclusively of senior civil servants; MPs; judges; bishops; bankers, newspaper editors and 'non-dom' international capitalists.

Absolute mobility *may* increase during periods of occupational change; indeed, it does tend to do so – but this is not inevitable. The expansion in numbers of highly skilled jobs (or more desirable social classes) can offer the prospect for upward mobility by recruiting from disadvantaged families – but not *unlimited* mobility, because some new jobs (certainly until now) are filled by children from the more advantaged classes who would otherwise have been downwardly mobile. Furthermore, when (as now) more of us *start* in the middle classes this reduces the number of those in the younger generation who are working class, thus by definition reducing the number who could become upwardly mobile (Payne and Roberts 2002). At the same time, the expansion of professional and managerial work sometimes slows (see chapter Nine), so that more of the younger generation born into the middle class must expect downward mobility.

In other words, *absolute* mobility can increase without there being more *upward* mobility. Absolute mobility cannot be used to promise 'each successive generation gaining better jobs' as Labour's White paper promises. '*Relative mobility*' (White Paper, para 1.21), on the other hand, is neither 'ensuring that everybody has the chance to achieve their potential and gain better jobs, no matter what their background' nor 'changes in position of individuals in relation to the rest of society' (Narey 2009, 13). It involves a more complex and abstract comparison of the chances of members from *two origin groups* being mobile. This is operationalised by social scientists as either a 'disparity' (or 'difference') ratio, which compares differences between the chances of becoming members of *one* destination group, or more commonly the 'odds ratio' comparison of chances of ending up in either of *two* contrasted destinations, from two origins (see Appendix).

Relative mobility is therefore essentially about selective *comparisons* (between specific classes, ethnic groups or genders), not about 'everybody' achieving 'their potential ... regardless of background', because differential backgrounds and achievements are central to that comparison. Odds ratios usually address designated destinations, better *and worse* – not 'gaining better jobs'. Without considering downward mobility, the picture is incomplete. Only in the very indirect sense of showing how far away we are from a utopian state of social equality can relative mobility mean what the White Paper claims. Therefore, when *New Opportunities* reports research by Goldthorpe and Mills (2008) and several papers by Blanden et al, it misrepresents them. Assertions that 'absolute social mobility remained stable after 1970' (TSO 2009, para 1.26), that 'rates of relative social mobility, for both men and women, have remained *broadly* constant since the war' (para 1.28; emphasis added) and that there was 'a decline in relative social mobility (when measured by income)' (para 1.29) are disconnected from the meanings used in the original sources. The original research may indeed have painted a somewhat pessimistic picture, but the way the White Paper draws on these highly relevant studies is unsatisfactory.

The Liberal Democrats' Independent Commission on Social Mobility

Drawing on the same sources, the low mobility story is repeated in the Liberal Democrats' Report: 'social mobility in Britain has declined and the extent of mobility is low relative to other developed countries' (Narey 2009, 4, 12). In addition to its introduction and summary recommendations, this 50,000-word document consists of six chapters on inequalities relating to child poverty; pre-school years; education; employment, health and local communities. Like those in Labour's White Paper, these are relevant to mobility; however, there is no chapter explicitly connecting them to mobility, discussing social mobility in its own right or attempting a systematic presentation of empirical sociological evidence about contemporary mobility patterns in the UK – using proper definitions.

The Commission redefines social mobility as 'equality of opportunity' (16); that is, not mobility *outcomes* or the number of people moving between social classes. It selects 'the measurable gaps in educational attainment, in differential employment opportunities and in health inequalities' as indicators of the 'barriers' that 'impede progress' for 'children born to poorer homes' (Narey 2009, 5[1]). It invokes 'a recent analysis by the Joseph Rowntree Foundation ... [of] the Government's record across a range of indicators of *social exclusion*' (Narey 2009, 5; emphasis added) as being further evidence of mobility. There is little wrong in this documenting of social *inequality*, so long as we remain clear that it is not a description of social *mobility*.

Educational attainment; health status; social exclusion, income and wealth play a part in mobility *outcomes*; however, as joint products of class differences, they are neither entirely independent variables nor mobility per se. By addressing mobility in terms of social inequality, the report runs together probable cause and outcome. The Commission is confused about what constitutes evidence, and how inequalities evidence connects with mobility.

The Commission has also foreclosed on a full structural explanation. By concentrating on the disadvantages of poorer groups, the *continued advantage* of some other groups is not problematised. It is as if the existence of the rich or elite, with all their advantages, were not part of the same problem. They do not even feature as potential victims of downward mobility. The intermediate range of society is also defined out of the picture, thus ignoring a substantial tranche of the class structure that does achieve close to its proportionate 'share' of mobility outcomes.

A useful analogy here is modern train travel in Britain. The privatised trains are overcrowded; not everybody can get on, let alone have a seat. If we sell more tickets, it does not mean that more people will be able get on board or have seats. To improve travel requires investment in more frequent services, more trains and better national coordination – or alternatively, that *some of the current travellers get off the train*. Improving schooling, health, community solidarity and so on for poorer families does not mean that there will be more upward mobility. That would require either a precisely matching expansion in the number of highly skilled jobs, or – more plausibly – downward mobility on the part of people presently getting those jobs not because of, but despite, their levels of ability.

While all of these documents pay a disproportionate amount of attention to education and young people, the Lib Dems' report does so to a greater extent than the others. This is probably due to the membership of the Commission and the influence of its background literature search. Although the ten members of the Commission have between them qualifications in social policy, economics and PPE, none of them is identified as having graduated in sociology; apart from economist Stephen Machin, who has researched income mobility, there is almost no hands-on familiarity with mobility analysis. Instead, six of the ten have backgrounds in working with children. Martin Narey and Di McNeish both worked for Barnardo's; Sonia Sodha lists her first two areas of expertise as children and young people's emotional wellbeing and education, Hilary Fisher and Jason Strelitz come from the Campaign to End Child Poverty and John Bangs is a former teacher representing the National Union of Teachers (NUT). Furthermore, Graeme Cooke – who 'wrote an initial literature review which was very significant in informing the Commission's work' (Narey 2009, 83; see IPPR 2008) – has written about poverty with an emphasis on families and children (for example, Cooke and Lawton 2008).

The Institute for Public Policy Review (IPPR) literature review used by the Commission lists 55 sources, although significantly these include two Labour Party statements and four research surveys from within government departments, specifically the Department for Education and Skills (DfES), Department for Work and Pensions (DWP) and the Cabinet Office. It is not immediately obvious how the Commission has incorporated these exercises into its text, but this illustrates how selective evidence and 'knowledge' about mobility is recycled within administrative circles in self-supporting perpetuation. Allowing for a degree of approximation in classification, the Review contains only about ten direct references to UK mobility research; half of these are to income mobility research carried out by the economists Blanden and Machin (see chapter Seven) and half are to products of what Savage has called 'the Nuffield paradigm' of mobility analysis (Savage and Egerton 1997, 645–7). A Cabinet Office Policy Unit seminar coordinated by John Goldthorpe (Aldridge 2001) is also acknowledged in the main report. The only outlier source is Platt's (2005) work on minority ethnic communities. More than half of the other sources deal with children and education rather than mobility per se – a feature replicated in the main body of the IPPR text, in which six of its 20 pages address childhood while five address social policies. In all this, the labour market receives only two paragraphs.

The Conservative Party's mobility documents

The Conservative Party's mobility documents (2008a, 5; 2008b, 3) demonstrate such a lack of concern for definitions and so few references to academic research that a cynical reader might accuse them of constituting window dressing rather than policy statements. *Building Skills, Transforming Lives* (Conservative Party 2008a) is really about extracting more worker productivity rather than social mobility;

its proposals are about training, apprenticeships, vocational further education and a careers service to help employers locate prospective employees. Apart from an introductory gloss about 'giving everyone the chance to defy the circumstances of their birth, climb the ladder and change their lives for the better' (2008a, 3) and the bald statement that 'skills build social mobility' (2008a, 5), there is no definition of mobility or details of its measurement. Most of the 59 separate sources in its 79 footnotes (2008a, 31) deal with social inequality; only one explicitly addresses mobility: the Centre for Economic Performance's *Intergenerational Mobility in Europe and North America* (Blanden et al 2005).

Their second publication that year, *Through the Glass Ceiling: a Conservative Agenda for Social Mobility*, again lacked formal definitions. The closest we come is: 'Britain is no longer a socially mobile nation. We fall far behind many of our international competitors in offering people a route up the social ladder, even though past generations in this country did have such a route' (Conservative Party 2008b, 2).

Much like the aforementioned publications, it switches almost immediately to policy areas: problem families; early years; schooling, job skills and back-to-work schemes. Its supporting evidence, largely from economics, deals with social inequalities without explaining how mobility will actually reduce them. Neither document shows any awareness of rates of downward mobility.

Only a handful of the publication's 93 footnotes reference sources that tackle mobility to any degree, the most often-cited sources being the Cabinet Office's (2008a) document *Getting On, Getting Ahead* and the DWP's (2007) *Factors Influencing Social Mobility*. It could be argued that these are omnibus reviews of other studies, but they are used as sources of data on social inequality rather than mobility. Despite the plundering of the glass ceiling metaphor for the publication's title, feminist readers will be disappointed by the single explicit mention of gender. Even this sole reference to gender implies that the real problem is the educational failure of boys rather than the academic success of girls (2008b, 22). Elsewhere, 'children', 'pupils', 'parents', 'employees' and so on remain undifferentiated by gender.

The Coalition government's official statement on social mobility

Whereas Labour had elevated mobility policy to the level of a White Paper, the Coalition Government's *Opening Doors, Breaking Barriers: A Strategy for Social Mobility* (Cabinet Office 2011) was accorded the lower status of a Cabinet Office strategy statement. Interestingly, nowhere in the statement is the Liberal Democrats' much heralded *Report of the Independent Commission on Social Mobility* (Narey 2009) mentioned by name, despite Nick Clegg using the Foreword to promise that 'improving social mobility is the principal goal of the Coalition Government's social policy' (Cabinet Office 2011, 3). Nor is there room for the two aforementioned Conservative Party documents, possibly a result of conventions for working in coalition. Whereas there was little to be lost from excluding the two Conservative documents, the Independent Commission had at least assembled some interesting data on education.

Four of the opening seven bullet points in *Opening Doors, Breaking Barriers* (2011, 5) deal with education, three of which give statistics about 'unfairness' in *education* (rather than mobility per se) and one that reports the unfair advantages of private education (without suggesting that anything should be done about public schools). Of the other three that deal directly with mobility, two refer to *relative* intergenerational mobility (not *absolute* mobility) in terms of income and only one in terms of occupational class.

The Introduction's clarion call for fairness includes a single sentence saying that 'there is a strong ethical imperative to improve social mobility' (2011, 11), which is immediately qualified by: 'But there is an economic dimension too' and four further paragraphs of elaboration about the need for prosperity and the economic benefits of mobility (ignoring downward mobility). An added justification for doing something about mobility follows in the form of our old friend, the emerging underclass:

> We have a group of people in our society who have become detached, unable to play a productive role *in the workplace*, in their families or in their communities. They are also trapped by addiction, debt, educational failure, family breakdown or *welfare dependency*. (2011, 11; emphasis added)

Although this quotation illustrates the economic thread running throughout the document, it also flags family, community and social disadvantages (however, little of the concern for the underclass expressed in this April publication would be heard in the House of Commons following the Tottenham urban riots only a few months later).

The preamble is followed by a short selective review that concentrates on intergenerational relative income mobility, emphasising inequalities

– especially in educational outcomes – and the UK's less-than-competitive position internationally. Despite asserting that it will be 'a ruthlessly evidence-based approach' (2011, 12), there is reference in this section to only *a single* article from the multitude of sociological sources; the rest are presumably dismissed under the statement: 'The evidence on social mobility is complex and sometimes contradictory. But the broad picture is … ' (2011, 16). Even the Department for Business, Innovation and Skills (BIS) paper (BIS 2011a) that lies behind the White Paper on Higher Education considered half a dozen sources from the sociological literature.

There is also a commitment to supporting research in the form of longitudinal cohort studies, but no proposal for a baseline survey of occupational mobility against which to measure the government's achievements. Gender, ethnicity and health do receive a brief mention on pages 21–2, but throughout the publication the definitional details – which, as we have seen, are so crucial – are sketchy, leaving us with selective generalities. Of course, no White Paper or major strategy statement can be expected to address the precise meanings of academic research results in the way a monograph can, but if vast swathes of research are ignored, details obscured and 'facts' cherry-picked the 'evidence-based approach' is not worth the white paper on which it is written.

To be fair, in contrast to the two Conservative policy documents, the Coalition's statement does at least attempt definitions – and indeed some of those presented are basically correct, albeit in a less than obvious way. There are not only implicit statements of meaning (for example, 2011, 5, 7) but also several formal definitions, three of which are accurate:

> Social mobility – the degree to which the patterns of advantage and disadvantage in one generation are passed onto the next. (2011, 11)

> Intergenerational social mobility is the extent to which people's *success* in life is determined by who their parents are … Relative social mobility refers to the comparative chances of people with different backgrounds ending up in certain social or income groups. (2011, 15; emphasis added)

However, the second of these definitions is used to refer only to success, not failure. Sadly, their copybook is blotted by the additional claim that:

> Absolute social mobility refers to the extent to which people are able to do *better than* their parents … The Government's focus is on relative social mobility. For any given level of skill and ambition, regardless of an individual's background, everybody should have an *equal* chance of *getting the job they want* or reaching a *higher* income bracket. (2011, 15; emphases added)

First, absolute mobility actually includes the *downward* mobility of those who do not succeed. Second, the problem with the elaboration of relative mobility is that while it could be said to work for upward comparisons, as measured by *difference ratios*, it does not hold for *odds ratios* (explained earlier). Furthermore, the data on social inequalities (for example, 18–20) that try to pass for mobility data are presented predominantly in a simple description and are not organised into a format that allows comparison of chances, or fairness.

Before leaving *Opening Doors, Breaking Barriers* we should note how it breaks away from not only with the Independent Commission's report but also from the earlier sources of evidence. A new range of research findings is predominantly drawn from economists' accounts of income mobility, such as the contribution of Blanden and her associates and a review by Crawford et al (2011). The latter review does not mention earlier civil service briefings such as the 'Aldridge papers' (which we shall come to shortly); as with much of the new content it is a product of work done for BIS, which seems to have become the lead ministry. Only a handful of sociological references are given; whereas the sociology can be turgid and technical, the economics lives in an abstract world of symbols and formulae impenetrable to the typical politician or advisor. However, the broad approach used in *Opening Doors, Breaking Barriers* is sufficiently reminiscent of the earlier civil service briefings to suggest that their influence has continued, albeit without explicit acknowledgement.

Education and mobility

The Coalition government's White Paper *Higher Education: Students at the Heart of the System* (BIS 2011b) – produced not by one of the departments for education but by the BIS, which then had control of HE – provides a further example of how mobility has been used to legitimate other social policies. The Introduction, signed off by Vince Cable and David Willetts, concludes that the Coalition will 'reform the financing of higher education, promote a better student experience and foster social mobility' (2011b, 3), but the bulk of document addresses the first, and to some extent the second, of these goals (see also Loveday 2014). In fairness, this is a document about HE, not mobility per se; however, given that its authors have chosen to link the two, it is reasonable to expect a proper treatment of both issues. Thus, while allocating six of the 24 main points in the Executive Summary to 'increasing social mobility' seems a promising start, one might anticipate that a fuller account would follow in the report itself.

Of these six key points, paragraph 15 is a statement of an undesirable aspect of present policy: 'The most disadvantaged young people are seven times less likely than the most advantaged to attend the most selective [university] institutions. This is not good enough.' Paragraph 16 notes that 'people from poorer backgrounds with no history of participating in higher education' face problems, which maintenance grants and loans and the efforts of the Office for Fair Access will try to ameliorate. Paragraphs 17, 18 and 20 do not actually mention social mobility – they are instead concerned with technicalities of administration, which at best might tangentially improve fairer access to HE – leaving paragraph 19 to talk about 'the best way to widen participation'. Here we find the promise to uphold the Robbins Report (1963) principle that 'higher education should be available for all those who are qualified by ability and attainment to pursue them' – although this would now be 'subject to expenditure constraints' (2011b, 6–8).

Again, although one of the six chapters of the White Paper is called 'Improved social mobility through fairer access', the connection to social mobility is still little more than implicit. The (not unreasonable) underlying assumption is that if more children from disadvantaged families can get into higher education their degree qualifications will help them enter the professions, although the chain connecting initial disadvantage to specific occupational achievement (see chapter Twelve) does not receive a great deal of attention. Paragraphs 5.13 and 5.14 do mention 'schools as engines of social mobility', with the latter expressing concern that the English Baccalaureate should be more narrowly determined by the recruitment needs of Russell Group universities. The following paragraph then identifies access to 'high quality, aspirational information, advice and guidance' as a means of supporting progression. There is no discussion of the effect that more competition may have on the current 'winners' in the mobility competition.

Instead, we are presented with a few facts about university access and invited to condemn evident inequalities between the very top and very bottom of the social scale (2011b, 55, 56). The differences between top and bottom *are* important; indeed, it is precisely in these contrasting pockets that immobility is most intransigent. However, this leaves out the less dramatic cases in the middle range.

It is appropriate that, as a policy document, the chapter (and the White Paper as whole) should devote much of its content to practical steps like setting up the Office of Fair Access, the new careers service, access agreements and funding, rather than social mobility per se. Even so, when it comes to defining mobility *Students at the Heart of the System* is a curate's egg, first offering two accurate definitions but then immediately shifting its focus onto relative mobility because high absolute mobility 'can go hand in hand with a society in which background still has an unfair influence on life chances' (2011, 54). While this statement is valid, it makes little sense as a justification for ignoring absolute rates of mobility – one half of the problem. It is equivalent to saying: 'There are two kinds of fruit, apples and oranges: because apples are not oranges we will ignore them and define "fruit" as consisting exclusively of oranges'. The expansion of occupational opportunities is closely linked to how much mobility there is; the question of who takes up the opportunities needs to be answered not only in terms of who has the better chances but also in terms of the scale of opportunities for which there is competition.

An example is the coverage of the expansion of HE. *Students at the Heart of the System* offers graphs to show how overall participation rates have increased (2011, 49) and how proportions of students from 'disadvantaged' backgrounds (not from 'the working class': Coulson et al 2017) entering HE have improved (2011, 55, 56). But it does not show how the proportions of students from *advantaged* backgrounds have also improved – and indeed, improved at such a rate that the student population is now probably (depending on which datasets are used; for example, House of Commons 2010) more middle class than it was 40 years ago. Given the document's stated intention to focus on relative mobility and fairness of chances, this omission is intriguing. There no discussion of whether the present *class mix* of the undergraduate population is desirable, and the subsequent policy recommendations – unsurprisingly – do not include setting access quotas to increase diversity of intakes to HE, particularly to the 'elite' Russell Group universities.

The introduction to the document's most relevant chapter is even stranger. Having defined 'absolute' and 'relative' mobility (more accurately than in most other official documents), the text makes a flying leap of connecting its technical definitions of mobility to the issue of university access, with the basic assertion that:

> Higher education *can* be a powerful engine of social mobility
> enabling *able* young people from low-income backgrounds
> to earn more than their parents and providing a route into
> *the professions* for people of non-professional backgrounds
> … there are significant barriers in the way of *bright* young
> people from the most disadvantaged backgrounds. (2011,
> 54; emphasis added)

The added emphasis here draws attention to how the Coalition's actual concerns with mobility do not address the less 'able' or less 'bright' students; neither do they address middle-class occupations other than 'the professions'. Leaving these out distorts our picture of how the rest of society works.

Although the problem of definitions does not go away, it would be unfair to treat all statements emanating from Whitehall as following the same line (or, indeed, to claim that this chapter can do full justice to each of the publications). The HE paper does at least get some of the definitions right. Prior to this, the final report of the Panel on Fair Access to the Professions (2009), *Unleashing Aspiration*, introduced a slightly more nuanced view of mobility rates; however, it repeats the garbled definitions in two bullet points:

> social mobility means:
> • better jobs for each generation, so that our children can
>   do better than us
> • fair chances, so that everyone has an opportunity to
>   access those jobs and so realise their potential.
> (2009, 26)

After stating that 'social mobility has slowed down in our country. Birth, not worth, has become more and more a determinant of people's life chances', Alan Milburn's Introduction suggests: 'that may be changing. There is now evidence that the long-running decline in social mobility has bottomed out' (2009, 5). The discussion of access routes into the professions, while perhaps overly optimistic about the potential for rapid change, shows a much more grounded and sophisticated appreciation of mobility processes. While the Labour government's response (Panel on Fair Access to the Professions 2010) was generally favourable to the report's recommendations, the General Election that year cut short further action – although one positive outcome was the setting up of the Social Mobility Commission (now the Social Mobility and Child Poverty Commission (SMCPC)). Future annual reports from the

SMCPC (re-named with little fanfare the Social Mobility Commission in May 2016) may provide further insights into how our ruling elite thinks about social mobility (for example, one of the very few accurate definitional statements appears in the SMCPC's Third Annual Report (2015c, 2)). In the meantime, it is possible to extend this analysis of 'official thinking' by exploring where contemporary political opinions have come from – in other words, to see where the civil servants and Special Advisers (SPADs) got their ideas.

Note

[1] All page references for Narey (2009) refer the to the original PDF version of the report, which has since mysteriously disappeared from all Liberal Democrat websites. The author is grateful to Julian Birch for finding a surviving version on Martin Narey's own web page (see References for URL).

FIVE

Tracing the origins

The way that mobility has been politicised in speeches and documents prompts the question: from where did their incorrect notions and inaccurate definitions come? This is not an easy question to answer. There are no publicly available records of who decided what, why and when. If elite or key informant interviews were now possible, the prospect of achieving complete and accurate recall of events during more than a decade of drafting these papers would still be remote. The process behind acquiring and adapting ideas for policy is not open to inspection; because ready access to the people involved is not available, the text of published documents has to be relied upon. Even then an added degree of uncertainty comes from limits to how far textual analysis can take us, because the referencing standards of the documents is so poor that tracking origins and influences is difficult.

Incorrect definitions and lack of attention to research data assumed importance partly because of the sparsity of mobility studies. After the flourish of work in the 1970s, there were no new national sample surveys of UK mobility for three decades (other than spinoffs from the quinquennial British Election Surveys up to 1997 and Paterson and Iannelli's (2007) work on Scotland). This was probably because of a sense that mobility had been 'done', together with concerns about the high cost of major programmes of research. This left a data vacuum, which was only partly filled by reanalysis of older longitudinal datasets. Thus documents that did respect definitions and research findings had relatively few sources on which to draw – such as the National Equality Panel report on economic inequalities, which quoted only six research studies (Hill et al 2010, 319–29) – and were otherwise dependent on the recycling of earlier documents:

> We have also been able to draw on two other recent exercises that relate in particular to the links between generations: the Cabinet Office's review of social mobility and the subsequent White Paper, and the Panel on Fair Access to the Professions. (Hill et al 2010, 7)

Although the National Equality Panel report was not widely taken up in debates about mobility, it typifies the somewhat incestuous approach of re-cycling other summaries of mobility discussed in the last chapter. In consequence, such reports concentrate on repeating varieties of small-scale interventions while ignoring the core issues (Grusky 2015).

The regurgitation of distorted findings can be explored through simple comparisons between successive documents and following whatever formal acknowledges are apparent. In Figure 5.1, the thick arrows indicate the direct influence of explicit and/or multiple references to incorrect definitions in the reports' main cross-references and borrowings. The thin arrows indicate indirect influences or weaker correspondences in which interconnections can be less explicitly demonstrated from the texts.

Figure 5.1: Main sources of mis-definitions and research evidence

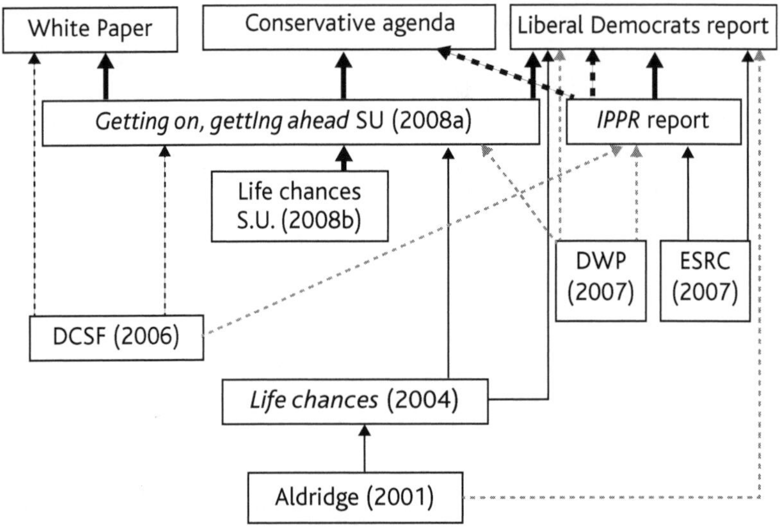

The dotted lines in Figure 5.1 show where research evidence – but *not* their definitions – has been imported from conventional mobility studies and then repeated. This is often filtered through the Cabinet Office Strategy Unit rather than coming directly from the research studies. The Cabinet Office's (2008a) *Getting On, Getting Ahead* provides a major linkage for all three parties – despite being solely published online rather than in hard copy like the other documents reviewed in the previous chapter.

Getting On, Getting Ahead

The Cabinet Office's (2008a) *Getting On, Getting Ahead* is an extraordinary document. It describes itself on page 11 as having three sections: the first aims to 'provide a clear definition of social mobility', the second to 'set out what has happened to social mobility over the past half century' and the third to consider the 'drivers' of mobility. Astonishingly, its first section then fails to give even a single proper definition!

Getting On, Getting Ahead firmly establishes the precedent for indirect – and therefore distorted and approximate – definitions, offering implicit meanings by juxtaposing 'mobility' with phrases like 'building people's capabilities so they can obtain better jobs', 'the creation of better jobs' and 'improving educational attainment' (Cabinet Office 2008a, 5, 6, 8). The closest we come to a specific definition is in the Introduction, which precedes the three main sections:

> Social mobility has two core aspects: ensuring there are better jobs for each successive generation, so our children can do better than us; [and] making sure that there are fairer chances, so that everyone has the opportunity to access those jobs in line with their potential.(Cabinet Office 2008a, 5)

These statements are repeated in almost identical words on page 11 as 'the definition' and are used as headings on each of the four following pages in section one. Readers may remember seeing a remarkably similar wording in the Labour Government White Paper (para 1.26) and the Coalition government's *Opening Doors, Breaking Barriers: A Strategy for Social Mobility* (Cabinet Office 2011, 15), and almost this exact form of words and layout in the Coalition's HE paper (BIS 2011, 26) quoted in the previous chapter.

The one specific definition in the second section informs us that: 'The percentage of those that are in a higher class than their father gives an indication of upward mobility, known as '*inter-generational upward absolute social mobility*' (Cabinet Office 2008a, 18; original emphasis).

If we ignore the somewhat old-fashioned method of indexing family background in terms of the father's occupation alone (that is, ignoring the effect of the mother), this is the only definition consistent with conventional social science usage. Unfortunately it is not used as a definition elsewhere in the text.

Figure 5.2, directly copied from the document, purports to differentiate between absolute and relative mobility: the former on the left, the latter on the right.

Figure 5.2: Mobility as claimed by the Cabinet Office #1

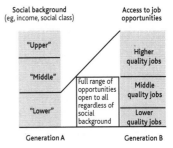

Better jobs: each successive generation gains more and higher quality jobs

Fairer chances: within each generation, everyone is able to realise their potential and access job opportunities

Source: Cabinet Office Strategy Unit (2008a, 13)

However, the left-hand panel shows no movement of *people*, only the *occupational structure* at two points in time, symbolising the growth of better *jobs*. The implication is presumably that the expansion of 'better' jobs means they will automatically be filled by those from below when the proportion of poorer jobs is reduced. This flies in the face of ample evidence – for example, from the Nuffield Mobility Study dataset (Goldthorpe 1987) – that while an expanded middle class has helped some (male) people to be upwardly mobile, it has also helped more sons of the middle class to cling onto the privileges and protection inherited from their parents and so to avoid downward mobility. The new jobs get shared out between people from the two origins.

The right-hand panel of Figure 5.2 claims to show relative mobility as potential individual movements from 'lower' backgrounds on the left to a full range of occupations on the right. The absence of any *comparison of chances* means this does *not* in fact show *relative* mobility as it claims; nor does it cover the full range of movements. If there is any doubt about this, we can compare Figure 5.2 with Figure 5.3.

Figure 5.3: Relative mobility as claimed by the Cabinet Office #2

Another strand in the academic literature measures the relative chances of people who grew up in families in different occupational classes moving to a particular class: 'intergenerational relative class mobility' or 'social fluidity'. This can be thought of as the importance of family background in determining the occupational class of someone later in life.

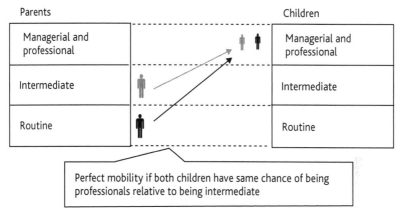

Source: Cabinet Office Strategy Unit (2008a, 25)

Following a recognition of disagreements between economists measuring income mobility and sociologists measuring class mobility and 'social fluidity' (but not reporting the differences of interpretation *among* sociologists about the amount of, and trends in, mobility), this diagram shows relative mobility of two origins and one destination – the basis of the 'disparity ratio' – portrayed by its two arrows (see Appendix). But even here there is further confusion.

Social fluidity is Goldthorpe's term not for comparing movements to *one* destination but rather for summarising movements to *pairs* of destinations, using 'odds ratios' (Goldthorpe 1987, 81–5). Although the boxed comment below the graphic refers to a second destination, it uses the term 'perfect mobility': a different statistical concept that David Glass (1954, 188, 222–3) introduced in the 1949 LSE mobility study. Both figures show one subset of *intergenerational upward absolute mobility* (and upward mobility is only one subset of *all* mobility). Where is the line to show us the *downward* mobility of the children from 'upper' social backgrounds?

The downwardly mobile do make a brief appearance on page 18 of *Getting On, Getting Ahead*, but even this is obfuscated by the statement that immediately follows it: 'Subtracting those that are in a lower class yields a measure of net upward mobility'. This is all the discussion downward mobility gets. Apart from two further passing references, downward mobility appears to remain hidden inside 'net upward mobility', but this specific term seldom reappears. Downward mobility is centrally important because unless new, high-level jobs are created to accommodate all the newly upwardly mobile, the latter will displace some of the children of the higher classes and force them into downward mobility. Admittedly, this new downward mobility will help to increase mobility rates, but as a policy it is not a great vote winner.

Like Labour's White Paper or the Coalition's use of Organisation for Economic Co-operation and Development (OECD) data in *Opening Doors, Breaking Barriers*, the emphasis in *Getting On, Getting Ahead* is on extracts from specific research studies and wider surveys of inequality, which adds to the blurring of the definitional picture. However, these headline accounts of research are not included in the definitional section of the documents; nor are their various specific operationalisations discussed. Not surprisingly in the light of these problems, the account of mobility trends in the document's second section is less than convincing. All three documents confuse evidence about *overall* patterns of mobility with the mobility experience of *subsets* of the population.

The core message in *Getting On, Getting Ahead* is that more (upward) mobility is needed because mobility rates have remained static or declined in recent years. These claims will be reviewed later in more detail; for now, there are three points to make. First, unless there is clarity about what mobility means and how it is measured it is impossible to say whether it is static, declining or increasing. Second, even if we could accept the garbled account in the document, none of the original research studies quoted on pages 26–7 (Goldthorpe 1987; Goldthorpe and Mills 2008; Heath and Payne, 1999;) define mobility in the same way as *Getting On, Getting Ahead,* so calling on the findings of these three studies is an abuse of the evidence. Third, the choice of studies is highly selective; there is no consideration of alternative findings, which show that mobility rates have increased for at least part of the time (for example, Lambert et al 2007). Padding out the coverage with charts showing aspects of occupational change or wider social inequalities does not directly address mobility and demonstrates a crude overreliance on projections of occupational change as a driver.

The Aldridge Reports

This superficial treatment is not inevitable, as one of the earlier sources, 'The Aldridge Report' (Aldridge 2001) shows. The Aldridge Report takes us further back to a seminar organised nearly a decade earlier by the Cabinet Office Strategy Unit and the revised briefing paper that arose from the seminar (Aldridge 2001). The seminar participants included mobility analysts and sociologists who were sufficient well-informed for the definitions in the resultant paper to *all* be based in conventional social science usage, although the large contingent working in the Nuffield paradigm (Savage and Egerton 1997, 645–7) may explain its restricted interpretations of the evidence. The Aldridge Report has been widely referred to in political speeches (along with the work in economics of Blanden, Gregg and Machin et al; Gorard 2008). Although only briefly and directly acknowledged via *Getting On, Getting Ahead*, it seems that the report was a major source of the somewhat negative baseline picture of mobility rates presented in later documents – prior to 2001, no obvious official publications addressed this topic.

Unfortunately, by the time of Aldridge's later contribution – the online *Life Chances and Social Mobility* (Cabinet Office Strategy Unit 2004) – the initial clarity of definitions had decayed, perhaps because the new focus is less on mobility than on life chances; that is, wider social inequalities. Despite having a correct definition of relative mobility, it includes a graphic supposedly to represent relative mobility that in fact shows the percentage of men remaining in the same class as their father by birth cohort, comparing Classes I and II with V–VII (Cabinet Office Strategy Unit 2004, slide 24). This may be a *comparison*, but it is a simple comparison of two *absolute* mobilities – or more strictly, comparative immobilities. These could be *part of a calculation* of relative mobility, but it is not expressed in the required format of relative chances, let alone social fluidity.

The 2004 presentation seems to be the key point at which incorrect definitions first enter the picture, confounding mobility per se with wider questions of social inequality and differential life experiences. Of its substantive slides, 45 address social inequality issues; almost two thirds concern *life chances* rather than social mobility. One slide (number 54) is the only point in the whole official literature in which a cautionary note is sounded about setting too high an expectation of increasing mobility as a cure-all silver bullet for all our social ills.

The Aldridge documents indicate where the mobility debate had reached at particular points in time. Not only are they the specific concrete sources from which later civil servants would (until about 2010) directly copy some of the detailed definitions and content for their subsequent briefing papers, but they also signal an underlying state of awareness of – or general assumptions about – mobility. Documents after the Aldridge reports retained the rhetoric of mobility as a *solution*, but shifted their focus back to the more traditional interests of the various individual state departments. The 2006 briefing from what is now the Department for Education (DfE) concentrated on education to such an extent that, in places, its definitions treat mobility as exclusively meaning enhanced education. The Department of Work and Pensions (DWP) turned to a team of consultant economists, who concentrated their review on income mobility and employment and showed little awareness of the sociological literature (DWP 2007).

This may help to explain the approach of the Cabinet Office Strategy Unit's background discussion in a second *Life Chances* document (2008b; quoted in Cabinet Office 2008a, 79), with its concentration on economic factors. Thus although the Aldridge reports receive relatively few direct mentions in the political parties' 2008–09 policy documents – or even in the two intervening influential publications, *Getting On, Getting Ahead* and the IPPR report – there is sufficient overlap to suggest that their influence may have been diffuse but was nonetheless considerable.

The policy result is that mobility is predominantly seen as a supply-side problem, best addressed by improving the competitive skills of those who are the current losers. Little attention is paid to mobility as a demand-led problem. In other words, it is assumed that occupational niches will be available for the new generation of better-qualified and more aspirational young people. While there is justification for this in the long-term expansion of white-collar employment, this expansion is not predictable, inevitable or a fast and furious social change (chapters Eight and Nine). In the absence of dramatic change in the labour market, openings in the more advantaged classes can only come at the expense of moving some of the current incumbents out into less desirable occupational roles.

None of the documents discussed in this chapter include the problem of downward mobility or the potential new frustrations of a more educated population if lack of economic growth denies them good prospects of employment. Similarly, although the discussions of class differentials in access to HE and the established professions do call for an opening up of opportunity, they do not advocate the abolition of public schools or control over the admission practices of elite universities – both of which lie at the heart of the problem. Nor would the proverbial Martian think that gender, ethnicity, age, disability or regional location make much difference to the life chances of British people. The diversity of the population and their disparate employment prospects receive scant attention. The idea of a complex and segmented labour market, in which a range of discriminatory recruitment practices combine with culturally reproduced variations in types of educational credentials to produce outcomes of marked dissimilarity, is sidelined.

Relying on official documents

While it is reasonable to use the official documents to demonstrate the failings of recent policy debates, they provide a poor guide to a proper understanding of mobility. Exploring the backgrounds of official documents helps to locate the more immediate origins of the mistaken ideas they present and how these sources shared, and contributed to, a very peculiar take on social mobility in Britain. This is to use an explanatory framework based upon very recent, visible and concrete causes, similar to the analysis of political speeches in chapter Four, which not only catalogued two decades of electoral politics but also implicitly suggested that the dynamics of party machinery were a probable cause of the new importance attached to mobility. However, bibliographic analysis can only go so far. Even if the practical limitations of the publications' poor referencing and difficulties accessing the memories of key civil servant and think-tank authors did not prevent a single-track slide into infinite regress in search of ever earlier sources, there are other ways to account for how mobility has come to be seen.

A completely different explanation that might in principle be advanced is that the change in the political agenda is purely *coincidental*. Thus the sudden popularity of mobility would be a random occurrence, requiring no special explanation other than the workings of chance. The conclusion in chapter Three – that 'the growth in coverage and interest in mobility in political speeches is too strong to be ignored as a mere coincidence' – was really a statement about the validity of the growth and its obsessive message of low rates of mobility, rather than a dismissal of the idea that the growth could have happened at the point and in the form in which it did by chance.

On the exact day when this section was first being drafted, mobility coincidentally featured in yet another news story. On Facebook, minutes after the withdraw of Mitt Romney from the race for the Republican presidential nomination, his rival Jeb Bush (the *third* member of the Bush family to run for President – against the 2016 candidature of the *second* member of the Clinton family) wrote: '

> I know that Mitt Romney will never stop advocating for renewal of America's promise through upward mobility ... I

look forward to working with him to ensure all Americans
have a chance to rise up. (Bush 2015)

The fact that his comments were reported in the UK was due to his
political prominence in the USA rather than the significance of social
mobility in this country. The timing was a result of presidential politics
and had absolutely nothing to do with developments in Britain.

The occurrence of random events like this may serve as cautionary
note but does not justify a wholesale non-causal model. The Bush
anecdote earns its place here because it also illustrates how easily
mobility can be incorporated into political philosophies to legitimate
a variety of systems and situations. The 'American way of life' may lack
a sense of irony but it is strong on opportunity as a core legitimation
symbol, which helps to explain why mobility has been part of a long
intellectual history about social and political order. The concept of
social mobility did not spring readymade into being at the turn of
this century.

SIX

Why low, why now?

It is not easy to separate the rise of political interest in mobility from the assumption that mobility rates have been too low. Put simply, the attraction of the latter is that something in society is broken and needs to be fixed. There would have been little mileage in talking about mobility as if there were no problem with mobility rates, whereas the call to increase mobility fitted well with a moderate reforming agenda, typified by Blair's 'education, education, education' refrain. But all of the political parties could invoke mobility – with its party-neutral associations of efficient use of talent, and moral fairness – in their own causes. Thus mobility could be bent to meet party needs, whether expressing Labour ideals of equality or Tory values of individual achievement or economic efficiency. Mobility could mean all things to all men (or women).

From the politicians' point of view, mobility offered two somewhat more cynical attractions. It provided a stick with which all parties could beat their opponents over their failure to promote mobility; a stick that could be wielded (by all parties) without having to go into technical details because the widespread, common-sense public perceptions were sufficient basis for generalisations and unfounded claims. For example, in reply to a question that implied social mobility rates were low, the Leader of the Liberal Democrats attacked Labour's assumption 'that people's life chances are blighted at birth. That is why I am so proud that this coalition Government – across the coalition – have dedicated so much time and resources in rectifying the mistakes of the previous Labour Government' (Clegg 2014) and subsequently offered a list of Coalition measures that would increase opportunities of social mobility.

Second, policies aimed at changing mobility rates – such as improving early childhood conditions, better educational access or even recruitment to the professions – all take a whole generation to bear fruit. By that time, the churn of ministerial appointments – the average tenure of office is down to 1.3 years (Cleary and Reeves 2009) – means that ministers will be long gone and therefore not answerable for their actions. Mobility was therefore a pretty safe card to play.

It also resonated with the life experiences of leading political figures. Older ministers and civil servants had lived through the 1960s and 1970s, experiencing first hand the social changes of that era. This not only provided ammunition for nostalgia for lost youth but also provided a heightened awareness that society had changed, even if making sense of those changes was difficult. The idea of a previous golden age of greater mobility was attractive (for example, Alex Salmon on BBC Scotland News 2011; see Black 2011), especially when major mobility studies could be read as currently emphasising a lack of mobility (chapter Seven). Admittedly these latter contributions were not widely known in detail, but they had filtered into the social and political networks of Whitehall, Oxford and LSE. A belief in low rates of social mobility was not entirely unreasonable.

The political usefulness of 'low mobility' to New Labour

More specific events within the party structures brought mobility to the fore. The historical decay of the industrial working class and consequent withering of Labour's traditional support led to the decay of its local party organisation. This opened the way for left-wing entryism and a crisis of conflict between Trotskyist militants, the party establishment and its 'modernising' wing. The capture of the party machinery by the latter in the form of New Labour created a problem for party ideology. The new party leadership did not wish to be seen as representing the trade unions or advocating its Clause Four aim of securing:

> for the workers by hand or by brain the full fruits of their industry and the most equitable distribution thereof that may be possible upon the basis of the common ownership of the means of production, distribution and exchange, and the best obtainable system of popular administration and control of each industry or service.

A new statement of intent and focus for action was needed.

Labour's five pledges in 1997 on education; employment; public spending, health and crime were one attempt to fill this gap (and of course to get elected to government). The rhetoric of social exclusion and joined-up government was another. Equalising opportunity and utilising all the talents of all the people contributed towards constructing a new ideological package, with the intention of attracting electoral support in the southeast of England. It also suited the New Labour leadership itself, increasingly drawn not from the traditional manual working class but from well-off middle-class homes and having less principled attachment to the old goals of equality and solidarity.

In short, Tony Blair's advocacy of social mobility can be seen as a direct response to Labour's internal feuding and collapse of the party's former role as a Left-of-centre party. The burst of mobility talk before the 2005 General Election probably indicated an expedient road testing of a possible 'Big Idea' for the upcoming election campaign. Ministers joined in this mobility shotgun approach to social dysfunction, using it as a convenient way of expressing concern, trailing the hope of amelioration and seeking 'core Labour values' around which interest groups on the centre-Left could coalesce.

Some versions of New Labour's view of mobility acknowledged an element of uncertainty about low rates of mobility and how they could be changed. James Purnell (2007) defended the government's track record with the argument that evaluating social mobility takes a generation. According to this minister – a *Labour* minister! – the blame for any contemporary problems explicitly lay with the Wilson or Callaghan governments. The then General Secretary of the Fabian Society dismissed claims of lower mobility rates by arguing that:

> there is no hard evidence either way. ... As Tony Giddens has said, 'it takes a minimum of 30 years to measure how socially mobile someone is, because we are comparing the jobs people are in today with those of their parents'. ... Try telling the newspaper editor needing to sum it up in a headline tomorrow that she will have to wait 30 years to report the facts on social mobility. (Katwala 2007)

In Ed Miliband's words, while he was a minister in the Brown administration:

> With the best will in the world, and the best strategy for lifelong learning in the world, it's hard for us to make a big difference to the social mobility of people who turned 27 when we came to power. ... This is the consensus I would like to see *in ten years' time:* a belief in social mobility that is strong enough to give children and parents the support they need. (Miliband 2008; emphasis added)

A similar future orientation came from Gordon Brown's (2008b) long-term focus: 'the years ahead ... a platform for a new era ... prospects for the future'. There is an attraction in drawing attention to contemporary mobility rates; present politicians are excused culpability for past errors and their own efforts can escape scrutiny until another generation has passed. The combination of idealism and cynical non-accountability in this future orientation, together with the potential electoral mileage from talking about low or falling rates, goes a long way towards explaining the popularity of social mobility as a political construct.

The political utility of 'low mobility' for opposition parties

Labour were not the only ones to play the mobility card, although they got into the game earlier and with more enthusiasm. The Conservatives' traditional One Nation 'squirearchy', who had run the local parties on the basis of inherited status combined with a sense of civic duty, lost ground to a younger generation of urban businessmen (and it was overwhelmingly men) – not least from the financial services: a new breed who defined themselves of self-made men and who embraced 'Thatcherism'. For many in both opposition and government, upward mobility was a good thing: it gratifyingly explained their own personal achievements (that is, those perceived as entirely due to their own hard work and abilities) and fitted with a masculinist culture of toughness, interpersonal rivalry and survival of the fittest (see Giazitzoglu and Down 2015 on businessmen performing masculinity). It also challenged the entrenched power of the old guard. This struggle continues; see, for example, concerns about the number of Old Etonians in the 2010–15 Coalition Cabinet and the lack of attention paid by the Conservatives to international comparisons of mobility rates, especially with the other countries of the European Union – not least during the EU Referendum campaign.

For the Conservatives in opposition, low social mobility also provided a new stick with which to beat the government. Attacks on poor levels of mobility carried indirect messages about the State's inability to provide solutions, lost grammar schools, frustrations of personal ambition and achievement and middle-class fears that their advantages might not be passed on to the next generation. It bound those who had succeeded through grammar schooling or bought their own council houses more closely to the Conservative Party. Increased mobility promised rewards for effort, a better-skilled work force and the reduction of the welfare costs of supporting an underclass.

The other main opposition party at the time used the Liberal Democrats Commission on Social Mobility to present itself as characteristically radical, demonstrating how both major parties were failing to tackle low mobility rates (Clegg 2008d). The capture of the party by the Right-of-centre 'Orange Book' faction (named after the 2004 book of essays inspired by 19th–century Liberalism) exacerbated the problem, similar to that of New Labour, of needing new legitimation symbols to hold together the party's Liberal and Social Democrat wings. Joining the Conservatives in government policies aimed at shrinking the State, and carrying forward a strong ideological commitment to individualism, the new Liberal Democrat leadership found the crusade against low social mobility every bit as attractive as their new allies in power.

Thus taking a negative view of mobility rates was no accident. It offered political payoff for *all* the parties in the form of a straw figure for counter-arguments and justification of partisan policies. They had vested interests in a pessimistic view of social mobility: the 'bad news is good news' rule extends beyond the media.

The result was confusion between mobility per se and other problems of social inequality and failing policies. For example, educational reform is not necessarily conditional on generating more mobility. Improvements in schooling (and so producing a skilled workforce and informed citizens better equipped for life) are desirable, independent of any reference to social mobility. New Labour linked educational failings to mobility as grounds for new policies, adding a moral justification for more resources from taxation to be directed towards disadvantaged families to create greater 'fairness'. The justification of increasing social mobility worked equally well for the Coalition parties, except that in their case the core purpose of educational reform was to reduce public expenditure and recapture control of the content of schooling.

New challenges, new anxieties

Although the previous section treated Britain's political leaders with some disdain – as self-serving carpetbaggers concerned only with justifying their own position – it has to be acknowledged that they have been faced with other substantial challenges: the consequences of accelerating globalisation, the spread of the 'terrorist threat', the banking crisis and its austerity regime 'solution' and growing inequalities between the very rich and the rest of society. A new and commonly held belief in a lack of social mobility opportunities is part of this mix. On its own it is, of course, an insufficient causal explanation for the contemporary zeitgeist of political discontent – but it is an important ingredient. That the proportion of those aged under 25 who voted in the 2010 General Election dropped to 44% from 76% in the 1960s (and was estimated by the British Election Study to be still less than 60% in 2015) is indicative of disillusionment with what 'life has to offer' the younger generation.

But it is not just the young who have begun to think of social mobility in a more general sense of hardships and handicaps. Many previously well-established citizens now *feel* less secure in their jobs and prospects, poorer than they were formerly, underachieving in their lives and thereby dishonoured by their failure to display the expected consumption and status behaviour normally associated with their station in society. So far, and for the most part, their disenchantment has been a muted one. On the other hand, those who are genuinely poorly paid or not on full-time contracts are cut off from the social and cultural rights enjoyed by the rest of society, with no sense of future opportunity. Their reaction has been more visible.

For illustrative convenience, if not for precision until later discussion, these two groups of people might be flagged as the 'squeezed middle' (the Oxford Dictionary's Word of the Year: Dent 2011) and the 'precariat' identified by Standing (2011). However, neither of these labels is entirely satisfactory. The idea of the squeezed middle classes, popularised in the early years of this century by the Democratic Party in the United States and taken up by Ed Miliband, has been applied to too many different groups to be deployed in serious research (see Lansley 2013). While not denying that the middle classes have problems or that many have a sense of failing to make progress (a kind of social immobility?), their situation would require further specification before it could be properly connected to social mobility. The idea of a precariat, however potentially useful, has been undermined by critics particularly on the Left who have rejected Standing's treatment of the precariat as a global *social class* (for example, Bremen 2013). Questions have also been raised about how far 'precarity' is reaching up the social ladder in the UK (Seymour 2012).

Although the internal power struggles of the political parties came to prominence in the 1980s and the resultant mobility policies date from the 1990s, the continuing relevance of mobility has been fuelled by these disaffected groups of electors. Recent policy proposals suggest particular concern over social cohesion and electoral swings, as well as new worries about security and potential terrorism among 'closed' Muslim communities and the threat to working-class families of 'immigration'. A key point in chapter Three was that underlying the vague calls for *general* mobility was a real but poorly articulated and under-evidenced concern about the least mobile groups at the bottom of the social scale.

While some of the politicians' concern for the latter was an expression of empathetic moral outrage that fellow human beings can be so isolated in deprivation, a second strand of concern has been a growing anxiety about the social unrest and potential political opposition that could come from 'the excluded' (perhaps a better term than 'precariat'). This is not to attribute all social unrest or electoral disaffection to a lack of social mobility, or to assert that immobility is the sole cause. As data presented in chapter Nine will show, there was indeed a problem 'at the bottom', manifesting in new challenges to the established political order through the rise of radical minority political parties, urban unrest and disaffection with the political elite. Support for Brexit comes disproportionately from disadvantaged areas of Britain, except for Scotland where opposition to the political elite in London is expressed through nationalism.Under New Labour, ministers extolled the virtues of upward mobility but warned of the potential growth of a new 'underclass' due to insufficient mobility. David Blunkett (2008: 14) cautioned about an emerging underclass because '2.5% of every generation seem to be stuck in a life cycle of disadvantage'. Alan Milburn had earlier reiterated one of the political class's traditional fears about what happens in a society with too little upward mobility:

> Families and sometimes whole communities permanently separated from mainstream society. A drug culture paid for by crime. Young men waging a war on their own neighbourhoods. Families living off the black economy. Too many people living a life of little hope and no ambition ... social resentment festers and grows. (Milburn 2004)

New Labour's 'underclass anxiety' has been expressed as a fear both for and of those excluded or isolated from mainstream society.

An immobile 'underclass'?

This strand of thinking about mobility, echoed by the other mainstream political parties, has a long pedigree stretching back to Marx and other early writers. Upward mobility – or a belief that a lot of *merited* upward mobility happens – supports the notion that society is run fairly and efficiently. Social systems ensure deserved success is rewarded, while the disadvantages of those at the bottom of the scale are justified. This view incorporates meritocracy – increasingly seen as merit evidenced by educational qualifications – but extends to a more general sense that people's social positions truly reflect their all-round worthiness. Upward mobility can also be seen as a way of removing potential leaders from the lower class and making them trusted members of the middle and ruling classes. An immobile lower class that still contained dissatisfied people of ability would otherwise be a greater source of disorder.

This disquiet coexists with a more high-minded moral sensitivity to the plight of one's fellow human beings. The political response, in the form of mobility policy proposals for ameliorating the circumstances of the disadvantaged, is therefore measures to allow the immobile to improve their lot and qualify for greater upward mobility. A more sceptical interpretation might be the wish to cut welfare budgets by bringing a growing and potentially 'dangerous underclass' (MacDonald 1997, 186) into employment. Amelioration would reduce the chances of civil unrest and stem the loss of mainstream votes to UKIP, the British Nationalist Party (BNP) and the English Defence League (EDL) should the underprivileged continue to embrace parties of the radical Right that are not part of the established order.

The idea of an emerging British underclass draws heavily on US debates over the poverty and IQ of minority ethnic groups (for example, Gans 1990; Herrnstein and Murray 1994; Wilson 1987). Whereas Blunkett and Milburn were sympathetic with those trapped on sink estates and isolated from mainstream society through little fault of their own, Herrnstein and Murray (1994) initially argued that a new underclass in the US (and by extension in other industrialised societies) consisted of those with low intelligence. They denied this underclass was due to social processes or racial discrimination. Rather than social problems producing low educational performance and test scores, social problems are seen as attributable to low intelligence. Critics were quick to point out that lower IQ scores among minority ethnic groups in fact took the authors' argument into the realms of racial superiority: it is no coincidence that the opening of *The Bell Curve* harks back to the pseudoscientific eugenics of a century ago (Herrnstein and Murray 1994; Iganski et al 1994).

UK sociology in the 1990s gave the idea of an underclass a predominantly negative reception – due mainly to its inadequate explanatory framework, but also to Britain's different cultural history and the boundaries and actual composition of the British lower classes (for example, Alcock 1997; Gallie 1994; Hall 2003; Heath 1992; Lister 1996; Moore 1993; Morris 1994; Murray 1990). Nonetheless, shorn of its racist and genetic assumptions, the term continues to provide a convenient – if far from perfect – shorthand when referring to the people who are most excluded from more desirable and conventional lifestyles and have least chance of upward mobility. It will therefore be used in this modified way in this chapter, but it must be stressed that *this does not imply that any of the members of such a class are inferior human beings.*

Milburn and Blunkett have been right to draw attention to an emerging sector of families that is doubly disadvantaged – not only the losers in a society marked by extensive and growing systemic economic and social inequality, but also facing little prospect that their children will escape the same fate. Some members of this underclass do act in antisocial ways or become the recruits of new extremist political parties. This is not to say that they are self-aware and hold up social mobility as an active and explicit grievance. Rather, their conditions – partly caused by immobility – make them more open to alternative forms of political action. The underclass has the potential to threaten political stability through activities like rioting or voting for extremist parties, or embracing radical and unworkable solutions such as Brexit. This uncomfortable fact goes some way towards explaining why the politicisation of social mobility has focused much of its energies on the supposed immobility of the underclass, particularly in the last few years.

Exclusion and riots

An excluded underclass, which by definition is not *incorporated* into mainstream society, is not only unfairly treated by contemporary mobility regimes but also not fully involved with the rest of society. People in the underclass are believed to be less likely to share dominant cultural values (having little respect for the mainstream's authority figures) and to have less interest in deferred gratification or planning. This view sits uneasily with urban riots, in which damage to other people's property is combined with a significant element of theft of consumer goods made desirable by a society-wide culture of consumerism. These thefts show that consumerist values are shared, albeit with alternative means of acquisition.

The main participants in the urban riots – which started in Tottenham and rapidly spread to other parts of London and other major UK cities in August 2011 – were taken to be Black adolescents and young adults, many of whom were unemployed or working in menial jobs, much like their parents. In other words, they were second- (or possibly third-) generation working-class families, immobile at the bottom of the social scale. Video footage shows the disturbances initially consisted of young males torching several cars and a bus, attacking and taunting an unprepared police force, breaking into shops and setting fire to a number of buildings. They also smashed cameras used by journalists covering the story.

The rioters were later joined by older men, and young women and children acting mainly as spectators, with rioters turning increasingly over the next few days from damaging parked cars and arson to the widespread theft of desirable goods: trainers, mobile phones, televisions and audio equipment, fashionable 'branded' clothing, and alcoholic drinks, i.e. the items held up by consumer society as most desirable to young people. The Mayor of London later condemned the rioters' 'extreme sense of entitlement' (in *The Guardian* and LSE 2011). Damage was extensive, with a number of homes above shops destroyed by fire, attacks on pubs and clubs, muggings, several deaths and many injuries.

Although the English (especially Londoners) have a history of mob violence (Hernon 2006; Hibbert 2004; see also Collins 2004 on Millwall football supporters), a new feature of the 2011 events was said to be the ability of rioters (who actually were only a few hundred people in each city) to communicate and plan actions via mobile phones, enabling them rapidly to assemble, disperse and reassemble in new districts faster than the police could organise their countermeasures. The underclass disobligingly declined to stay on their social housing estates and – rather than organising pre-notified and officially approved marches or demonstration in one location, or quietly supporting extremist but minority political parties – expressed their frustrations through property damage, theft and the great excitement of rioting on the streets and confronting the police (see Gorringe and Rosie, 2011; Grover 2011; Murji and Neal 2011; Roberts 2011; Solomos 2011). The backlash provoked by the rioting can be gauged from what is usually regarded as an unreliable source: the Wikipedia (2012) entry for '2011 England Riots' makes chilling reading, with its 300 references to contemporary political and media reactions.

In this moral panic, which included leading members of the ruling parties eventually having to return from their long holidays and the reconvening of Parliament, a public relations contest developed to 'explain' the riots. Not only the media but 'water-cooler talk' shifted blame between the Coalition Government for having abolished funding for youth work programmes, youth employment schemes and continuing education; the Labour Government for being too soft to have 'done something about it'; 'society' for ignoring the plight of young people; parents not bringing up their children properly; 'the liberal intelligentsia' and their 'sociological justifications' (Boris Johnson quoted in Milne (2012, 221)); the police (for not being able to shoot the rioters); the 'Black community' (for being Black), Polish workers (for being in Britain) and a lack of employment opportunity and upward social mobility (RCVP 2012). There was remarkably little memory of the riots of the 1980s (see Benyon and Solomos 1987; Solomos 2003). A widespread consensus among non-rioters emphasised the *criminality* of the riots rather than attempting any explanation (Cooper 2012).

Early reactions outside of academia expressed almost universal anger, fear and bewilderment (*The Guardian*/LSE 2011). The intensity of these feelings illustrates the significant role that a supposed underclass of immobile and excluded families can play. Such an underclass ceases to be an abstract bogeyman and becomes a force of considerable power, even if those involved in the riots were a tiny minority. The retribution and repression were responses to the underlying crisis that rioters created, showing they could challenge the established order. If the rioters were part of an underclass that had grown to the point at which it could break out in this way, it posed a deeply serious threat. When the threat is connected to the *immobility* of an underclass, then social mobility assumes a new importance.

It was only later that a more considered concern about a lack of occupational opportunities and alienation from mainstream society began to emerge in media accounts. This is not to claim that more upward mobility – or 'opportunities' – would actually provide a complete solution to civil disorder (any more than will Boris Johnson's (then London Mayor) rushed and expensive purchase of some elderly water cannons that nobody else wanted and that were not even licensed for use in Britain). However, the 2011 urban riots do serve to demonstrate that social mobility is not just a matter of arcane political philosophy or vague underclass anxiety, but rather has sharp contemporary relevance.

Voting instead of violence: Scottish separatism

Within a couple of years of the urban riots a new threat to the political order emerged in the form of highly visible support for alternative 'third parties': the Scottish Nationalist Party (SNP) and their fellow travellers, and the United Kingdom Independence Party (UKIP). Both parties challenged the very foundation of British society with new visions of citizenship, borders, legal frameworks and economic systems. During 2013–14, both parties' political campaigns fed (and fed off) public disillusionment with and alienation from the 'Whitehall elite'. While of course there are various motives for supporting nationalist parties, one reason they resonated with voters was their perception of a general lack of opportunity and social mobility, combined with a more specific view that 'elites' – with their family backgrounds and immobility at the top – were different from ordinary people.

Unlike the supposed underclass, supporters of the two independence parties came from all social classes and several different types of voter. In Scotland, the separatist movement received strong backing from the Scottish 'cultural community' of disillusioned middle-class Scots in the arts and media, from public sector workers stigmatised by English Conservatives and Liberal Democrats and from sectors of the local business community whose profits did not depend on Anglo–Scottish communications or English markets. But the campaign also engaged with many Scots more typical of an underclass, who had not voted before and indeed were previously not registered to vote. Some of this support carried over into the 2015 General Election, in which the SNP's electoral triumph was based on a turnout of over 71% (compared with less than 66% in England and Wales).

The registered electorate of 4,285,323 for the Scottish Independence referendum – 97% of the estimated eligible population (Queiro and Eardley 2014; ScotlandGov 2014) – was an increase of 8% on the electoral roll for the 2010 General Election (Rallings and Thrasher 2010). The 8% or 312,748 *exclude* the 109,533 16- and 17-year-olds enfranchised for the first time but not necessarily all registered or voting (Barford 2014). Turnout among this enlarged electorate rose from 63.8% to 84.6%. Even if we disregard the 16- and 17-year-olds we can see that, compared with the 2010 General Election, the combination of increased registration with higher turnout of eligible voters resulted in well over *1 million* more people – or about one quarter of the voting-age population of Scotland – becoming politically active to the extent of going to the polls.

There are two distinct issues here. First, for such a major increase in political activity to occur the extra voters must include substantial members of a proto-underclass, because it is they who – almost by definition – previously felt excluded from political influence to the extent that they were unlikely even to register to vote. Second, simple arithmetic suggests that many of the new 18+ voters must have included the socially immobile in the working class, although perhaps not to the extent represented in media concentration on vox-pop interviews from the notoriously deprived estate of Paisley's Ferguslie Park. Where else were the previous non-voters hiding? This point is not dependent on how the extra voters actually voted in the Scottish Independence referendum (or in the 2015 General Election, which is a secondary issue).

Although there is still some uncertainty about what proportion of these new voters wanted a separate Scottish state (Curtice 2014; Davidson 2014), it seems probable they tended to favour separatism. Even if the extra '1 million+' split along overall lines (55.3% 'No' and 44.7% 'Yes'), this still leaves about half a million people expressing discontent with the political status quo. There is a strong ecological association between non-registration and unemployment, social housing and deprivation. Areas characterised by the latter disadvantages returned a much higher 'Yes' vote.

The National Statistics Multiple Deprivation Index (2012) shows Dundee, Glasgow, North Lanarkshire and West Dunbartonshire – the only four areas with majorities in favour of separation – all had substantially more unemployment and families on low incomes than the Scottish average. Although there is not a perfect correlation between deprivation (and implied immobility) and support for separatism – West Dunbartonshire, for example, is slightly less educationally deprived than the other three and closer to other west of Scotland rust-bucket areas – a commentary on the Scottish Index of Multiple Deprivation two years ahead of the Independence referendum had observed that:

> Glasgow's local share of the 5% most education deprived datazones is almost a fifth (19.3%). The next highest local share belongs to North Lanarkshire, at 8.6%. Meanwhile, around 45% of Glasgow's datazones are in the 20% most education deprived with the next largest proportion in Dundee City (37.4%). (National Statistics 2012, tables 2.17 and 2.18)

The separatist movement was, of course, fuelled by many factors – not least nationalism – and these data are insufficient evidence to be absolutely certain that a large share of Scottish disaffection can be attributed to a lack of social mobility. However, the evidence is compatible with such an interpretation. Without qualifications or jobs, the prospects of upward mobility are bleak. When there is little hope of improvement under the established order, even for one's children, radical solutions like nationalism are likely to appear more attractive – even if these are channelled through 'constitutional' means rather than by taking to the streets. The structural social disadvantage of the socially immobile, which also helps to explain their rejection of austerity policies and 'the Whitehall elite', was lost in the noise of campaigning and media commentary. There are strong similarities in the Brexit campaign and its aftermath: the Remainers seriously misjudged the resentful mood of the nation, to the extent that Cameron had made no plans in case the outcome would require the fundamental constitutional and economic changes involved in leaving the EU.

Voting without violence: England

There are similarities with UKIP, where again we find more than one kind of supporter and therefore no simple profile of 'the typical voter'. Ford and Goodwin (2014a) argue that, whatever UKIP's origins as a splinter Conservative Party movement drawing on the relatively affluent suburban middle class, a new core loyalist grouping comes from the working class:

> It is the 'left behind', whose prospects for employment and social mobility have been receding for decades, who now find that their values and priorities are being pushed to the margins of debate. These voters have particularly distinct views on UKIP's radical right platform: on Europe, national identity, immigration and their views toward our politics. (Ford and Goodwin 2014).

Using YouGov polling data on voting intentions from February 2013, Kellner (2013) reported that about a third had no educational qualifications and 'just 13% of UKIP supporters have university degrees – half the national average' (Kellner 2013).

More than three quarters of UKIP supporters lived in households earning less than the 2011 national average of £40,000 a year. UKIP appealed to older, working-class former Tories, especially those who left school at 15 or 16 and earn less than £20,000 (Kellner 2014). Kellner's voter profile includes all types of UKIP supporters, not only those who would qualify for the underclass, thereby partly hiding the underclass element lacking the qualifications to achieve upward social mobility. They 'are a strongly motivated electorate; so angry and fed up that they are willing to back an untested radical alternative' (Ford and Goodwin 2014a; see also Ford and Goodwin 2014b), resenting the successes of the more cosmopolitan population. Such UKIP voters stand to lose most as a result of an increase in numbers of immigrant workers prepared to work in low-status, poorly paid jobs. This suggests that poor prospects of upward mobility for those 'left behind' is fuelling the rise of a movement that echoes the BNP and increasingly resembles the 'radical Right' ultra-nationalist parties of continental Europe; for example, the Dutch Party for Freedom, the Danish People's Party, the Austrian Freedom Party and the True Finns (Ford et al 2011). These recent developments give a fresh twist to earlier (and perhaps more abstract) concerns about social order. Not everything can be attributed to a lack of mobility opportunities in certain parts of British society; however, the urban riots, nationalist movements and the rise of radical Right parties' voting power (drawing substantially on the politically disaffected socially immobile) render the underclass into a more concrete and immediate form. The rise of nationalism in Scotland broke the Labour Party; English nationalism pushed the Conservatives (and the rest of us after the Brexit vote) into confronting the exit from the European Union. The considerable consequence for Britain has given politicians increased underclass anxiety and its knock-on effect of prioritising more upward mobility.

SEVEN

The pessimism of earlier academic mobility analysis

In previous chapters, politicians and the media were taken to task for misrepresenting the amounts of, and reasons for, mobility in Britain. The implication was that all specialist research studies by academic sociologists offered a better guide and that no blame could be laid at their door. While it is true that serious sociological research offers a more systematic and evidenced approach, it too has inadvertently contributed to an unduly narrow and negative impression that very little mobility has been taking place and that mobility rates have not improved. Problems have arisen from overreliance on research *techniques* now seen as questionable and the interpretation of the evidence from particular *perspectives*. These studies had little direct impact on the public consciousness, but when political commentators did seek empirical data and research-based judgements (as for the Aldridge Report) the apparent findings of low mobility rates fed into the public domain (for example, the impact of Blanden and colleagues' (2005) work on income mobility). This chapter therefore looks at limitations in three major studies, as exemplars of research on British mobility, to redress the balance of earlier criticism and further display the roots of current thinking. It concludes by also briefly considering geographical mobility and ethnicity, which have previously been largely ignored in mobility analysis – and indeed, which also receive only little discussion in this book due to limited space.

With apologies to the many colleagues who have added significantly to our understanding of social mobility, the three studies to be considered can be said to have dominated the British 'scene': the LSE (or 'David Glass') study in 1949, published in 1954 as *Social Mobility in Britain*; the 1972 Nuffield College survey, mainly first reported in 1980 in Goldthorpe's *Social Mobility and Class Structure in Modern Britain*; and the work of economists Jo Blanden, Paul Gregg, Stephen Machen and colleagues (2001; 2004) in papers on income mobility produced since the turn of the millennium. Each cluster of research included a key publication that was representative of considerable amounts of other research output. What these influential studies have in common is that they all convey an impression that rates of UK social mobility are low.

The LSE study: *Social Mobility in Britain*

Although the earliest British social mobility studies are usually credited to Chapman and Marquis (1912) and Chapman and Abbott (1913), neither actually used the term 'social mobility'. As already observed, it was not until 1949 that the project led by David Glass at LSE, published as *Social Mobility in Britain* in 1954, became the first 'proper' major study of its kind, setting the framework for British mobility analysis and for other European societies. Despite what are now seen as limitations in the Glass class categorisation scheme (the Hall-Jones Scale) compared to more recent schema, as well as its theoretical orientation towards elites in the civil service rather than class mobility and its particular emphasis on the results of post-war reforms in secondary education, the LSE study determined how the next generation of sociologists interpreted mobility – and class structures more generally.

Some of this wide influence was because British sociology was a much smaller profession in the 1950s and 1960s. The intellectual sway of the LSE department (the largest of the then only small number of academic departments) was impressively extensive and remained virtually undisputed until the mid 1970s (Payne, 2014). Former LSE lecturers and postgraduates staffed new sociology departments as they were set up, spreading the message of the low mobility rates found in Glass's classic study at a time when the volume of sociological research was still small.

As a result, in mobility analysis (as in other fields) some findings achieved prominence while others struggled to be heard. Long neglected UK contributions include local studies and work on the professions by Caradog Jones (1934), Carr-Saunders and Wilson (1933) and Lewis and Maud (1949), while early mobility evidence produced by Ginsberg (1929), Saunders (1931) and Benjamin (1958),which differed from the Glass findings, was disregarded. Much of this early tradition, including research by economists, emphasised the occupational dimension of mobility; it is interesting that recent publications by the SMCPC (2015) have echoed their concerns with recruitment to the professions. Despite the rival contributions (see also Bauman 1972), the Glass data and interpretation were adopted into mainstream British sociology – not least because the findings seemed plausible to sociologists, who tended to stand on the political Left.

Without alleging conscious bias or deliberate falsification of data, the LSE study 'found what it was looking for': low levels of mobility into and out of the upper echelons. The goal of the study had been to show the distinctiveness of the senior civil servants as an elite, and the survey data produced by the research justified the researchers' expectations. Their findings, and the way they presented their work, created an *impression* of low mobility rates and a rigid class structure.

It is certainly true the LSE study directly dominated mobility analysis for a generation, both in its methods and findings, and that this contributed to the general belief in low mobility rates. Sociologists (through no fault of the Glass team itself) neglected to carry out much further research on the topic for some time. The LSE data were deployed widely in discussions of social stratification, becoming major planks of British sociological thinking about social class between 1950 and 1980, which incorporated low mobility rates and rigid class boundaries. A typical interpretation was that:

> long distance movement especially – from bottom to top, as well as from top to bottom – is uncommon ... [with] no change of substance in the amount of movement up and down the social scale till about the time of World War II. And there seems now to have been little increase in social circulation after that either. (Westergaard and Resler 1975, 315, 302)

This view was seen as scotching the popular myth of a more open society and confirming 'what every sociologist knows' (Scase 1976, 515); it was widely repeated in the sociological literature and in most introductory sociology textbooks, which first began to be published in the 1970s and 1980s. The textbook 'used in about half the universities in the UK, in many colleges of various kinds, and even – to our surprise – in schools' (Worsley et al 1977, 15) taught the findings of the Glass survey:

> though there is a great deal of mobility, most of it is, in fact, very short range mobility. The myths of 'long distance' mobility – 'from log-cabin to President' – are, overwhelmingly, myths as far as the life chances of the mass of the population are concerned. (Worsley et al 1977, 432)

Very similar statements, placing the emphasis on the limitations of mobility, can be found among leading contributions including Miller (1960, 36–41), Bottomore (1965, 38); Miliband (1969, 34–44), Parkin 1971, 51–6) and Giddens (1973, 107, 181–2). An introduction to social class published as late as the early 1990s continued to state:

> There is a high degree of intergenerational inheritance
> of managerial and professional jobs on the one hand,
> and of manual occupations on the other. If there is any
> intergenerational openness, it is among lower grade
> technical, lesser professional and routine non-manual
> occupations. (Scase 1992, 53)

Although mobility rates are indeed worryingly lower at the top and bottom of the social scale, overstated conclusions such as these sit uncomfortably with research findings since 1980.

The LSE findings of little substantial mobility in fieldwork carried out some 70 years ago provided the basis for more general descriptions of the rigidity of the British class structure in the late 1960s and 1970s. Bottomore (1965) and Miliband (1969) invoked the metaphor of a pyramid, in which upward movement became increasing difficult as one neared the summit. Westergaard and Riesler (1975, 302) suggested the idea of an obstructive 'mobility threshold' between manual and non-manual classes. Parkin offered a more elaborated three-class model, in which an intermediate class acted as a social and cultural 'buffer zone' against direct movements from the working class to the professional and managerial classes and vice versa (1971, 56).

All these models expressed variations of the low mobility findings but neglected to observe the different makeup and sizes of class groupings in the two generations. A consistent finding in mobility research from industrialised countries in the 20th century was that parents' distribution of classes/occupations was dissimilar to those of their children. This 'asymmetry' took the form of a higher proportion of blue-collar and a lower proportion of white-collar classes/ occupations among the origins than in the destinations. There were two main reasons for this asymmetry. First, occupational change – or the 'occupational transition' of industrial society discussed in chapter Eight – gives the younger generation starting new careers more access to the new 'better' white-collar jobs than their parents, who started work in a less white-collar period. Second, a random sample of the younger generation (the sampling method adopted in studies following the LSE survey) contains more children from larger families because they are more likely to be picked than families that have only one child. The former type of family has several chances of being picked – one for each child – whereas the single-child family has only a single chance. Although class differentials in fertility have declined over a long historical period, blue-collar families were still on average larger, and therefore had a higher probability of being selected, which skews the apparent occupational balance in the distribution of origins. More fathers *appear* to be from blue-collar occupations (Allen and Bytheway 1973; Duncan 1966; Noble 1972).

Although the latter effect was subsequently shown to have been a relatively small factor in later studies (Payne 2003), occupational transition and class differentials in fertility together produced the asymmetrical occupational distributions for all industrialised countries – *with the key exception of the LSE study* (Glass 1954, 180–8), in which the distributions were almost exactly symmetrical, but its small asymmetry was in the *reverse direction* from other mobility studies. It is true that the expected asymmetry is apparent if the middle classes as an aggregate are compared to the manual class using Miller's (1960, 71) re-analysis (which splits Class 5 into routine office work and skilled manual trades). However, even then the difference between origins and destination is only three cases out of a total of 3,497.

The LSE study misled a whole generation of mobility and class analysts. The mobility rates reported could only have been true if there had been a *decrease* of 18% in white-collar employment between fathers and sons – but in fact white-collar employment had *increased* by 17%. Put plainly, the LSE data were incompatible with the evidence of occupational transition and differential fertility/sampling: the findings were wrong.

Why did the LSE study get it wrong?

A number of scholars recognised this peculiarity (for example, Hope 1975; Noble 1972; Ridge and Macdonald 1972 and indeed Glass himself (1954, 190–4)); however, they reconciled their doubt by reference to census data (but this confused age cohorts with long-term structural change) or by possible problems in the categories of the Hall-Jones occupational classification scheme. It was not until the mid 1970s that the findings of the LSE study were seriously questioned, both by data emerging from new mobility studies and by closer reanalysis of the LSE findings (for a fuller account see Payne 1987a, 88–117). Glass himself, in a most courteous and supportive personal correspondence with the author in 1977 that was typical of his admirable professional standards (unlike some later mobility analysts), acknowledged that he could find no adequate explanation for his results.

The reason for the misleading findings is intriguing and can now be made public for the first time. In a private conversation in 1978, after the author had raised his own doubts about the credibility of the Glass data, Professor Joe Banks talked about his experiences when he had been one of the 'coders' (data processors) while he was a postgraduate at LSE. He asked that his account be not published until after his death (which occurred in 2005), as it might cause hurt and embarrassment. Joe Banks recalled that the Glass questionnaire collected relatively full information about the respondent's occupation, but less on the father's occupation. This limitation, together with the imprecision of the Hall-Jones scale due to it not covering all occupations, sometimes made coding occupations into social classes difficult, particularly in the case of fathers, and with occupations having ambiguous generic titles like 'engineer' or 'manager'. Coders had to make judgements on insufficient information.

During the coding of the study there was often no senior or supervisor coder in the coders' room. Instead, coders were supposed to request adjudications by telephone from Ruth Glass (David Glass's wife, who also worked on the study). However, Ruth was notoriously short-tempered when interrupted while she was working on other things. So the coders sometimes took their own decisions, looking at the coding for the respondent's class (situated close to the question in the questionnaire about the father's occupation) and using that as a guide to coding the father (and occasionally vice versa). They worked on the assumption of 'what everybody knew' and what the study was expected to show – namely, that there was really little upward social mobility.

Although this was not a regular occurrence, said Joe, it introduced an element of unreliability – particularly in the coding of fathers' occupations. In ambiguous cases, the fathers' class was coded as too similar to their sons. This reduced the observed rate of mobility, not least long-distance mobility. As few as 200 of these miscodes – even in the large sample of 3,497 – would have produced more plausible asymmetrical distributions. The resulting exaggerated message of low mobility and sharp class/status differences became the orthodoxy for later models of class mobility in Britain.

The continued willingness within British academic sociology to accept the Glass findings over the following quarter of a century was unsurprising, given what else was known about social inequality and the stage at which the discipline had then developed. Additionally, British sociology has had limited quantitative expertise and a reluctance to re-examine data, let alone findings that which seem plausible. Saunders (1989, 4–5; 2010, 151) has gone further, controversially attributing the continued acceptance of the low mobility idea to Left-wing bias. His view is that the profession's concern for the underdog led to a lack of critical examination of the data and an unwillingness to consider alternative explanations. While this latter claim is somewhat exaggerated, it is nonetheless true that sociologists writing about class in the 1960s and 1970s were predisposed to accept the Glass results because the findings were compatible with evidence of other social inequalities and the profession's pre-existing view of British society as deeply inequitable.

British sociology is often seen as having characteristically 'Fabian' roots (Holmwood and Scott 2014, 130, 201–2). As noted earlier, the Glass study was certainly supported by the Labour government and while it ranged over a number of issues one of its core motivations was to explore the impact of the post-war welfare reforms. These were the reasons why a mobility study was carried out – or, to use a term from the next significant contribution to mobility analysis, these constituted the 'interest' of the researchers in social mobility.

The Nuffield Mobility Study

Completed in 1972, the second major contribution to mobility research was the large-scale survey of England and Wales by a team at Nuffield College, Oxford: the largest of similar national studies covering Scotland, Ulster and Eire. Initially conceived as 'Glass, one generation on', its results were radically different from its predecessor and it progressively replaced Glass as the key reference point for most subsequent studies of mobility and class until the turn of the century. One of the strengths of the Nuffield project was preliminary work to improve occupational categorisation: the Hope-Goldthorpe Scale (Goldthorpe and Hope 1974). Its ranking of the 'desirability' of occupations contributed to the detailed grouping of occupations within the class framework superimposed by Goldthorpe in his categorical class schema. The main Nuffield study results were published as Halsey et al (1980), which concentrated on educational access as a means of mobility, and Goldthorpe (1980/1987), which addressed class mobility as an end result. The latter publication has a long orienting chapter discussing how mobility had been treated in earlier social and political debates. While:

> there is no *necessary* connection between a research interest in mobility, and any specific ideological attachment ... mobility research is an ideologically loaded area – in the sense that underlying a research interest in it, one must expect there to be also an 'interest' of a different kind, which in some way derives from the researcher's own socio-

political experience, values and commitments. (Goldthorpe
1987, 2; original italics)

The Nuffield interest in this latter sense was twofold. It self-identified as
having an explicitly 'Marxian or least a *marxisant* character' (Goldthorpe
1987, 28; original italics), addressing mobility's implications for class
formation, class relations and class action without commitment to the
historical inevitability of the proletarian revolution. This ideological
stance saw 'a particular pattern of mobility as representing a goal
that is to be pursued – the pattern that would characterise greater
openness' (Goldthorpe 1987, 28). This goal is 'only likely to be brought
about through collective class action on the part of those in inferior
positions' (Goldthorpe 1987, 29). The second, associated interest was
the provision of an empirical description of current rates of mobility,
showing how far British society falls short of openness. Both interests
orient the account of mobility towards stressing that more mobility
is desirable.

This was amplified by the attention paid to relative mobility, despite
absolute mobility (running at over 70% even in 1972) forming 'the
greater part of the analyses' (Goldthorpe 1987, 29) of the study.
Absolute mobility is useful for describing current rates of mobility
and class formation in the 'class demographic' terms of class size,
continuity of membership and de facto movements between classes.
Relative mobility as a comparison with 'some norm or standard'
(Goldthorpe 1987,29) and using techniques then just introduced in
the USA by Hauser et al (1975a; 1975b) was more useful – not only
in demonstrating the gulf between actual mobility and the goal of
genuine equality of outcome for all citizens, but also in elaborating
absolute mobility. However, rather than the 'optimistic' view derived
from high absolute mobility rates, indexes of relative mobility – when
used to show the limitations of absolute mobility and the gulf between
actual mobility and the goal of openness – present a more pessimistic
picture, as explained in the Appendix. Relative mobility, to which
the study would 'give a good deal of attention' (Goldthorpe 1987,
29), given its marxisant orientation, places an emphasis on the need
for greater mobility.

This approach had two accidental and less direct consequences. First,
it added further technicalities to social mobility, already a technically
complex area. This made it harder for non-specialists to follow the
detailed case as presented, probably contributing to the political class's
misunderstandings. But despite the considerable coverage given to
absolute mobility, the comparisons with relative mobility generated

a more subtle shift of emphasis through the exposition's frequent juxtaposition and balancing of the two types of mobility. This rhetorical effect tended to downplay the full extent of the absolute mobility and contributed to the widely received message that rates of mobility needed to be raised.

Nuffield on changing rates of mobility

Goldthorpe's (1987, 327) conclusion is that the goal of openness 'is still far off and, moreover, there is little evidence of progress having been made towards it' due to the 'flexibility and effectiveness with which the more powerful and advantaged groupings in society can use the resources at their disposal to preserve their privileged positions' (1987, 328). The 'strategy of egalitarian reform that was pursued during the post-war period: in effect, that of seeking to attack social inequalities via legislation and administrative measures' (1987, 328) has failed because it tried to work within a political consensus. Without disagreeing that the advantaged classes have considerable capacity to protect their self-interests, the sweeping dismissal of both of policies and changes in mobility rates only makes sense in terms of Goldthorpe's prioritisation of relative mobility. As Saunders (2010,158) has noted, Goldthorpe's key test is the failure to achieve 'any equalisation of relative mobility chances' – that is to say, relative mobility defined in terms of odds ratios and separate from structural change and absolute mobility.

Of course, it is not possible to know if mobility would have been *even lower* in the absence of those policies. However, the study was overambitious about the capacity of the data to sustain analysis of trends over time. The 1972 study provides a weak basis on its own for interpretations of trends because it was carried out at a single point in time. The effects of social change could not be explored as adequately as when there are two or more studies completed at different times.

The way around this problem of having only a single study was to compare older and younger members of the same sample (a method the author has also used in the past (1987b)), but this is an unreliable method. The underlying logic of comparing people of different ages within one sample (or 'pseudo-cohorts') is only valid *other things being equal*. But *ceteris paribus* does not hold true: each pseudo-cohort represents mobility at a given historical phase. Each pseudo-cohort is unique; its mobility destination a product of a three-way interaction:

- its site in history, which is unique to that cohort;
- the stage the cohort has reached in its collective career;

- the evolving changes in the labour market and class system, which simultaneously effect all cohorts, but not in identical ways.

These factors interact, and indeed partially counterbalance each other, so that taking the data from a single survey is a less than optimal method, as Goldthorpe (1987, 69–70, 73–4) acknowledges.

For example, if mobility rates had increased, younger informants should be more mobile, having lived only in the later period of higher mobility rates. The expansion of white-collar work creates better opportunities, especially for younger workers, while older people would have experienced less mobility, having started at a point when rates were lower. Conversely, cohorts follow each other through similar career profiles, so that older workers tend to be more mobile (having had longer to achieve their full *intra*generational mobility) and make more progress in achieving managerial or supervisory roles than younger workers. Even though most manual occupations have a very flat career structure, the two effects tend to cancel each other. Internal comparisons of pseudo-cohorts provide a poor indication of changing mobility rates.

There is the added complication of major historical upheavals: some of the Nuffield sample had the unique experience of having been young men during the Second World War. War service interrupted their early careers and killed many of their counterparts. When the survivors were demobbed, they competed for post-war employment with the flow of younger people who had been too young for military service and whose employment and class position was thus initially rendered 'atypical'. If mobility rates have changed so little, the 'finding' that a major World War did not disrupt them would indeed be a major sociological discovery.

There are no typical or constant historical conditions; each generation has entered work at specific points in world events and economic cycles of boom and bust. In this sense, each cohort is unique. These disruptions sit alongside the slower evolution of labour markets or reforms of the school systems to produce new generations of educated young people to fill highly skilled occupations, as well as the development of cultural attitudes about gender and employment. It follows that claims about a *lack of change* in mobility rates, whether absolute or relative, need to be treated with caution. In much the same way as in the earlier response to the LSE study, little detailed reanalysis of the data behind Goldthorpe's conclusions has taken place (although see Saunders 2010).

There has been further work to investigate changes in mobility routes that goes beyond pseudo-cohorts, in particular Goldthorpe and Jackson (2007), Goldthorpe and Mills (2008) and Bukodi et al (2015). The first (Goldthorpe and Jackson 2007) examined absolute and relative mobility among men and women, comparing those in the National Child Development Study born in 1958 with those in the British Cohort Study born in 1970. The authors report almost no change in mobility rates; just a few percentage points more absolute upward mobility and a few percentage points less downward mobility. Their models, using odds ratios, indicate that openness has remained 'very much the same' (Goldthorpe and Jackson 2007, 539).

The second paper (Goldthorpe and Mills 2008) used more datasets to explore mobility rates between 1972 and 2005, finding slightly less upward mobility for men (but not for women) but overall little change. The authors' conclusion is slightly more nuanced, however. Their evaluation is a cautious one:

> In sum, while there are no strong grounds for regarding Britain today as being a more mobile society than it was in 1970…there are no grounds at all for taking the opposite view. (Goldthorpe and Mills 2008, 94–95)

Whereas they stress that 'there are no grounds at all' for taking the view that mobility rates have fallen, they are more cautious about possible increases in mobility, saying only that 'there are no *strong* grounds for regarding Britain today as being a more mobile society than it was in the 1970s. (emphasis added)

The third study (Bukodi et al 2015), again using longitudinal comparisons, suggests even more change (in line with hints in Heath and Payne's (1999) analysis of the British Election Survey series):

> Among the members of successive cohorts, the experience of absolute upward mobility is becoming less common and that of absolute downward mobility more common; and class-linked inequalities in relative chances of mobility and immobility appear wider than previously thought. (Bukodi et al 2015, 93)

The inclusion of women in later studies has also helped to draw attention to small-scale changes that previously went unperceived, but these newer findings have had little impact on the *idée fixe* of the political class that mobility rates (implicitly meaning *male* mobility rates) are low and declining.

Although these findings are a welcome fit with the author's own position, they should still be interpreted with care. Their relative mobility findings depend on odds ratios, while those using data from the NCDS – widely used in the social sciences in the absence of any alternative – suffer from several limitations, not least a loss of informants over several decades. The comparisons are for people in their early thirties, an age at which many have reached 'occupational maturity'; however, as Bühlmann (2010) has shown for the service class, for some (particularly women) there is more class mobility to come – certainly up to the age of 40 (and perhaps beyond?). Not all occupations have the same career profiles. The idea of occupational and class maturity is underresearched.

The original Nuffield Mobility Study, like its LSE predecessor, made a substantial contribution to the belief that mobility rates were low and not improving. As noted in chapter Five, the influential Aldridge Seminar for the Cabinet Office in 2001 was dominated by contributors from the Nuffield school. It is of course a delicious irony that these influential contributions come from Nuffield College – the centre of mobility analysis in Britain – at Oxford University – the bastion of protected privilege (chapter Eleven).

The economists' income mobility

The third prominent contribution, Blanden et al's (2005) *Intergenerational Mobility in Europe and North America*, stands out among a cluster of allied articles produced by that research team over several years. Unlike its two predecessors, its income mobility dataset has been subsequently reanalysed and comes from a team less explicit about its 'interests'. However, here the mobility addressed is *income* mobility. The other two contributions described class mobility rates as probably stable, but this more recent research asserts that income mobility in declining:

> Intergenerational income mobility and intergenerational class mobility are of course different phenomena, and there is no *a priori* reason why they should change in tandem. ... None the less, the question of why the one should appear to be declining while the other does not is of evident interest – not only in regard to current political debates. (Erikson and Goldthorpe 2010, 211)

Much of the disagreement between the studies, and other studies, comes down to issues about the available data. Missing data led to Blanden et al (2005) excluding 'income data provided by small proprietors and the self-employed as being too unreliable to use' (Goldthorpe 2012, 4). The economists also missed the significance for earnings of national and historical variations in demography and cultural change that has seen more families in the second generation dependent on *both* adult partners, with more women continuing in paid employment after entering into marriage or a partner relationship. This did not prevent rapid and extensive take-up of the findings about a lack of *income* mobility and its conversion into factoids about *social* mobility more generally.

Income mobility results not only received extensive media coverage, thanks to promotion by both LSE and the Sutton Trust (see chapter Three), but also had 'a remarkable impact, becoming the empirical basis for the view that levels of social mobility have fallen to a disturbing degree' (Goldthorpe 2012, 2). For non-specialists, Blanden et al (2005) confirmed the impression from the Glass and Nuffield studies of no improvement in (class) mobility rates. Blanden et al's paper has been the most widely quoted (or misquoted) research source in the documents and speeches reviewed in chapters Three and Four. As Gorard (2008, 318) notes in an excellent critique, their interpretation of income mobility found its way into 'a UNICEF report, is explicitly channelled by the Institute for Public Policy Research, the Social Market Foundation and other think tanks, and is now accepted as fact by many social and media commentators'.

Although unreferenced, David Cameron's 2015 Conservative Party Conference statement – 'Britain has the lowest social mobility in the developed world. Here, the salary you earn is more linked to what your father got paid than in any other major country' – seems to draw on this one piece of research, a source identified and dismissed by even the Right-wing Institute of Economic Affairs (IEA) (IEA 2015).

The now widely believed claim that mobility rates have fallen, and that Britain has lower mobility rates than comparable nations, is largely based on data from Blanden et al (2005) showing closer association of income levels between parents and their sons in more recent years than for those born in 1958. Whereas the authors start by talking about intergenerational mobility of parents and children, this quickly morphs into income differences between generations. The data for men in their early thirties compare two datasets from the National Child Development Study (which we have already observed has some limitations) and the British Cohort Study (1970). To take those born in one week in a single year (April 1958) is to rely on a very small slice of this complexity whose experience in the labour market is not necessarily representative of 1958 births, let alone the period around that time.

Longitudinal studies suffer from loss of contact with their original birth cohorts, a problem that grows worse the older the study. People die, emigrate, refuse to continue or simply disappear. Gorard (2008, 319) reports that 20% of the 1970 sample has already gone missing. Similarly, 48% of the NCDS cases were non-contactable by 2004. It is not possible to know how 'the missing' differ from 'the survivors'. Even if they can be shown to be similar on some social characteristics, or the survivors can be weighted up (for example, Carpenter and Plewis 2011), this does not mean they are identical on every variable or that the adjusted data meet the conditions of a proper random sample. This has repercussions for any statistical technique based on the assumption of a random sample: the economists' data are no longer random, so any invocation of support from significance tests is unreliable.

But instead, the economists selected only 2,000 sons from each study. Gorard (2008, 320) suggests this reduced the proportion of the original informants to 13% of the NCDS and 12% of the BCS, equivalent to an attrition rate of 87%–88%. The BCS has data on family earnings – parents' combined incomes – whereas an equivalent indicator for the NCDS had to be constructed from separate measurements of fathers', mothers' and 'other' income. An analysis of the full 1958 data, including daughters, found that when alternative measurements of income were deployed a wide range of coefficient values was generated (Hobcraft 2001). This is evidence of the sensitivity of measurement construction, indicating that the Blanden et al results are highly definition-dependent.

Blanden et al's case that income mobility has fallen is based on the calculation of partial correlations between the two generations: 0.17 for the 1958 cohort and 0.28 for the 1970 cohort; neither particularly large. While this does suggest (subject to the data quality constraints already mentioned) that parents' and sons' incomes are a little more similar in the later study, the question remains whether this small difference justifies the conclusions or the faith subsequently shown in them by policy makers and commentators. Nor is it absolutely clear that Britain has less income mobility than comparable countries. Blanden et al's comparison uses the 1970 figure (actually 0.27, rather than the 0.28 stated) because the average parental income data are better. But had they chosen the 1958 cohort's figure, which would not have been incompatible with the timing of most of the other countries' data, the lower figure of 0.17 would have placed Britain much closer to the European average.

The comparison is further weakened by variation in national career spans. Gorard (2008, 322) points out that, 'In Norway, the sons were measured at age 34 or 41, and so were an average of eight years older than their British counterparts', with the age gaps for Denmark, Sweden and Finland also greater than in Britain. If the amount of mobility is related to the length of time the men have had to become intragenerationally mobile, then the apparent greater mobility in the Scandinavian countries may be explained away by the age of the informants and their greater career progression rather than differences in national mobility regimes. We might add that, applying this insight, a ranking of the countries by sons' ages in the samples accurately predicts national income mobility rank order for six of the eight nations. The complexity of handling eight different welfare state systems over several different time periods, in addition to changing demographic factors, means that comparing income mobility between countries becomes a major (and possibly unmanageable) enterprise.

A final observation on income mobility is that even if all of the technical issues could be explained away and we were to trust the data despite all the previous objections, the conclusion drawn by Blanden et al (2005) is unnecessarily pessimistic:

> In both cohorts around 17% of those born to the poorest 25% of families end up in the richest quadrant, and *vice versa*. If there were no financial inheritance, no inheritance of talent, no nepotism, and *perfect* social mobility, then the maximum this figure could be is 25%. (Gorard 2008, 323; emphasis in original)

As Gorard (2008, 323) observes, these (albeit unreliable) figures show very high rates of intergenerational movement; indeed, that 'Britain has a quite staggering level of social mobility'.

These three major studies cannot perfectly represent the extensive mainstream literature. Nonetheless, their influence justifies their use here to demonstrate that the core message of academic sociological research has been one of low general mobility rates that need increasing. This is a one-sided view of the real mobility taking place. Contemporary mobility combines high overall mobility rates (once downward mobility is included) with pockets of undesirably high immobility.

The authors of the three studies cannot be held responsible for politicians' subsequent misrepresentations – but they are accountable for their 'interests', any technical failings of analysis and the way they presented their interpretations. It would therefore be wrong to lay all the blame for recent and current misunderstandings of mobility on the politicians. However, these key studies also helped to define which dimensions of mobility would come to the fore and which would receive less attention.

The limitations of conventional mobility analysis

Perhaps the most obvious gap is the absence of a spatial dimension. In most mobility analysis the prime interest has been the national picture, but of course this is made up of a series of more *local labour markets* in which local class competition takes place. Localised opportunity structures are clearly visible in Table 7.1, which illustrates the differences in employment and class outcomes among residents. If there is a smaller middle class to move into, mobility possibilities are limited.

Table 7.1: Variations in labour markets: usual residents, 16-74 SeC Classes*

SeC Classes	England (%)	South East (%)	North East (%)	Middlesbrough
1 & 2	36.7	40.9	30.6	26.3
3 & 4	26.0	27.1	23.5	21.8
5, 6 & 7	37.3	32.0	45.9	51.9

Note: *% excluding 'never worked and long-term unemployed'
Source: 2011 Census, Table KS611UK

Given that a basic infrastructure is common to all areas, these variations are indicative of distinctive regional economic histories and class cultures. For example, mobility in Scotland, although broadly similar to England and Wales *in shape*, has lower rates of upward mobility, reflecting its characteristic historical dependence on heavy industry and state employment (Payne 1987b). Of course, residents move between areas, either commuting to work across boundaries or moving home from one region to another (as frequently happens on entering or after completing HE, particularly for middle-class students). Among studies on internal migration, Savage (1988) referred to the 'the missing link' between physical and social mobility, while Fielding (1992) has argued that the South East is an 'escalator' region in which mobility gains in early career are more rapidly advanced. Champion (2013) is more sceptical about the escalator region hypothesis, but using income and longitudinal data he reports substantial employment and geographical effects, notably for younger workers in highly skilled occupations (Champion et al 2013). These patterns can be seen as geographical extension of the occupational transition idea discussed later.

Spatial location and distance have another kind of significance for social mobility. At a more personal level, geographical mobility also involves breaking old social relationships and making new ones. Getting 'better' jobs may depend on migration, with consequences for social ties (Bell 1968; Watson 1964). Individuals are not free-floating units of labour but human beings with family, friendship and community ties and needs for housing. The 'incomer/local' dichotomy reported in many locality studies involves class, mobility, migration and local social integration (Payne 1973). In other words, the geographical becomes both personal and 'communal'.

Internal migrants may be more or less visible in their new locations (via, for example, regional accents), but *international* migration raises new issues. This is an important subfield of mobility research, which again cannot be tackled here due to restrictions of length. Ethnicity; changing levels of immigration; border controls; work permits; generational cohorts, demographics and differences in origin and education experience would all need to be taken account. Mobility analysis says little about migration studies, and vice versa.

The same applies to research on race and ethnicity. Somewhat similarly to gender, minority ethnic identities play into mobility in terms of social exclusion and types of work available. First-generation immigrants to the UK from the Caribbean and Asia were channelled into low-skill employment in transport, textiles and the NHS, and spatially concentrated, so that their subsequent mobility experience was highly likely to be distinctive – even without further racial discrimination. Iganski et al (1999; 2001) argued from census data that the *offspring* of this first generation were achieving an occupational profile close to that of the white non-migrants, so that their mobility experiences would increasingly converge. Exceptions seem likely to be Pakistani and Bangladeshi women, and to a lesser extent, young males from Caribbean families.

In a more sophisticated analysis of historical and demographic conditions, Platt (2005) indirectly confirmed this hypothesis. However, like Heath and McMahon (2005), she found that occupationally successful members of resident minority ethnic groups had to overcome an 'ethnic penalty' by being better qualified than equivalent white non-migrants, and that unemployment rates are higher for most minority ethnic groups. Mason (2006, 117–19) has also urged caution in assuming that mobility and occupations operate in the same way across all ethnicities, suggesting that for some groups employment and upward mobility may depend on opportunities *within* a person's own ethnic group, which differ from the main national pattern.

Recent international political developments and climate change in the Middle East and North Africa have complicated the situation of minority ethnic groups. There is little reason to expect the conditions that have driven refugee migration northward to disappear in the foreseeable future. During the EU Membership Referendum, free movement of labour became even more a central issue in British politics, with exaggerated claims of resultant depressed wage levels and unemployment fuelling anti-immigration policies. Migration Observatory (2015) figures indicate that about 17% of the labour force was not born in Britain. It is plausible to suggest that local concentrations of in-migrants (a headline in *The Guardian* on 23 January 2016 read: 'Nearly 40% of Londoners were born abroad') alter local mobility outcomes. Conversely, approximately 2 million UK citizens of working age (the age range used in mobility analysis) are employed abroad and so do not show up in mobility statistics. This poses several questions, not least whether nations are adequate units of analysis and how mobility will be calculated after Brexit (assuming, that is, that 'control over migration' is compatible with membership of the European free market).

In a globalised world, conventional mobility analysis requires further modification. Once it is recognised that class mobility is largely dependent on labour market conditions, a connection emerges with the international transfer of jobs. Relocation of call centres abroad may be the example most obvious to middle-class consumers, but the decline of the British textile industry and transfers of production or research and development facilities by multinationals have carved large holes in the national occupational opportunity structures of both exporters and importers of employment. At the time of writing, the employment fate of steel and oil workers in the UK is being determined by world trade pressures.

In contrast to these worldwide effects, a final topic in need of fuller treatment is the definitional framing of mobility itself. Discussion has already touched on the lack of information about the elite and the longer perspective given by three generations. Similarly, unemployment, part-time employment and underemployment as risk factors need a better theoretical integration into the mobility pattern.

The changing nature of work itself, and the creation of a new precariat, feed back into social mobility. Because mobility takes place within employing organisations we need a more detailed and contextualised perspective, as advocated by Breiger (1990). And even if we are to retain an employment definition of class and mobility, newer, more cultural visions of social class call for greater consideration as part of re-addressing the personal experience and meaning of being mobile at the individual level. Do high rates of mobility weaken specific class cultures and help to explain the consumption patterns and tastes reported in the Great British Class Survey (Savage et al 2015)? The task of redefining the new mobility is still far from complete.

EIGHT

The emergence of a new society

In their different ways, the three major mobility studies discussed in the previous chapter all struggled with incorporating the idea of social change overtime. They were not alone. Despite an interest in whether mobility rates were rising or falling, comparisons were complicated by the fact that mobility tables for different times (and different societies) had varying proportions in both the origin and the destination categories. Rather than treating these structural differences as important, most analysts used statistical techniques to discount these variations as 'noise in the system' (for example, Bibby 1975) in order to concentrate on the 'real' mobility going on, 'independently' of the changing distributions of classes or jobs.

Mobility analysis should have taken more, and more careful, account of social change for two reasons. First, historical industrial and occupational transformation in a demographic sense – that is, the size and composition of industrial sectors and occupational groupings – are connected to class mobility. If mobility is measured as movements between groupings of occupations, mobility and occupations are by definition connected (even when the categorisation into groupings is informed by theories of social class). This is one way of beginning to rectify the shortcomings of earlier research frameworks. Second, even if the underlying mobility processes – differentials in access to education, recruitment practices and so on – change relatively little, the flows of people must necessarily change to fill new opportunities (in an expanding middle class) or to reduce the flow into industries and occupations that are beginning to disappear (in a contracting working class). This fact of mobility is every bit as real, and requires just as much explanation, as any other kind of mobility. It is therefore important that the evolution of labour markets and occupational groupings, the playing fields on which the mobility game is played out, are explored as part of mobility regimes.

However, 'occupational groupings' are not as obvious as it first seems. Cannadine (1998) points to early uses of 'social class' to mean the collective interests of industries (for example, 'the farming interest') rather than the types of workers (farmers; agricultural labourers).

19th century Census classifications confused industrial output (what is produced) with types of occupations (the work tasks people do). In some cases this mattered little (agricultural labourers worked in farming, pitmen in the mining industry and so on), but as the social division of labour increasingly produced new, more specialised jobs, this occupation–industry connection broke down. While industrial sectors still matter, as the source of employment, occupational groups became a more useful focus.

Industrial and occupational demographics: sectoral changes

In 1700 Britain, a majority of the (male) population still worked as agricultural labourers. Only a minority worked as skilled craftsmen, or were merchants, or administrators in the Church or the State, the latter being the equivalent of white-collar workers in modern society. The Industrial Revolution created a demand for factory workers, miners and skilled technical trades, together with new occupations to service the material needs of the emerging urban workforce. By the early years of Queen Victoria's reign, the concomitant but often forgotten Agrarian Revolution was well underway, driving farm labourers and tenant smallholders off the land and creating a supply of labour to fill the new factory jobs. Writing in and about the mid 1880s, Charles Booth concluded that the 1881 Census had shown 'that in the last thirty years England has changed from a population about half agricultural and half manufacturing, to one in which manufacture is double of Agriculture (Booth 1886, reprinted in Routh 1987, 11).

In a period of rapid population growth, 'support had been found ... in other ways than tilling the soil, for a new population of $8^1/_2$ million souls'.(Booth 1886, reprinted in Routh 1987, 12).Today, primary production (agriculture, fishing and mining) accounts for one tenth of the jobs it provided a century ago, while manufacturing has crashed from 40.4% (1921 Census) to 8.4%. The occupational and industrial landscapes have changed fundamentally. Even 20 years ago it was being said that 'Britain has around 8,000 curry houses with a £1.5 billion turnover, which employ around 70,000 people – more than steel, coal and shipbuilding put together' (Keegan 1998). Data from the 2011 Census show that employment is now dominated by the characteristic jobs of a consumer society (sales, distribution, hospitality, leisure and finance) and those of a welfare society (education, health and public administration); despite privatisation and outsourcing policies, 'public services' has grown from 6% to 36%. Notwithstanding a few nations proving exceptions (Bauer and Yamey 1951; Triantes 1953; Oshima 1971), the early 1970s saw the Fisher-Clark thesis – that economic activity shifts from the primary, agricultural sector, into manufacturing industry, and subsequently into the tertiary, services sector – became well-established in the social science canon. In sociology it had been sufficiently well-demonstrated and debated to become an established phenomenon of sociological interest, if not consensus: see Bell (1973) Touraine (1974); Browning and Singlemann (1975); Gershuny (1978); Espring-Andersen (1993).

Although it was recognised that economic/industrial sectors employ different mixes of occupations, and that their expansions and contractions therefore alter the labour market, most commentators (such as Block 1990; Mehta 2004; Theobald 1996) stayed within the basic economic paradigm of industrial-sector analysis. Early critics made accusations of ideological bias against modernisation and development theory, while a second strand of criticism began to identify technical problems in having only three industrial sectors (a trichotomy first used in the Swiss Census of 1888) and with the way industries were grouped in their classification into the sectors (Browning and Singelmann 1978). Cohen and Zysmen (1987) attacked the basic formulation of the supposed transition: what matters is not the sectors per se but the *linkage* between them (if nobody farms, why would we need to manufacture tractors, let alone have a tertiary sector to distribute and retail food or run a pork futures market?). Gershuny (1983) argued that the underlying shift of economic processes need not be continuous, due to expanding 'self-servicing' in the household. Household members provide many of their own services inside the home rather than buying them (which would have added new occupational demand). Instead, households self-service by using domestic machinery, knowledge resources (such as books and TV) and their own cars for transport.

A common difficulty underlying much of the sociological debate was that the classification of industries into sectors was initially borrowed too uncritically from economic ideas. Industrial sectors may be useful to economists to measure GDP or economic growth, but they are ill adapted to understanding occupations and mobility. This applies most strongly to the 'basic ambiguity of the tertiary sector' (Singelmann 1978, 1225); that is, basing the 'services' sector on the arbitrary and unnecessary distinction made by classical economics between products (which are tangible) and services (which are consumed at the moment of their generation: *incorporeal,* to use J.S. Mills' term). This distinction is hard to sustain. Cohen and Zysmen (1987), after a review of attempts to define services, quote Shelp's 'admirable candour':

> I can offer no solid definition of services. … The most that can be said at the general level is that services encompasses an extremely heterogeneous group of economic activities often having little in common other than that their principal outputs are for the most part intangible products. (Shelp 1981, 52, quoted in Cohen and Zysmen 1987, 52)

But Cohen and Zysmen (1987, 51) reject even this intangibility test: not all intangibles (for instance, interest payments) are services, nor are all services concerned with intangibles: 'architecture, product design and shipping take their finality in goods; they are part of the production of tangible things'. Thus even the basic trichotomy of industry sectors breaks down.

Their examples of product design and transport have implications beyond the service sector: industry and occupation are increasingly loosely connected. Manufacturing involves employees with no direct hands-on contact with raw materials, the making process or end products. Whereas old-style managers could multi-task, businesses now need specialists, employed either in-house or contracted out: maintenance engineers; lab technicians; buyers; designers; marketing researchers; salespersons; accountants; lawyers; IT, PR, HR, and R and D departments; and, despite the digital revolution, general office staff. Universities are increasingly dominated by staff who neither teach or research. Proportions of employees only indirectly involved in production rise as new automated technologies replace workers and new sociotechnical skills emerge. The 'services' sector may employ more white collar and highly skilled personnel (paramedics, teachers, care workers, entertainers, or bankers, in the welfare state or financial services) but all industrial sectors have seen this other major occupational transition.

Rather than becoming fixated on economic activity, a more sociological approach is to turn directly to *occupations* (we have already seen how occupations, social classes and mobility mesh together). This helps to solve the 'who does what?' classification problem within each industry. Thus there are two sources of occupational change going on. One is the balance between industrial sectors identified in the Fisher-Clark account (even if the precise form of this change is open to dispute). The other is modification of how paid labour is carried out. Although automated production, digitisation of expertise and management policies to reduce dependence on skilled workers – Braverman's (1974) 'de-skilling' thesis – reduce the quality of work experience and constrain craft trades, the net consequence has been steady relative expansion of white-collar work. This basic change does not depend on rigid stages of evolution, the same pace of change across all nations or industries or time periods, nor the spread of American pluralist democracy, but it cannot be ignored.

Occupational transition: the long-term picture

The 'expansion of the tertiary sector' that impinges on social mobility therefore becomes less a statement about capital or productivity, and instead a summary of work-force proportions doing kinds of work; a way of thinking about the sizes of 'social' classes and how they are recruited. This connection with social mobility, originally made with respect to industrial sectors by Foote and Hatt (1953) in 'an article, unjustly neglected' that deeply influenced the work of Daniel Bell, as Bell himself acknowledged (1973, 35). While there is little support among sociologists for Bell's vision of a post-industrial society run by scientists and experts, his work indicated the importance of how the occupational composition of society was changing. *The Coming of Post-Industrial Society* rightly identified the need to explore the knock-on social consequences of that change in terms of political power and relationships between classes.

The way in which occupations required for retailing, welfare, finance and administration supplanted industrial and manufacturing occupations during the twentieth century is often called 'occupational transition'. Occupational transition should not be confused with individual or group *movements between* occupational classes, which is social mobility. Rather, it resembles 'demographic transition' – that other major historical change (in length of life, population numbers and family sizes) which summarises, and sometimes oversimplifies, the difference between older and more recent types of society.

Changes in employment have direct consequences for rates of social mobility. Low level of social mobility can be identified from the time when administrative records began (Kaelble 1985; Lambert et al 2007; Miles and Vincent 1993; Miles 1999; Prandy and Bottero 1998, 2000a, 2000b), while higher rates of movement are found in the latter part of the Victorian era. However, the world the late Victorians knew and the social circumstances of British life that existed between the two World Wars were, in turn, very different from the UK today.

Rejecting theories of evolutionary stages of human progress – let alone those expressed in terms of only a few industrial sectors – calls for an alternative account. This should ideally involve a proper investigation, looking at each era and country in closer detail. Smaller, historically concrete changes (like the establishment of the state secondary school system in the UK, or the marketization of the NHS) would concentrate on levels of employment and types of occupations rather than economic performance or profitability of industrial sectors. Such a major undertaking is not feasible here, but a sense of long-term socioeconomic change can be obtained by refocusing on occupation and connecting it to mobility, measured as movements between occupational statuses.

Unfortunately, limitations in official statistics – particularly the many revisions to occupational classifications – necessitate a broad-brush account. Exact comparisons over a century are problematic (Payne 1999). Time series involve complex approximations. Figure 8.1 draws

Figure 8.1: Occupational transition since the First World War

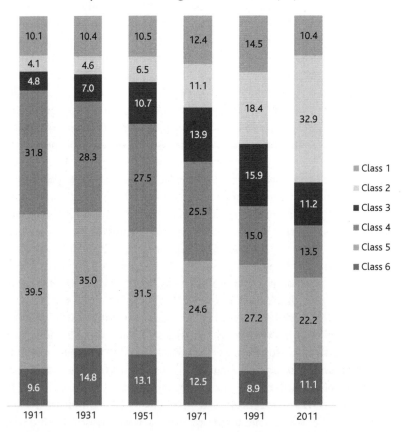

Occupational change 1911–2011 (%)

Legend:
- Class 1
- Class 2
- Class 3
- Class 4
- Class 5
- Class 6

Sources: Author's calculations from data in Routh (1987: tables 3.1 and 4.3) for years 1911-1981; from LFS (1992: table 6.11) for 1991;and from ONS (2011: table EMP16) for 2011.

114

on the most widely accepted version (Routh 1987), which covers much of the last century and offers uniform data points for 20-year intervals. Routh's Census-based time series has here been extended to 2011 by data from the Labour Force Survey (LFS) (LFS 2011) but in a simplified format of six 'occupational classes' because of limitations in comparability: *the classes in Figure 8.1 are not the same as those in the NS-SeC* (see Johnson 2011; Rose and Pevalin 2010). The data should therefore be taken as indicative rather than definitive.

In 1911, manual jobs (Classes 4, 5, and 6 in Figure 8.1) accounted for well over three quarters of all paid employment, whereas today they comprise less than half. Before the Great War, professional and managerial work (occupational Classes 1 and 2) accounted for less than 15% of the workforce but has since expanded nearly threefold to 43%. In round figures, even when those now reaching 'retirement age' first started work the comparable figure was only about one quarter.

This broad-brush summary hides considerable variation. There is no reason for changes to be consistent across all time points (for example, the fluctuations in the size of Class 6 in Figure 8.1). Skilled manual work (Class 4) has declined the most and most consistently. The semiskilled Class 5 has been partly sustained by the expansion in the retailing, distribution and the hospitality industries, while its former types of work in manufacturing have declined. The steady expansion of clerical work (Class 3) seems to have plateaued in the last couple of decades. At the same time, the leap in professional employment has been concentrated in the 'associate professions' such as education and health care, in which the labour force is largely female. Other, more detailed changes are also invisible at this level. In 1921, 7% of all work was domestic employment; farmers were another 7%, and miners again about 7% of the work force. Today, all three *combined* contribute a total of less than 1% of UK employment. Change accelerated during the 1950s, shortly before questions about intergenerational mobility began to be increasingly salient in academic circles, if not yet for the general public. Many children literally could not follow their parents into the same type of work even if they wanted to, because the old types of paid employment were disappearing. The social upheavals of the Second World War and their electoral and social policy consequences for post-war welfare institutions (most notably in provision of secondary education and free healthcare) disrupted the confidence of the old 'gentlemanly' political order and contributed to shifts in public awareness and aspirations (Savage 2010). Conversely, new types of work were being created for the first time and thus by definition could not initially be 'handed down'.

Occupational transition: the recent picture

Although there are still problems of comparability between datasets, these have become less of an issue in recent years. It is possible to combine tabulations from the LFS for 1997, 2005 and 2014 with Census data for 2001 and 2011, but *now using the NS-SeC schema* employed earlier to present the mobility data. This still involves variation due to the fine detail of occupational classification, sampling and age ranges. LFS is a smaller sample but covers the whole UK, whereas the Census datasets are much larger but include only England and Wales. One result is that the censuses for 2001 and 2011 tend to report slightly different *levels* than the LFS data for 1997, 2007 and 2014, but Census sources report very similar patterns to those in the LFS (Johnson 2011).

The results, shown in Figure 8.2, should again be treated as indicative rather than precise and definitive. Within these constraints, Figure 8.2 provides more recent and closer time points for 1997–2014 than for the 20-year intervals since 1911. It is also more directly compatible with the data on mobility rates, showing ongoing occupational transition.

The broad trends of the previous 100 years are continuing, most notably with Classes 1 and 2 increasing from 33% to 43%. Other classes show fluctuations, but over the 17 years that Figure 8.2 covers the working classes (5, 6 and 7) shrunk from 41% to 32%. Class 3 may be seeing a stabilisation, or indeed contraction, in its proportion of the workforce after 100 years of expansion. Class 4 (own account and small business owners) – the marginal case between white- and blue-collar work – also seems to deviate from earlier trends. Its employment share might best be described as stable, despite recent public debate about redundant skilled manual workers being forced into poorly paid self-employment.

Comparing the decade 1997–2007 to the years 2007–14 indicates that, around the 1990s, the long-term trend briefly slowed before picking up again. This requires further consideration of how fast occupation transition is taking place and what the effects for class and mobility of a new pattern would be, rather than reducing the importance of occupational transition. Given occupational structure is one effect in mobility rates, this is indirect evidence of a decade in which upward mobility slowed – or even possibly stalled – which in turn helps explain why social mobility became an issue of greater public concern around this time. On the other hand, the underlying trend in transition is rather stronger.

Figure 8.2: Recent occupational transition: NS-SeC Classes (excluding 'never worked')

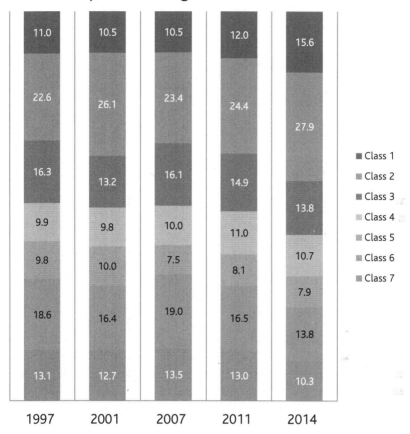

Occupational change 1997–2014

Legend:
- Class 1
- Class 2
- Class 3
- Class 4
- Class 5
- Class 6
- Class 7

	1997	2001	2007	2011	2014
	11.0	10.5	10.5	12.0	15.6
	22.6	26.1	23.4	24.4	27.9
	16.3	13.2	16.1	14.9	13.8
	9.9	9.8	10.0	11.0	10.7
	9.8	10.0	7.5	8.1	7.9
	18.6	16.4	19.0	16.5	13.8
	13.1	12.7	13.5	13.0	10.3

Sources: author's re-calculations from:
1997: Rose and Pevalin (2010) LFS data, table 4;
2001: Census 2001 table S43;
2007: Rose and Pevalin (2010) LFS data, table 4;
2011: Census 2011: table KS611EW;
2014: LFS (2015) table EMP11.

For simplicity of exposition, up to this point the labour force has been treated as homogenous; but, of course, it consists of different types of work and workers. Gender is one of these important subdivisions. As Figure 8.3 shows, men and women end up in different proportions in the social classes (as Chapman 1990a and Chapman 1900b show) and so have distinctive mobility patterns.

Nor are these distributions constant; some occupations, like retailing (Cox and Hobley 2014) and office work (Lockwood 1989) have largely ceased to be work done by men, who were increasingly replaced first by unmarried women and later joined by women after they had married.

Figure 8.3: The gendered class distribution: NS-SeC 2015

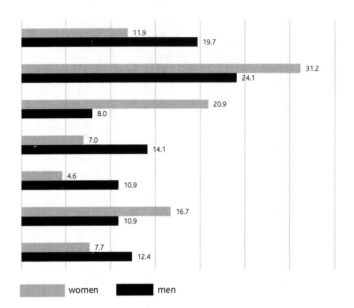

Source: LFS July-September 2015, seasonally unadjusted. Table EMP11

Because many specific occupations tend to be numerically dominated by either male or female employees (Abbott 2013, 92–5), changes in the labour market do not have an equal impact on men and women. Occupational transition can consist of expansion or contraction of opportunity for men, but not women. For instance, the increase in (largely male) senior managerial and professional employment and the decrease in (also largely male) skilled manual trades have more of an impact on men. The expansion of lower professional occupations or (more recently) the contraction of intermediate jobs affects women more than men. Figure 8.4 gives a picture of the gendered nature of occupational transition.

In the period since 1997, LFS data suggest the proportion of males in Class 1 has increased by about 3.5 percentage points. However, most of this occurs after 2007, following a flattening off in the middle years, before an increase in the 2014 data. The Census shows a small reduction in the first decade of this century. The same pattern is found in Class 2, the lower professional and managerial sector.

For females, the Class 1 increase was larger – about 5.5 percentage points – and growth continued between the 2001 and 2011 Census years. The Class 2 increase from 1997 to 2014 was 6.2 percentage points for females, whereas for men the figure was only 2.8, although the small drop reported in the Census is similar. The lower classes' contraction was sharper for women; for example, Classes 6 and 7 decreased from 36.1% to 24.7% in the LFS (32.7% to 31.7% in the censuses), while among men the decrease was only 3.7 percentage points in the LFS and there was actually a marginal increase in the Census data.

The implications for social mobility are that, if new job opportunities among the higher social classes increase and those in the lower classes

Figure 8.4: Gender differences in recent occupational transition: NS-SeC Classes (excluding 'never worked')

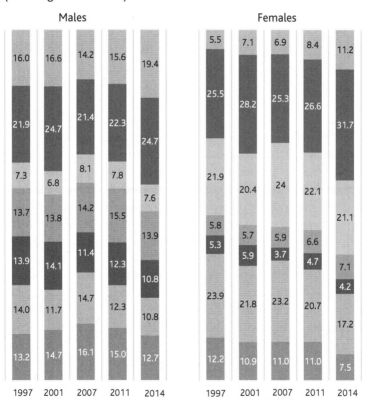

Sources: author's re-calculations from:
1997: Rose and Pevalin with O'Reilly (2005) LFS data, table 5;
2001: Census 2001 tables KS14bEW and 14cEW for 2001;
2007: Rose and Pevalin (2010) LFS data, table 5;
2011: Census 2011: table KS611EW; and
2014: LFS (2015) table EMP11.

decrease, disparate possibilities of upward social mobility are opened up for women and men. This is not the same as saying that upward mobility is the only outcome, because children born into the higher classes – who might otherwise have been downwardly socially mobile – can take up some of the new opportunities. However, to the extent that occupational transition tends to be associated with upward occupation movements across generations, the long-term evolution in employment helps to explain why social mobility is now more of an issue. But we now see that occupational transition has a differential impact on men and women.

In a male-dominated society, the continued improvement in women's employment and mobility receives little attention. As chapter Four observed, gender is seldom mentioned in official publications on mobility – although see former Conservative Minister David Willetts' (2011) public statement, in which he claimed that women who would otherwise have been housewives had taken university places and well-paid jobs that could have gone to ambitious working-class men (or indeed, ambitious but less able young men from middle-class homes, who receive less of his attention!). The public perception that (male) upward mobility rates have fallen in recent times may well be a response to a sense that opportunities for *men* – the traditional breadwinners in old-fashioned minds – have ceased to improve at the same rate.

Since the long-term occupational shift which became evident after 1950, more recent changes began to take a new turn. Those entering the job market in the 1960s and 1970s, and who are now parents or grandparents, commonly experienced their own upward social mobility, and that of people they knew. Life for many of them got better, as the professional and managerial classes expanded. But the enlarged middle classes this created then needed to find opportunities for *their children*: there seems to have been a slight slowing of occupational transition, particularly for sons, around the turn of this century.

Greater competition for the more desirable occupations was fed by the expansion of university education and a new vision of the role of women. Private education, commercial tutors and selection to high-status Russell Group universities (chapters Ten and Eleven) became the means by which a new and stronger class line – between the upper-middle classes and the newer associate-professional/middle-managerial classes – could be reconstructed. On the upper side there was still status anxiety; on the lower side was much greater frustration and underachievement. The progressive accumulation of new jobs (and its mirror image, the disappearance of older types of work), and the reduction in job security in a neo-liberal labour market where 'jobs for life' are no longer to be expected, served to foster concern about opportunity and immobility. By early 2015, one in six young people aged between 16 and 24 and not in education had no job at all, let alone 'career prospects'. The Office for National Statistics (ONS) count of zero-hours contracts rose from around 200,000 to 1,800,000 during the Coalition Government, whose austerity policy reduced the number of jobs in local government by eliminating services for less advantaged families and individuals (libraries, youth work, elder care and so on.). There was a growing sense of a shortage of 'graduate jobs', with reports that as many as 40% of graduates were without work six months after graduation (Totaljobs.com 2014).

These employment issues do not stand in isolation. Steeply rising housing costs, largely caused by a housing shortage created by the sale and non-replacement of council houses, restricted geographical movement in search of work and ate into disposable income. With would-be first-time house buyers unable to accumulate deposits in a period of static wage levels (in 2015, Milburn reported that the average age of first-time buyers in London had reached 41) and rent increases, many among the younger generation were unable to leave their parental homes. A headline in *ConservativeHome* (which describes itself as 'Britain's leading Conservative blog for news, comment, analysis and campaigns') asked 'How can we stop house prices from strangling social mobility?' (Franklin 2015).Mobility shades into wider social problems. With rising expectations thwarted and intergenerational lifestyle improvements unlikely, it is unsurprising that lack of mobility became an issue for the 'squeezed middle'. But with poorer public services and welfare benefits the prospects of the younger generation in other classes also began to recede. If more of the sons of the middle class are downwardly mobile (discussed later) they compete for employment lower down the scale, adding pressure on those from working-class families.

Occupational transition: the new hidden hand

Up to this point occupational transition has been treated as a simple change in job opportunities available from generation to generation, which normally benefited those entering the labour market. However, there is a secondary effect that has largely been ignored. British sociology was slow to acknowledge the consequences of occupational transition in the *parents'* generation (Payne and Roberts 2002). If there is an increase in the *rate* of occupational transition, as in the 1950s and (particularly) the early 1970s, that change has a ripple effect one generation later. When the 1970s generation of children grew up to be the next parental generation, the higher rate of white-collar employment they had gained meant they would later pass on a higher rate of *white-collar origins* for their own children. Other things being equal, if there are more middle-class origins then by definition fewer people can be upwardly mobile into the middle class, because the working class is smaller. Conversely, the larger number starting with middle-class origins may increase the prospects of downward mobility because there are more of them competing to remain in the middle class.

Despite the technical limitations of mobility samples – a random sample of children, asked to describe their parents, does not yield a random sample of parents – parental shift can be seen in data mainly from successive British Election Studies (BES) in the 1980s and 1990s. Table 8.1 shows the occupational changes among the children and their parents, using three collapsed social classes due to limitations of data comparability. The data refer to fathers because data on mothers is not available in the earlier studies. It would be useful if later studies could be included, but there are so many differences that their data would be more likely to confuse than illuminate.

The left-hand side of the table shows the now-familiar occupational transition among randomly sampled sons and daughters. The right-hand side of the table is more interesting here because it shows the social classes of their fathers/parents, which also follow the same trends but of course lag a little behind, because occupational change manifests itself more strongly in the younger workforce. In the early studies, managerial and professional fathers (that is, Class 1 origins in Table 8.1) were well short of a fifth of cases. In the later studies, this class had risen to around one quarter. In the early studies, manual work (Class 3 here) accounted for more than half of all origins; now it is less than 40%.

Thus, whereas in the 1970s the generational differences between proportions in origins and destination were seen as a characteristic feature facilitating upward mobility (particularly for men), this time series suggests that proportions among the origins have also responded to occupational transition, so reducing the origin/destination differential. However, the origins are those *reported* by the informants. Today's oldest informants would be talking about origins around 1970 whereas the youngest would be referring to the first decade of this century. Even if the origins were set at the average point – not the most reliable indicator – in, say, the late 1980s, this would not adequately reflect the impact of more recent changes.

Table 8.1: Trends in parent–child class differentials

Male class distributions in mobility studies, 1972–2005 (%)

	Sons			Fathers		
	1	2	3	1	2	3
1972	26.4	25.4	48.2	14.5	28.5	57.0
1983	33.6	26.7	39.7	17.9	29.6	52.5
1987	34.8	26.3	38.9	18.7	31.4	50.0
1992	38.4	24.3	37.3	21.2	27.2	51.6
1997	36.4	28.9	34.6	23.6	35.0	41.4

Female class distributions in mobility studies, 1983–2005 (%)

	Daughters			Fathers		
	1	2	3	1	2	3
1983	17.6	49.8	32.6	20.1	27.8	52.1
1987	20.4	48.7	30.9	20.4	28.1	51.5
1992	26.5	46.8	26.7	23.2	28.7	48.2
1997	32.0	44.4	23.6	27.6	35.5	36.9

Source: Author's recalculations from Payne and Roberts 2002, tables 1 and 2. Classes 1972–1997 are Goldthorpe Class Schema classes I and II; III, IV and V; VI and VII.

While Table 8.1 does not show mobility directly, it provides information about the prospects for male mobility. For instance, what were the chances of upward mobility from Class 3 to Class 1 in 1972? To qualify for that move, it was first 'necessary' to have a working-class origin (fathers), which 57 of every 100 sons had. They competed for the 26 of every 100 managerial and professional posts (sons' destinations). By 1997, the equivalent numbers were 41 working-class origins and 36 managerial and professional destinations. In other words, although there were *more* professional and managerial positions, there were actually *fewer* men from the working class who could (in principle) enter them. The Li and Devine (2011) study (not included in Table 8.1 because some of its classes are constructed in a non-comparable way) is broadly comparable for Classes 1 and 2 (its 1991 data for these two classes do closely match the BES 1992 figures). These data show a further closing of the parent–child gap of nearly 4% for men and a little less for women between 1991 and 2005.

This can be read in two ways. *If* – and it is a significant if – one starts as working class, there are fewer working-class competitors and more higher-class destinations to go round, so the chances of reaching such a destination are improved. But that omits the fact that the competition is not only with others from the working class but also with all classes.

The expansion of origins from Classes 1 and 2 means there are more competitors: 23 (instead of 15) with the advantages of starting in a higher class than Class 3, competing for 36 of every 100 destinations.

These moves make up the rates of mobility that commentators claim to be declining. Whether they are indeed declining depends both on the nature of the measurement (rather than any deliberate policy of social amelioration) and how long policies take to have an effect. It is perfectly possible for the social processes that plausibly have an impact on mobility rates (schooling, child health, aspirations and so on) to remain either unchanged or yet to make an impact, but for the amount of mobility (as conventionally measured) to increase or decrease because the 'demographic' structure of the employment classes has changed. Figure 8.5 offers a visual representation of this.

Again, Figure 8.5 does not show mobility per se (despite having origins and destinations) but rather how the proportions of origins and destinations evolved between 1972 and 2005. Reading the top and

Figure 8.5: Changes in male origins and destinations 1972-2005 (%: to scale)

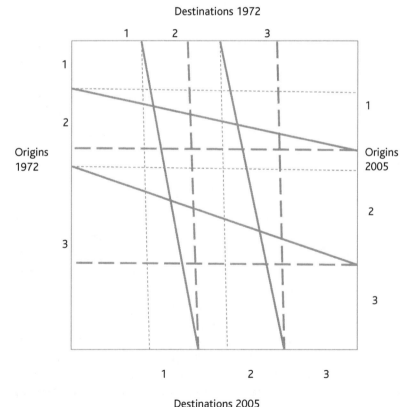

left-hand legends and the faint dotted lines shows the situation in 1972, while reading the bottom and right-hand legends and the stronger dotted lines shows the situation in 2005. The firm lines emphasise how the playing field has changed by showing the changing shapes and areas in which mobility can take place. As would be expected from the data in Table 8.1, the shrinkage in manual work is the most striking feature; although greater across the destinations, this is also clearly visible among the origins. The intermediate Class 2 shows a much smaller expansion, but sufficient to mean that the pattern for Class 1 is not simply the mirror image of the (working-) Class 3.

However, if mobility rates did not fall around the turn of the century (which is hard to demonstrate due to lack of data), the conclusion must be that this is *despite* the decline in the occupational transition effect; that is, that other processes generating mobility have increased in effectiveness. Occupational transition is not the only contributor to social mobility.

This argument about changing class distributions in the fathers' generation also extends to mobility measured as similarity of *incomes* between father and sons; for example, in the work of Blanden and Machen (2007). The expansion of the better-off middle classes in the now-parents' generation means that, in the middle of the income distribution, the incomes of the two generations are likely to be closer. This interpretation would imply that it is not income per se that is producing the income mobility effect, but rather the underlying occupation transition and distribution of *occupations*, thus providing an added reason to use occupation and class measurements rather than incomes.

Necessary but not sufficient

This chapter has documented the central process of occupational transition and drawn attention to the recent emergence of a new and different playing field on which the competition for mobility now takes place. The easiest way to think about this is to split mobility into two parts. On the one hand, there are the systems of selection, recruitment and reproduction that allocate people to their social destinations – such as educational qualifications, gender inequalities or inheritance of capital. On the other hand, there is the structural availability of origins and destinations; for example, there are a limited number of elite positions into which people can move. This analytical distinction is somewhat arbitrary because the two parts interact, but it resembles the older convention of splitting mobility into 'pure' and 'structural' mobilities. However, the key difference here is that structure effects are treated neither as an inconvenient arithmetical feature nor as less important than the systems of selection.

If we measure mobility in terms of occupations (whether or not these are grouped into social classes), there can be no upward mobility unless there are employment opportunities to provide destinations. However, demonstrating the connection between occupation transition and mobility is not straightforward, because whereas the Census data deal with *destinations* at specific time points and can be thought of as drawn effectively from a random sample, mobility data has to deal with *origins* across a period of over 40 years and are not taken from a random sample (see chapter Seven). Nonetheless, the connection between occupational change and mobility, insofar as it can be shown, works only in one direction.

Upward mobility requires available destinations, but a supply of destinations does not directly and automatically cause upward mobility to take place. The new middle-class occupations created during occupational transition can also be filled from among those (sons) at the top of society who would otherwise have been downwardly mobile, or those (daughters) who would previously have been excluded from the more desirable sectors of the labour market. Availability of occupational destinations is a *necessary*, but not a *sufficient*, condition for upward mobility. Policies to create equality of opportunity can only succeed in raising mobility rates if occupational transition generates precisely sufficient numbers of new jobs, at the right time and in the right places, to meet this new demand.

In parallel, the contraction of the old occupations makes immobility less common and contributes to reducing downward mobility by shrinking the available (and less desirable) occupations. But a lack of employment opportunities does not turn people into professionals and managers; there is always the possibility of unemployment or retreat from the labour market. Although rates of relative mobility are important, too much concern with them misses this central contribution that structural change and absolute mobility make to the formation of contemporary society. This limitation helps to explain why mainstream mobility analysis has inadvertently contributed to the misconception of mobility among politicians (discussed in the previous chapter).

NINE

The new mobility regime

One of this book's core messages is that British mobility rates are relatively high but unevenly distributed. Adding numerical flesh to the bones of this broad-brush argument is best done by concentrating mainly on a single representative dataset, thus avoiding repetition and potential confusion between studies that differ in small ways because their operational definitions are not strictly comparable (see Appendix).

Data from the 2014 LFS survey have been chosen because it is the most recent dataset at the time of writing. Its tabulations are increasingly becoming available to the public and were assembled from data collected by well-established methods from over 30,000 informants with incomes – a relatively large sample. Indeed, the LFS sample is sufficiently large that it can be treated as two subsamples of females and males, which allows the argument of a gendered labour force from the previous chapter to be followed through.[1]

Analysis of the data demonstrates that mobility has to take account of several, interconnected processes. The most obvious is that there are inequalities of outcome in the mobility competition, which can be attributed to social advantages or disadvantages ('class' differences) or to individual 'abilities' (see chapter Ten). The second element is the availability of employment, within which the mobility competition takes place: how important are the labour market changes under occupational transition? Third, the previous chapter identified gender differences in employment patterns, which may reasonably be expected to play into mobility outcomes. The analysis here is not intended to give a definitive answer but rather to show that all three of these elements make substantial contributions not only to overall mobility rates but also to particular occupational groupings. It follows that the mobility regime is not uniform: there are pockets of high and low mobility, and people experience a variety of outcomes. A number of other explanatory factors such as education (discussed in the next chapter), ethnicity and geographical variations are acknowledged, but discussion of these goes beyond the scope of the present chapter.

Women, paid work and female class

To develop this perspective of alternative interacting explanations, the example of mobility of men and women offers two main alternative interpretations. On the one hand, it can argued that the core processes that generate mobility – qualifications; recruitment; general social advantages and disadvantages; 'ability' – apply to both women and men in a similar way; in other words, that social class is the key feature. On the other hand there is a case to be made that the jobs that women tend to do are different from those taken by men; in the previous chapter, attention was drawn to the gendered patterns of types of work – and, by implication, mobility. It can be argued that these 'female' occupations have distinctively different processes of recruitment/allocation. The difference is not simply which ideological stance is preferred. Addressing class leads to a more generalised account, whereas starting with gender suggests a more detailed level of analysis. The mobility evidence alone does not provide a basis for dismissing either approach. Class and gender 'intersect', or interact.

However, a further line of argument has been that women do not have class identities in the same way as men because they are less involved with their employment situation and, for married women, living a lifestyle that is more determined by their male partners. In the 1970s and 1980s, work from the Nuffield school (the 1972 Nuffield Study having concentrated on male mobility) argued strongly that married women should be allocated not to the classes indicated by their occupations but to the classes of their husbands, and need not be studied separately (for example, Goldthorpe 1983; 1984). Fewer women were in paid employment, particularly full-time employment, and whether or not they worked depended on their husbands' class, so that the connection between occupation and class was weaker for women. Recognising that the fathers' social class was on average higher than their daughters (because the labour market is gendered) and claiming that cross-class marriages had little net effect, 'a woman's "class fate" is more loosely linked to her social origins than is a man's' (Heath 1981, 14; see also Goldthorpe and Payne 1986, 539; McRae 1986).

The argument about low numbers of women in paid employment was a strong one. At the time of the national mobility studies of the early 1970s, many would have lived through an earlier period in which relatively few married women had jobs. Women's occupations would have been indexed from their 'last jobs' – those before marriage or childbirth – which they had often long since given up. These included being 'in domestic service' as a temporary employment for young unmarried women (which was not perceived as a career destination in the same way as those for 'breadwinner' men) and war-time work as replacements for men who had been taken into the military, from which women were displaced when the men returned after the cessation of hostilities. In 1931, about 10% of married women were in paid employment. Even by the 1960s, only just over 40% were in paid employment (Payne and Abbott 1990, 14). Today more than two thirds of married women are in paid work and dual-income families are the norm. Although more married women than men work part-time, this makes little difference to classed attitudes (Abbott and Sapsford 1987). Eventually, the Nuffield school quietly accepted the need first to include unmarried women (Goldthorpe and Payne 1986) and then all women (for example, Bukodi et al 2015), classifying them – in line with standard practice in current official statistics – by their own occupations.

However, advocates of studying female mobility face the inconsistency of differential treatment of a woman's class in her own employment and her parental roles (for a fuller account of issues in female social mobility, see Payne and Abbott 1990). Miller and Hayes (1990) – among others – have shown that mothers' work and education has an impact on their children's schooling and occupation destinations separate to that of the fathers. Although the former method of defining origins by the father's occupation has been replaced by the 'dominance method', which defines origins using the mother's occupation and class when it is higher than the father's, the adult daughter's destination occupation is taken as fully determining her class position. The dominance method still results in the father's occupation being used in somewhere between 75% and 80% of origin classifications (for example, Li and Devine 2011, 3.2)

Gender differences in rates of occupational change and absolute mobility

Typical careers for women (Chapman 1990b) have involved a mobility drop from male origin to first entry to the (female) employment market. This is because their origins are mainly taken from their fathers and male occupations are on average of a higher position than female occupations. Women's average class position then rises in early career before falling during the childrearing phase. This is followed by some recovery – although this is often partial, and probably less pronounced for those who enter part-time paid employment. This has been described as the 'W-shaped' mobility profile (Payne and Abbott 1990, 163–5). It might be expected that men and women would share the same *origin* pattern, but in the LFS data slightly more women have managerial or professional backgrounds and slightly fewer come from working class origins (Table 9.1). This may simply be sampling error, but the same effect has been reported in other studies (for example, Li and Devine 2011). A more likely explanation is that women who are in paid employment differ in some respects from those not in employment due to coming from slightly different origins. This might lead to a stronger 'career' orientation among those raised in Classes 1 and 2 (Domenico and Jones 2006; Laughland-Booÿ et al 2015) and a greater tendency for women from these origins to be active in the labour force.

However, the gender differences in *destinations* are striking, as Table 9.1's column percentages show. The narrowest gender gap among destination classes is in Class 7: five percentage points. The largest is Class 3 (13.6%), while the net average difference across the seven destination classes exceeds eight percentage points. Classes 1, 4 and 5 have roughly twice the proportions of males, whereas in Classes 3 and 6 the proportion of females is double that of males. While the marginal totals demonstrate fairly straightforward occupational transition effects for men, effects for women are more complicated. Men and women live in divergent occupational worlds, but mobility analysts have been slow to take this fully into account.

The outcome of gendered employment suggests further elaboration of the concepts of both occupational transition and mobility. Men demonstrate the occupational transition effect most clearly in Classes 1 and 2 (expansion) and Classes 6 and 7 (contraction) – the upper and lower ends of the social scale – and to a lesser extent in Class 5. However, the male intermediate occupations ('white-collar, lower level administrative and higher level technical work' and 'self-employment/ small businesses') deviate from occupational transition expectations. Among women, the expected changes appear more strongly in expanding Classes 2 and 3 and contracting Classes 5 and 7. But occupational transition appears neither in women's Class 1 nor in Class 6, in which – contrary to expectations – semi-routine employment shows a marginal increase (although like the men, the female working classes as a whole have contracted).

The sharpest deviation (given its relatively small size) is the own account and small business class (Class 4), which appears to have contracted slightly for men (from 15.0% to 13.7%) and halved for women (from 15.2% to 6.8%). The recent rise in self-employment – up two percentage points between 2008 and 2014 in ONS data (Monaghan 2014; ONS 2014) – has yet to make an overall impact on mobility

Table 9.1: Male and female social mobility, 2014

Origins	1	2	3	4	5	6	7	Row Totals	Row %
					Destinations				
1 Higher managerial and professional	867	696	182	210	141	104	121	**2,321**	**14.5**
	534	1,018	447	190	62	235	73	2,559	15.2
2 Lower managerial and professional	726	792	194	251	178	176	177	**2,494**	**15.6**
	399	1,112	514	178	104	330	86	2,723	16.2
3 Intermediate occupations	426	500	155	203	141	134	155	**1,714**	**10.7**
	246	600	417	114	62	260	91	1,790	10.6
4 Small employers & own account workers	376	508	155	581	266	200	323	**2,409**	**15.0**
	216	754	504	231	117	504	230	2,556	15.2
5 Lower supervisory and technical	398	494	147	270	272	200	265	**2,046**	**12.8**
	202	622	522	137	95	381	141	2,100	12.5
6 Semi-routine occupations	299	425	139	271	268	266	331	**1,999**	**12.5**
	129	568	448	132	118	433	213	2,041	12.1
7 Routine occupations	389	575	218	414	414	443	602	**3,055**	**19.1**
	176	718	681	168	163	752	398	3,056	18.2
Column totals	**3,481**	**3,990**	**1,190**	**2,200**	**1,680**	**1,523**	**1,974**	**16,036**	
	1,902	5,392	3,533	1,150	721	2,895	1,232	16,825	
Column %	**21.7**	**24.9**	**7.4**	**13.7**	**10.5**	**9.5**	**12.3**		**100**
	11.3	32.1	21.0	6.8	4.3	17.2	7.32		100

rates. It may be that small businesses are not passed on so readily to daughters, especially in recent difficult economic circumstances. A further possibility is that self-employment depends on gendered manual skills acquired during previous employee work; for example, in the construction trades (the most common form of self-employment, along with taxi-driving; ONS 2014). The dataset may also exclude some self-employed people due to missing income data.

The mobility effect attributable to occupational transition is clearest in Classes 1 and 2 (the upper part of the white-collar sector) and Classes 6 and 7 (the core of blue-collar work). Because more of the labour force is made up of men, the male pattern shows up more strongly in the overall picture of occupational transition. Some analysts have suggested that the lower end of Class 3 – intermediate white-collar work – is the female class equivalent of skilled manual work for men (for example, Erikson and Goldthorpe 1992; Li and Devine 2011; McRae 1986), but the expansion of Class 3 and contraction of Class 5 suggests this is not the best choice in mobility analysis.

The mobility data for the classes tend to support the idea that the results of class advantage and disadvantage seem to be modified – but not overridden by – gendered occupational transition effects. When one's origin is in a contracting class, 'inheritance' of that destination is less likely than if one's origin is in an expanding class. Levels of immobility should be higher in shrinking classes than expanding ones.

If we use the exogenous evidence from the previous chapter instead of the endogenous information from Table 9.1, the seven classes fall neatly into three groups according to the amount of expansion they have experienced. In the last 20 years or so, Classes 1 and 2 have expanded most: from a range of just under 3% to just over 6%. Classes 3 and 4, and Class 5 for women and Class 7 for men, have not seen much change: between 1.2% and –1.1%. Class 6 and Class 7 for women and Class 5 for men have experienced larger reductions: from about 3% to over 6% (% here meaning percentage points).

Comparing these groupings with the mobility table, the expanding group shows the highest levels of immobility, with the exception of Class 1 for women. However, three other categories also show immobility rates in excess of 20%: small employers and own account workers for men, and intermediate and semi-routine occupations for women. The earlier commentary drew attention to the relative difficulty women have in obtaining Class 1 and Class 4 destinations and the heavy predominance of women in Class 3. These particular characteristics of the exceptions suggest that, in recent years, gender may have played a stronger part than occupational transition in their formation.

There is little systematic difference between those classes that have shown little change and those with most shrinkage. Indeed, apart from the exceptions already mentioned, the no-change category has slightly lower self-recruitment than the shrinking classes, which are all 'working class'. Here, the class dimension would seem to have more impact, with more mobility being possible in the middle of the mobility table, whereas more people seem to be hampered by their origins in Classes 5, 6 and 7. These differences are not visible in discussions of mobility as an undifferentiated rate. Thus, at first sight, the amounts of absolute intergenerational mobility in Table 9.1 are very similar: 78.0% for men and 80.1% for women. Upward mobility is almost identical at about 49%. Downward mobility for men is 32%, with women two percentage points lower. However, small variations of a few percentage points of gender difference accumulate; the blue-collar classes provide more of the current male managers and professionals than females (31.2% and 26.7% respectively). All destination classes for both genders show a majority of new mobile entrants, ranging from just below 70% in Class 7 to the high 80s for both genders in Class 3. On the other hand, they also show higher internal recruitment than would be expected if origin had no association with destination. The latter is more obvious in the top and bottom classes and for men rather than women.

The constituent parts of these mobilities show distinctive gender patterns, suggesting that the gendered experience of being mobile is therefore also different. The destination Classes 1 and 5, for example, contribute twice as much to male mobility as they do to female mobility, while the reverse is true for Class 2. Another quick way of documenting this is a simple comparison of self-recruitment/ immobility rankings for each gender, shown in Table 9.2.

Table 9.2 Self-recruitment levels and class size

Item ranked	Classes ranked in order of magnitude						
a) Immobile men	1	2	7	4	5	6	3
b) Men's origins	7	2	4	1	5	6	3
c) Men's destinations	2	1	4	7	5	6	3
d) Immobile women	2	1	6	3	7	4	5
e) Women's origins	7	6	1	4	5	6	3
f) Women's destinations	2	3	6	1	7	4	5

Brief inspection shows that male immobility ranking (row a) is a little closer to the ranking of their origins (row b) than women's immobility (row d) is to their origins (row e). This follows from the unavoidable use of fathers' (male) class to index their daughters' origins in about three quarters of cases, even when the dominance method is deployed. Women's immobility is very similar to *destination* class size, except for Classes 1 and 3 – women seem to find it harder to enter Class 1 (see chapter Eight), and Class 3 has both the fewest men and the widest gender gap.

This is a combination of four effects. The social processes that create differential connections between classes as origins and destinations and the changing size of the classes due to occupational transition give the mobility table its underlying shape. The higher classes retain more of their advantage intergenerationally, although it is Class 1 that does the heavy lifting for men and Class 2 for women. However, more women than men are mobile – both because of the 'maleness' of women's origins and the 'femaleness' of their destinations and because of specific gendered factors in class size and availability of entry routes. This suggests that measuring mobility as overall openness ('we need more social mobility'), which implies a similar picture for men and women and disregards the variations between specific origins and destinations, hides a lot of what is actually going on (and therefore what would need to be changed if policy solutions were sought). Despite the relatively small gender differences in terms of total percentages, male and female mobility do differ and need to be explored separately.

Gender differences in comparative mobility chances

When we look at outflow mobility by comparing disparity ratios separately for men and women, no single simple pattern of class advantage emerges. This suggests that the gender differences in destinations are sufficiently strong to disrupt underlying non-gendered class advantage effects. Most disparity ratio values for both genders lie between 1.1 and 2.6, particularly in the middle of the table. Among women, the chances of upward mobility tend to be poorer – but conversely, the risks of downward mobility are slightly lower. For both men and women, the biggest differences are in the chances of those from Class 1 staying in Class 1 compared to those moving from Class 7 up to Class 1 – 2.9:1.0 in favour of men from Class 1 but 3.6:1.0 for women from Class 1. For every one chance of moving from Class 2 to Class 7, the chances of men staying in Class 7 are 2.8 and the chances are 4.1 for women.

It should be remembered that these disparities have been expressed by standardising chances *within* each gender, not as a direct comparison of men and women's chances. If a direct comparison of gender differences is made, men are found to have a 2.2 times better chance of moving from Class 7 to Class 1 than women and a 1.8 times better chance of staying in Class 1. Conversely, the chances of men's downward mobility from Class 1 to Class 7 are 1.8 times greater than those of women. These disparity ratio figures are lower than those derived from odds ratios (the more conventional method of calculating relative mobility). Although this account eschews reliance on odds ratios (see Appendix), Bukodi et al (2015, 112) report comparable results from a collapsed three-class model for three successive cohorts of men and women, each at the age of 38; the ratios for men 'could be reasonably thought to lie somewhere between 5 and 10, with those for women probably falling somewhere below this range for younger cohorts'. In the 2014 data, the odds ratios are 5.2:1 for men and 4.8:1 for women; that is, there is a degree of congruence between the two studies despite their different methodologies.

Before leaving the comparison of mobility chances, it is worth thinking about chances in a rather different way. Both disparity and odds ratios tell us something about what one's prospects are *once we have started from given origins*. But they do not take account of the chances of getting those origins in the first place – indeed, this is one of the attractions of odds ratios for further statistical techniques. An alternative way of characterising relative mobility, or rather *comparative chances of mobility*, is the 'conditional disparity ratio'. This incorporates *two* logical conditions: (a) chances of being *present in the origin class*, and (b) *arriving (or not arriving) at a destination*. The first takes the proportion of the overall total who have a specific origin; the second, the proportion of a given destination class who come from that origin. The combination of the two conditions can be thought of as the percentage of the whole sample meeting the two logical conditions. The chances, for example, of being a 'second-generation' female member of Class 1 are 4.27% (compared to 3.60% for men); that is, the chances of women holding on to their Class 1 status are higher than men, provided their chances of starting there are factored in. Using the conditional disparity ratio, men show higher probabilities overall of upward mobility, while women are more likely to be downwardly mobile unless their origin is in Class 1 or Class 2.

Standardised conditional disparity ratios are smaller than the odds ratios and a little lower than those given by simple disparity ratios. This does not mean that the inequalities in mobility chances should be treated as unimportant. Rather, the new values indicate the scale of inequality *when the realities of the occupational and class shape of UK society are taken into account*. It is useful to be able to see immediately how occupational transition (the chances of being in an origin) has altered relative mobility rates. In this sense, the conditional disparity ratio gives a more grounded picture of what is happening. This measurement makes comparisons between studies more viable, provided they share operational definitions. Whichever ratio is deployed, what matters about relative chances is the interpretive importance given to them in terms of moral unfairness of outcome. Odds ratios can give apparently large numbers, and so convey an impression of greater inequality. Is an advantage or disadvantage of, say, a two or three or four times better (or worse) chance of mobility indicative of high or low levels of inequality? Even if the numbers are this small, they still indicate outcomes substantially different than would be anticipated in a fairer system.

The problem with demonstrating trends in mobility rates

The claim that mobility rates are declining has been touched on several times in earlier chapters. Variations in operational definitions (see Appendix) make many comparisons unreliable, even if there were agreement about which measurement to use and how to take account of structural changes. However, there is some circumstantial evidence that mobility rates are not in decline.

Those who have asserted – with little solid evidence, save the Blanden and Machen (2005) income studies criticised in chapter Seven – that mobility rates are too low and are falling have not included in their claims statements of *what would be acceptable or target rates.* It is therefore difficult to engage with their arguments because rates are so imprecisely specified. Without saying present levels are satisfactory, evidence presented earlier from a variety of sociological studies has shown that absolute intergenerational mobility rates are 'high'; that is, ranging from somewhere between the mid 70%s to the low 80%s. If there had been a decline, *at some previous point mobility rates must have been even higher.* In other words, starting from known current rates around 80% it is not possible to simultaneously claim that rates are falling and that rates have been low – it must be one or the other, given the available evidence.

In fact, the more direct evidence on trends does *not* point to a decline. The British Election Study data, collected in a standardised way between 1983 and 1997, found no evidence of decline, and on the contrary, one analysis cautiously suggested the possibility that 'there has been a real, albeit small, increase in the openness of British society' (Heath and Payne 2000, 273–5). In Northern Ireland, Breen (2000, 403) found a parallel pattern of 'a rather weaker association between origins and destinations' between 1973 and 1996. Payne and Roberts (2002) confirmed the rising mobility rates for men in the British Election Study data but suggested that the late 1990s may have seen this levelling off, or even a small decline.

In a time series extending into the 21st century based on cohorts at the age of 38 (the youngest born between 1980–84), Bukodi et al (2015) found no evidence for a decline in intergenerational mobility whether considered in absolute or in relative terms. They did, however, suggest that the composition of this mobility was changing. Male absolute upward mobility is tending to fall and downward mobility to increase, while relative mobility inequalities are being reduced among women.

Disaggregation of overall mobility by gender and specific classes, taken together with the occupational transition effect, provides a more precise – but still elaborate – picture of what has been determining recent trends. The expansion of white-collar employment has increased mobility chances for both men and women – Class 1 in particular for men and Classes 2 and 3 for women. However, this increase slowed for about a decade overlapping the turn of the century, thus probably dampening down mobility until faster growth resumed. In the same period, the occupational transition that had benefitted the sons' generation in the 1970s was progressively spreading into older people as they became parents, thus increasing the proportion of white-collar origins, reducing the possibility of further upward mobility and increasing the likelihood of more downward mobility. Finally, access to qualifications, and expectations that married women should be in paid employment, brought more women into the labour market as employment opportunities for them increased, again particularly in Classes 2 and 3.

If there have been 'losers' as a result of these trends it has been the sons of Classes 1 and 2, who – despite actually still retaining considerable advantages (like a lower risk of long-distance downward mobility) – are now finding the competition for managerial and professional jobs harder than their parents did a generation before. This failing of family expectations is fertile ground for the idea that all other mobility rates are falling. Fear of downward mobility inspires calls for 'more mobility'. The other loser group is the much more disadvantaged second-generation men in Class 7, who – while perhaps not yet constituting an underclass – seem increasingly isolated from the potential goods of modern society.

It is hard to say whether this pattern will continue or for how long. Future patterns of mobility are difficult to predict because the outcome will depend on the balance between, and the individual strength of, these effects. Leaving aside the wilder speculations of futurologists' robotics dreams, occupational transition cannot go on forever, even if it has continued for longer than expected (Noble 2000). As occupational transition slows, the gap in class distributions between parents and their children is likely to go on shrinking and will become more important. If the labour market becomes less gender-segregated – as is slowly becoming likely – the pressure on the children of middle-class families will be modified.

Of course, this system of interacting effects has also had an impact on overall mobility. Although the emphasis in this chapter has been on disaggregation, especially by gender, a basic mobility regime still emerges. In the centre of the mobility table, short-distance mobility is common despite the special characteristics of Class 4 (the self-employed). Analysts have largely ignored these short-distance movements as unimportant compared to long-distance mobility and the greater degree of inequality at the top and bottom of the social scale. However, both short-and long-distance mobility deserve to be taken seriously. This is why this book has talked about both the high levels of movement and the relatively closed nature of Classes 1 and 7.

Note

[1] This chapter would not have been possible without the generosity of Daniel Laurison and Sam Friedman, to whom the author is greatly indebted for sharing their pre-publication results. They are, of course, not responsible for my interpretations and indeed would take a different approach – see, for example, their work on elites and income (Laurison and Friedman 2015).

TEN

Misconceptions of schooling and meritocracy

Earlier chapters showed that explanations of mobility draw heavily on assumptions about individual ability and achievement, rather than structural constraints on opportunity, to account for class outcomes. That individualistic discourse says achieving upward mobility and its consequent social benefits is fair because those who are downwardly mobile, or immobile at the bottom of the social hierarchy, deserve to fail since they are lesser human beings who lack 'ability'. Educational *qualifications* (partly because they seem to come in a standardised, comparable form, and we have all experienced the academic testing which is integral to our schooling) have become the proxy for the *ability* assumed to explain mobility outcomes. It is therefore necessary to consider how mobility is linked to education, both because of its prevalence and as the cornerstone of the individualistic discourse of mobility outcomes. In Boris Johnson's (2013) somewhat complicated metaphor, education is essential if the cornflakes with individual talents and high IQs are to get to the top of the box.

The idea of a meritocratic society, with individual merit accounting for mobility, has become widespread (Hennessy 2014). Common sense says many technical and white-collar jobs involve complex skills and hence require extensive prior education to acquire them, while manual jobs need less training. Not everybody can do the more demanding jobs. Even mobility analysts using a social class framework see education as a key vector through which class is reproduced. The introduction of secondary education following the 1944 Education Act was a major issue in the LSE study (Glass 1954: chapters by Floud, Himmelweit, Martin, Kelsall and Hall and Glass) – a tradition continued in the Nuffield study (Halsey et al 1980). The education–mobility link remains central to research from pressure groups (for example, Atherton 2015; SMCPC 2015c, 27–54; Sutton Trust 2015a; Sutton Trust 2015b). Documents and statistical releases from ONS, the government's Departments for Education, and Business Innovation and Skills provide such extensive illustration of inequalities in educational outcome that there is a risk of disappearing in a sea of evidence.

There are in fact considerable local and historical variations in English education, which are almost impossible to cover even at book length (for example, see Ball 2013; Basit and Tomlinson 2014; Dench 2006; McNamee and Miller 2013). In addition, Scotland and Northern Ireland have had their own educational systems. Qualifications are not as standardised as is generally believed. This chapter therefore provides illustrations rather than systematic coverage, drawn mainly from primary and secondary schooling, while the following chapter deals with post-secondary education and entry to work. Both chapters unpack education's causal link with mobility, in particular the idea of meritocracy, but this chapter seeks to show how academic progress in school determines access to later qualifications, whereas the following chapter raises doubts about the link between employment and academic credentials. This abbreviated consideration of upbringing and schooling does not imply that they are unimportant – they have an impact on *all* children (Lareau 2003) and underpin subsequent competition for university places, which will be discussed in more detail. As the focus of arguments about what causes mobility, the education system itself take a central place in the explanation of social mobility.

Connecting ability, education and occupational outcome

Figure 10.1 is an often-used summary representing the linkages between origin (O), education (E) and destination (D) as a simple triangle. How far does O influence D directly or indirectly through E? If the influence of E grows, the influence of O reduces. If there is a strong connection between O and D, then E is weaker and a society is less meritocratic.

The model can, of course, be elaborated with other variables like the education of parent, grandparents and so on or by subdividing groups by gender, age or ethnicity. The more complex the model, the greater scope for debate; elaborate statistical arguments have developed to simplify the field's complexity. Statistical modelling to test 'the effect

Figure 10.1: The origin/education/destination triangle

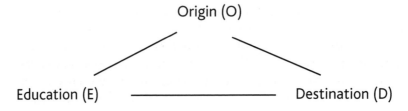

of education' on mobility outcomes (for example, Bond and Saunders 1999; Breen and Goldthorpe 1999; 2001; 2002; Marshall and Swift 1996; Paterson and Iannelli 2007; Saunders 1995; 1997; 2002; 2010, 88–94) is useful but constrained by the nature of the raw data and the level of detail measured. How many differences in education should be measured? Being a graduate has advantages over not having a degree, but Oxbridge degrees are not the same mobility tickets as those from Neasden University, while physics degrees differ from those in cultural studies.

During the 40 years covered by a typical mobility study, types of institutions and qualifications change. In the early 1960s, 'secondary modern' schools predominated before comprehensive schools took over, which in turn are increasingly being replaced by unofficially entry-selective 'free schools' and 'academies', which on average receive 62% higher funding than state schools (Mansell 2015). At the time of today's older people's schooling, around 500,000 A-levels were sat each year: currently the equivalent is over 850,000. If more people pass A-levels, the market advantage of A levels tends to reduce. In the 1970s, about 25% of passes were at grade B or better; now it is over 50%. One need not join in media complaints about exams getting easier and grade inflation every August to see that the currency of a 'good pass' is likely to be devalued if the supply is doubled. Add occupational transition to this and we have continual, shifting mismatches between the supply of school qualifications and the demand of types of occupational opportunities. Lower-level qualifications may be required to access higher-level education but educational qualifications are often necessary, but not sufficient, preconditions for employment.

Education systems may develop mental capacities without inculcating vocational skills. They certify acquired academic performance levels, progressively filtering out 'unsuitable' candidates to prevent them obtaining higher qualifications. Only those deemed suitable pass through to graduating from Higher Education, or even from an 'elite' university. The unsuitable – who lack intellectual ability, motivation, aspiration, or material, social and cultural capital, depending on one's choice of explanatory framework – are sieved out at successive stages formally because they have failed to achieve the qualifications necessary to proceed, but also because of other social circumstances and lack of cultural capital.

The issue turns on how far Britain is, or should be, a true meritocracy. Meritocracy means a society ruled by those with 'merit', but in the context of social mobility it has come to mean a social system in which occupational outcomes – with their differential economic, political and social rewards – have a close and justifiable association with prior *educational* performance. For practical political purposes, what matters are people's *beliefs* about the extent of meritocracy rather than the reality, as belief legitimates the status quo. Although more than two thirds of us recognise that Britain is not fully meritocratic (British Social Attitudes Survey 2013), we still pay lip service to educational merit. A 2011 YouGov poll for Policy Exchange found 85% of the UK public agrees that 'in a fair society, people's incomes should depend on how hard they work and how talented they are' (Policy Exchange 2011, 3).

Accounting for meritocracy: SAD or DIM

The problem is deciding what is talent, how many talented people there are, how their qualifications reflect this and whether academic credentials determine class outcomes. Most accounts of British mobility have emphasised inequalities in gaining desirable destinations, which implies there is a pool of under-educated and therefore under-utilised talent – although, as Saunders (2010) has observed, there has been relatively little sociological research into the supposed general distribution of ability. Sociologists normally treat ability as culturally defined rather than innate, so the *potential* to be described as having 'ability' is initially distributed more or less randomly across the population. However, the subsequent differential acquisition of socially valued characteristics in later life is then attributed to environmental forces that both progressively and immediately from birth (or indeed *in utero*) redefine individuals' abilities and disabilities.

Environmental social factors in early life such as healthy diet; good housing conditions; an intellectually stimulating home life favouring early conversation in infancy and encouragement to learn to read; material security, aspirational parents and high-quality schooling – or the opposites of all these – create, shape and continue to modify the personalities and abilities of each new generation. Because these factors are not randomly shared across the population, culturally valued attributes are allocated in an unfair way. In this view, individual differences are the *result* of what happens to us rather than the *cause*. In particular, 'intelligence' is a product; levels of intelligence can and do change. IQ tests are an unreliable measurement because I.Q. testing cannot escape its cultural biases (for example, see Baker et al 2015 and Kendler et al 2015 on 'malleable intelligence').

In contrast, among some branches of psychology, a faith in IQ testing and a belief that individual differences are resistant to change point towards a social hierarchy based on inherited 'ability' or 'intelligence' as being both 'normal' and desirable. Greater social mobility would therefore be undesirable and dysfunctional because it would promote less 'able' people. This was implicit in the psychological theory underpinning the introduction of selective secondary education in the Education Act 1944, which effectively deprived the 70% of children in secondary moderns of a syllabus leading to the educational qualifications required for sixth-form studies or university entry (Mitchell 1988). Some evolutionary psychologists still claim that holding an advantaged social position is a natural outcome of being a genetically superior person (THES 2008), or that certain national populations with different colour skins are more intelligent or that men are cleverer than women (for example, see the debate between Lynn (2005a; 2005b) and his critics (Wicherts et al 2010a; 2010b) or the controversy over Herrnstein and Murray's (1994) *The Bell Curve*). Claims of genetic superiority often elide into a circular claim in which an advantaged position becomes part of the *evidence* for genetic superiority.

Unusually among sociologists, Peter Saunders (1996, 2010, 2012) has taken differences in IQ scores seriously, attributing mobility outcomes chiefly to personal ability. He defends IQ tests as measuring intelligence (Saunders 2010, 49–66) and uses genetic inheritance to suggest that, if 'ability' is *not* uniformly distributed across the population, those at the top of society will be more able; they 'merit' their position and can pass on their abilities to their children. He demonstrates that observed patterns of mobility and immobility are close to what would be predicted by known IQ scores of people in various social classes. Saunders rejects the standard sociological explanation that '"social advantage and disadvantage" conferred at birth is what shapes people's destinies', which he calls the 'SAD' thesis (Saunders 2010, 3). For convenience we can refer to Saunders' own explanation as the 'DIM' thesis; that is, the *D*ue to *I*nnate *M*erit thesis.

As the title of his 1996 book *Unequal But Fair?* suggests, Saunders argues that inequality is morally *fair* because those at the top of society are more able people and deserve their rewards. He does, however, accept that the opportunities leading to mobility outcomes are inequitable and that development of potentially available talent is not maximised by current social processes. They do not work well for 'recruitment into the very top ('elite') positions of British society' nor is enough known about the underclass. He does

> not claim that Britain is a *perfect* meritocracy. The various
> advantages and disadvantages associated with different
> social class origins do still play some part in influencing

people's occupational chances – sociologists have not been completely wrong or deluded. (1996, 1–2)

In addition to elite and underclass recruitment, he acknowledges that mainstream schooling does not provide an entirely level playing field; for instance, for minority ethnic groups. Nonetheless, the distinctive feature of his analysis lies in his challenge to the more usual assumption that intelligence/talent/ability is randomly inherited and distributed across the population, and the thrust of his argument is that ability is the major component determining mobility outcomes.

It is extremely difficult to define and measure ability – even if we confine ourselves to 'intelligence'. Despite continued refinements of IQ testing (for example, Kaufman 2009), it has fallen from favour outside of psychology because it cannot be purged of its cultural biases. The 'general intelligence' that IQ tests are supposed to measure has become better understood as numerous different intelligences, such as short-term memory, reasoning and verbal agility (in an extensive literature, see Murdoch 2007 and Hampshire et al 2012, for examples). Many advocates of 'nature' in today's 'nature vs nurture' debate accept that there is an interaction between the two. Some adults do indeed perform complex thinking and tasks better than others, particularly at the extremes of performance, but that does not necessitate theories of social order in which such differences take logical precedence. It is therefore possible to acknowledge Saunders' complaint – that sociological accounts of mobility outcomes depend on a relatively untested idea – without accepting his alternative explanation.

Of course, 'merit' need not be indexed purely by IQ scores – or, indeed, educational qualifications. Michael Young's (1958) famous formulation of $M = I + E$ (Merit equals Intelligence, measured by IQ tests, plus Effort) not only identifies cognitive performance and hard work but also implies that these produce the educational outcomes used to sort people into jobs. Working hard at a task is likely to result in a different outcome than idling one's time away; however, other things being equal, 'effort' (like intelligence) does not lend itself to simple definition or direct systematic measurement. People develop their abilities (and sadly eventually lose them) at different rates as they move through the life course. Intelligence, effort and personal characteristics are not individual constants and therefore would need repeated testing, if such tests existed. These measurement difficulties have encouraged the use of educational outcome (however questionable) as the main proxy indicator of 'ability'.

But educational credentials are not the only badge of ability, if ability is seen as outcomes. The winners of Miss World competitions, *Strictly*, the Premier League or Olympic gold medals do not also need to possess five GCSEs at grades A★–C. Socially-valued characteristics such as physique, physical coordination, self-confidence, and adaptability, and in some cases substance abuse play their parts. More jobs are filled with little regard to educational qualifications than dreamt of by academics – who spend their lives inside the education system.

This lack of match between certain careers and schooling does not mean inequalities in education can be ignored. A brief illustration of these inequalities shows their extent, although on its own this provides neither a clear adjudication between SAD and DIM theses nor a full explanation of the 'tightening bond' between schooling and employment that T.H. Marshall first identified in 1949 (Marshall 1965). It is important to distinguish between evidence of inequalities in educational outcome (for a good discussion, see Cassen and Kingdon 2007) and the possible consequences of such inequalities for obtaining jobs and achieving (or not achieving) upward social mobility.

Schooling inequalities

Differential performance comes into play early. In the 1970 British Cohort Study, children rated 'less bright' in cognitive ability tests at 22 months who were from professional/managerial occupational backgrounds scored higher in tests at ages of 5 and 10 (that is, after nursery and primary education) than children rated 'bright' at 22 months who were from semiskilled/unskilled manual occupation backgrounds (Feinstein 2003). Low-scoring offspring of less wealthy or poorly educated parents seldom caught up (Feinstein 2003). Favourable home conditions in infancy are associated with school performance:

> By the time children start at school there are already wide variations in ability between children from different backgrounds ... Only 75% of the poorest children reach the expected level by the time they leave primary school, compared to 97% of the richest children. (Cabinet Office 2011, 24, 34)

In 2012–13, by the age of 11, 37% of children receiving free school meals (FSM) or the 'pupil premium' (widely used but crude indicators of social disadvantage) failed to achieve the expected Key Stage (KS) 2, level 4 in literacy and numeracy, compared to 19% of other pupils

(DfE 2014). By KS 4, just 20% of children from the poorest families gained five GCSEs including English and Maths at grades A★–C, compared to 75% of the richest children (Cabinet Office 2011, 34). Almost 60% of more generally 'disadvantaged' children failed to obtain five A★–C GCSEs including English and Maths, compared to 32% of other pupils (DfE 2014, 3–4). Among the disadvantaged, 66% of the top fifth of performers at KS 2 were missing from the top fifth of GCSE performers. Among other pupils, the discrepancy was 42%. A further half of the surviving top-performing disadvantaged students at age 16 have dropped out by the age of 18 (Sutton Trust 2008, 4–5).

Older participants in mobility studies were educated well before present schooling arrangements, when the secondary-modern/ grammar school system was dominant, in contrast to the 164 grammar schools that remain in 'a handful of counties and local authorities in England' (Richardson 2015). Selection by intelligence testing and interview in the state system disadvantaged many, who were labelled failures, and yet did little to benefit many of the minority from lower class backgrounds who were supposed to be sponsored through the system. In the earlier period (when about 40% of children came from semi- or unskilled families) only 16% got to grammar school (Hart et al 2012). 18% of all pupils achieved five O-level passes and 6% achieved three A-levels (Coughlan 2015a), but over 56% of those entering grammar school from semi- and un-skilled families failed to get three O-level passes and over 30% had left before the end of their fifth year (Gurney-Dixon Report 1954, 34). After grammar schools were restricted to 36 local authorities (Hansard 2007), about 2% of their pupils received Free School Meals compared to the national average of 18% (Carvel 1999).

With a tightening bond between qualifications and employability, direct and covert selection ruined many lives. But despite the extremely powerful case against selective education at an early age (for example, Benn and Downes 2015; Hart et al 2012; Rubinstein and Simon 1969; Skipp et al 2013; Stewart 2015), the argument continues (Coughlan 2015a; Hinsliff 2015). In 2007, the overwhelming majority of several hundred listeners responding to John Humphrys' special feature on social mobility on the BBC Radio 4 *Today* programme wrote to the website about the virtues of grammar schools; there was almost no mention of secondary moderns (in which pupils could not study for academic subjects) and little about social mobility per se.

Responding to Conservative calls for more grammar schools, the head of OFSTED, Sir Michael Wilshaw, complained that grammar schools failed to increase social mobility because 'academic selection works well for a tiny minority of pupils while consigning large numbers of other children to educational failure' (in Paton, 2013). Grammar schooling does not significantly increase the probability of getting a degree or graduating from an 'elite' institution, but advantaged social origins and private schooling do raise the chances of graduation – especially from an elite university – above and beyond cognitive and examination attainment (Sullivan and Swift 2011).

This evidence has not prevented well-off parents from using their assets to gain what they perceive as educational advantage. The most obvious examples are moving house into the catchment areas of favourable schools, attending church to gain entry for their children in high status 'church schools' and using their social capital to improve their children's prospects. It is not simply that they seek better qualifications; as Devine (2004) convincingly shows, the desired schools often resemble the schools the parents attended, with stricter codes of manners and fewer pupils from lower-class families.

Recent years have also seen an increase in an army of private tutors, many helping pupils to prepare for grammar school entry tests. There are no really reliable data, but the *Times Educational Supplement* reported that 'There are twice as many tutors as there are school teachers in England' (an IPSOS Mori poll put the figure at around 1.5 million (Hurst 20130), while *The Telegraph* estimated that nearly a quarter of all pupils have private tuition – a figure rising to 40% in London (Wallop 2013). At £40 an hour, as claimed by Cohen 2013, this obviously favours the wealthy: a Sutton Trust poll (2014) found the richest fifth of households are four times more likely to pay for extra classes outside school than the poorest fifth.

This more recent form of private education sits alongside traditional fee-paying schools. These may be 'independent', 'direct grant' or 'Headmasters Conference' schools; for boarding or day pupils; single-sex or coeducational, denominational or non-religious – and, of course, some have changed their characteristics during the last 40 years. There were nearly 580,000 independent school pupils in 2012 (DfE 2012, Table 1c) – 7.1% of all pupils in England – but the Conservative policy of replacing state-administered schooling with 'academies' and 'free schools' makes this an increasingly complex figure to monitor. It can also be misleading to report private school fee levels – not only because they vary between schools, but also because monetary values change over time. Firms selling investment advice report that current average costs (including 'extras') for 5 years at a private boarding school are in the region of £750,000; non-boarding attendance would take 36% of an average doctor's salary or 73% of a plumber's salary – three times greater than the levels in 1990 (Killik 2014). Even mainstream 'professionals risk being priced out of private schools, as fees continue to rise' (CEBR 2015; see also Lloyds 2012).

Parents offer various reasons for paying these large sums. Columnists for *The Telegraph* (for example Learner 2012) and participants in online forums such as Mumsnet talk about individual attention; parental involvement; class size; broader learning programmes; high-quality teachers; school spirit, better facilities and independence from public controls or funding levels. While there is occasional reference to 'getting higher grades' (which is indeed what private education delivers: public school pupils are 3.5 times more likely than those on free schools meals to attain 5 GCSEs including English and Maths at grades A★–C), there is little direct mention of gaining advantages over less well-off families or links with elite universities' admissions tutors. Nobody refers to posh accents; self-esteem and confidence; proper etiquette and middle-class standards; learning to exercise leadership, building influential networks for later in life or avoidance of lower-class pupils – yet these are also on offer. As the later discussion of Higher Education and access to elite professions will show, a public school education offers payoffs after it has been completed. Selection by ability to pay favours the few, but must thereby disadvantage others.

This brief discussion of backgrounds, primary and secondary education and meritocracy has provided sufficient information about inequalities in scholastic progress to suggest that the DIM thesis is improbable, and certainly incomplete. However, the evidence does not constitute a logically complete critique; some of the educational outcomes could still be partially explained on the basis of talent. On the other hand, this talent would seem to work not so much directly in the *child* as through other forms of social advantage acquired by the *parents* – such as material resources or the parents' educational backgrounds impacting on home circumstances. Nor does the individual child's ability fully account for selection processes and decisions by schools. Having parents with the ability to pay for an elite education is not a good indicator of children's talent.

It is striking how little of the available governmental evidence is in the form of the seven SeC classes. Instead, it is presented in more limited terminology such as poverty, access to free school milk, or (implicitly) the middle-class cultural capital of knowledge about how schools operate. This limitation makes it harder to make direct connections between qualifications and class mobility. The problem is little better when it comes to higher education and how qualifications actually connect to occupation.

ELEVEN

Tightening bonds and professional access

Lengthy education and vocational training are de rigueur for the 'professional' occupations that make up much of NS-SeC Class I and II. At the extremes, after A-levels medics must undertake a further nine years of preparation, and solicitors a further six or seven years. Entry rules are often enshrined in law and governed by members of the professions themselves, thus reducing labour market competition by demanding educational credentials that only those able to afford long periods of study can obtain (which also contributes to the development of a distinctive collective identity and social status). 'Opportunity hoarding' (Tilly 1998) by reducing the supply of qualified workers secures higher incomes and the social prestige of exclusive occupations. This middle-class 'social closure' is often discussed in terms of human or educational capital and called 'professionalisation'. In working-class craft trade unions, control over job entry through 5-year apprenticeships and 'who does what?' disputes was called the 'closed shop'.

The market advantage of the older professions has come under attack in recent years. What were once doctors' prerogatives are being opened up to (cheaper) specialist nurses and local pharmacists. Large legal conglomerates have driven out local family firms of 'high-street solicitors', reducing many lawyers to the status of employees rather than self-supervising independent professionals, while more straightforward legal services like conveyancing are now offered by agencies and even Tesco. However, despite this more competitive environment, the new agencies support the idea of prolonged training because they can use it to extract greater profits by controlling the supply of legal services.

The 'new professions' in Class 2 have been less successful in establishing social closure. Despite raising entry qualifications from 'diplomas' to degree level in teaching, nursing, librarianship and social work – all mainly in the state sector – training requirements have been reduced by government intervention. 'Free schools' are no longer obliged to use qualified teachers; training in the form of accelerated in-the-classroom experience is replacing postgraduate educational studies, while the numerical expansion and abuse of the role of Teaching Assistant has diminished the distinctive status of teachers. The latter have been vilified by a recent education minister as part of 'the Blob' of Marxists; academics; educationalists; democratically elected local councillors, liberals and teaching trade unions, who should have no say in curriculum content or teaching methods (Gove 2013). Probation and social work have had their hard-won degree entry requirements watered down, with an emphasis on hands-on, 'watching Nelly' training – also increasingly called for in nurses' training. Government cuts to public libraries have resulted in amateur volunteers having to replace the expertise of qualified librarians in many of those libraries that managed to survive.

The professions' labour market strategy of using educational requirements to achieve occupational and social closure also created an unforeseen problem. In assuming their own children would be equally adept (and able to afford the prolonged training, or now unpaid internships – unlike aspirants from the working class), the middle class was 'guilty of grievous errors and miscalculations in its reproductive designs' (Parkin 1971, 62). Direct transmission of advantaged occupational positions to the next generation would prove difficult:

> Dense children of the professional middle class ... will continue to stumble at the intellectual assault course set up largely for their *parents'* own protection. Conversely, large numbers of bright children of the culturally dispossessed will sail through to claim the prize of professional entry. (Parkin 1971, 6; original emphasis)

Despite his criticism of social closure, Parkin's basic position implies a belief in a reserve pool of underutilised talent, as well as that Britain is ultimately meritocratic.

However, in 2009, the Cabinet Office Panel on Fair Access to the Professions reported that the professions 'had actually become more – not less – socially exclusive over time. *Unleashing Aspiration* found that tomorrow's professional is growing up in a family richer than seven in ten of all families in the UK' (in SMCPC 2012, 2). Milburn's progress report 3 years later lamented that 'The general picture seems to be of mainly minor changes in the social composition of the professions. At the top especially, the professions remain dominated by a social elite' (SMCPC 2012, 3). A further three years on, another SMCPC study (2015a, 6) of 'the barriers to entry for people from less privileged socioeconomic backgrounds' found elite law and accountancy firms 'continue to be heavily dominated at entry level by people from more privileged socioeconomic backgrounds'. The 'Parkin effect' may contribute to *downward* mobility of dense children who fail, but 35 years after he was writing it is not preventing a high degree of occupational 'inheritance', nor guaranteeing upward mobility of new entrants.

Unlike most older professions, vacancies for many lower-level or 'service' professions in public sector bureaucracies are typically filled through a routinised, relatively transparent system in which formal qualifications can be explicitly used to sort applicants. In this limited sense, the values of achievement rather than ascription and universalism rather than particularism are more evident than in the private sector or other professions that feature a greater variety of specialisms, career routes and levels. Vacancies for less skilled employment are, however, usually filled from a local labour market in which word of mouth can play a larger part; as such, regional variation is normal. This contrasts with other posts, which are more likely to draw from a national – indeed, sometimes international – pool of potential recruits. Notice of high earning vacancies are often less precise, so the earnings figures in Table 11.1 depend on some approximation.

Other factors lie behind the apparent credentialism of recruitment. Based on job advertisements, careers sites and official bodies that control particular occupations, the posts listed include 'person specifications' such as reliability; honesty; confidence; good timekeeping; communication skills; adaptability; flexibility; strength; dexterity; accountability; drive; ambition; passion; fairness; local geographical knowledge; team playing; safeguarding, commitment to equal opportunities and anti-oppressive practice in all aspects or work – and, of course, prior experience and positive references. And this was just for the cleaners, lollipop ladies, assistant gardeners and caretakers! For recruitment into many Class I jobs,

> firms define "talent" according to a number of factors such as drive, resilience, strong communication skills and above all confidence and "polish", which participants in the research acknowledged can be mapped on to middle-class status and socialisation. (SMCPC 2015a, 6)

In addition to formal qualifications typically obtained in 'elite' universities, candidates are assessed on their social and cultural capital. Person specifications – and opaque social network connections – provide intangible recruitment justifications that have little to do with

Table 11.1: Qualifications and approximate earnings for occupations, September 2015

Job title	Formal educational qualifications[1]	Pay (per annum)[2]
Cleaner (part-time)	None / 'good standard of education' / British Institute of Cleaning Science	£13,144
School Crossing Patrol (part-time)	Four GCSEs, including English	£13,523
Assistant Gardener	NVQ L2 in Amenity Horticulture	£14,378[3]
Hair and Beauty Receptionist	NVQ L2 in Customer Service; GCSEs (grade C) in Maths and English	£15,779
Passenger Assistant	NVQ L2 in Health and Social Care	£16,231
Caretaker (Temporary)	NVQ in General Maintenance and Housekeeping	£17,774
Newspaper Journalist	Degree	£24,656[4]
General Practitioner (GP)	5-year medical degree; 2-year Foundation Programme; 3-year special GP training	£50,781
Solicitor	LL.B. or degree + conversion course (or 5-year Chartered Institute of Legal Executives); 1-year Legal Practice course; 2-year training contract (including Professional Skills course)	£54,100
Banker (Front Office)	Degree	£55,000[5]
Member of Parliament (MP)	None	£67,060

Notes
1 GCSE = General Certificate of Secondary Education; NVQ L2 = National Vocational Qualification Level 2 (equivalent to a GCSE grade A*–C).
2 National average early career earnings excluding expenses, allowances and/or bonuses. Where appropriate, grossed up from part-time or short-term contract hourly rates to annual equivalents, 2015.
3 This post is a zero-hours contract – that is, it offers no guaranteed hours – and is paid at an hourly rate of £7.90.
4 Varies widely; elite columnists earn six-figure fees per annum.
5 Unlike most other non-professional occupations in this table, reliable information on investment bankers' incomes (excluding bonuses) is extremely hard to obtain.

the formal educational qualifications stated on job application forms (Jackson 2001).

However, among the 'non-professional' members of NS-SeC Classes I and II – the managers – formal qualifications have not been the absolute norm for recruitment. 50% of men in Classes 1 and 2 in the Nuffield study did not enter their employment directly (by implication, due to educational selection) but rather were *intra-*

generationally upwardly mobile. The *People in Society* study showed a further variation of the education/employment/mobility linkage among women (Abbott 1990). In 2006, a national study found that more than 40% of British managers did not even have educational qualifications equivalent to GCSE at grades A*– C or NVQ Level 2 (Leitch 2006, 89–90). These key people, who carry out highly skilled functions on which the success of the British economy depends, lacked the *formal* qualifications required to supervise school crossings, help cut the grass in the park or change a light bulb.

Higher education for higher occupations

Connections between mobility and formal education are looser than usually assumed, even at the upper end of the qualifications and occupations range. 56% of Classes I and II jobs are open to non-graduates, as is three quarters of all employment (Ball 2013). In the mid 1980s, only 10% of jobs had the specific entry requirement of a first degree; even by 2012, this had increased to only 26% (Felstead et al 2013). Unfortunately, the categories used in official statistics make it hard to explore the relationship between university qualifications and employment and therefore who has been to which universities – let alone why that matters. The often repeated claim that 'nearly half of young people now go to university' in fact refers to the Higher Education Initial Participation Rate (HEIPR), currently running at about 49%. At first sight, this appears to be the proportion of undergraduates or those obtaining bachelor's degrees, but it turns out to be another *Alice in Wonderland* Civil Service measurement: 'we use the word "graduates" to refer to those people who have left education with qualifications above A level standard' (ONS 2013, 1); or since 2006–07, the proportion of '17-30 year old English domiciled first-time HE entrants to UK HE institutions and English, Welsh and Scottish FE colleges who remain in HE for at least six months' (Department for Business Innovation and Skills 2011).

HEIPR therefore does not refer to those people holding or studying for a first degree but rather to all Level 4 NVQ or equivalent courses at accredited institutions, including BTEC Professional Certificates; Higher National Certificates; Certificates of Higher Education (equivalent to the First Year of a degree); various diplomas and Foundation degrees, as well as conventional bachelor's degree programs and postgraduate degrees. It is not a straightforward count of bodies, but rather a more elaborate calculation designed to estimate (a) the *probability* of (b) a 17 year old now or at some point in the future (c) *starting* a course lasting six months or more, (d) *by the age of 30* and (e) *remaining a student* for at least half a year. Being a HEIPR 'graduate' does not necessarily qualify somebody for jobs that require a degree. That requires completing a proper degree program at a university.

The HEIPR's predecessor, the Age Participation Index (API), had technical limitations (for example, excluding part-timers) but did at least try to measure university degree participation – calculated as the under-21, home-domiciled, full-time and sandwich students entering HE for the first time, expressed as a percentage of the 18- to 19-year-old population. Recalibrated on several occasions (Parliamentary Briefing 2015), this ran at 5% in 1960 (Finegold 2006) and rose to about 30% in the 1990s; there was little further improvement among young men, but a few percentage points increase over a decade for women. In contrast, after a peak at 49% in 2011–12, the new HEIPR declined to 42% three years later, dropping by 6.3% when £9,000 university fees were introduced by the Conservative-led Coalition government (Universities UK 2014, 5). If the HEIPR/API differential were constant, the API would now be 11 points lower, currently at about 31%.

Earlier, Figure 8.2 showed that NS-SeC Classes I and II increased from 33% to 43% of the workforce in the 17 years to 2014. This is generally symmetrical with the HEIPR changes, but we already know from Felstead et al (2013) that more than half of the posts in these classes do not require a degree, although a quarter of jobs in other classes *do* require degree or equivalent qualifications (Ball 2013). But at the time of their UCAS applications, how do 18-year-olds know about the distribution of degree-requiring jobs 3, 4 or 30 years in the future? There is no *neat* fit between the output of 'graduates', employment opportunities and social mobility.

Increased participation rates also raise problems for Saunders' DIM thesis. It seems unlikely that the ability levels for which the qualifications are a proxy have suddenly increased in the last quarter of a century. Did the British population rapidly become brighter and/or more hardworking? If so, psychological ideas of relatively fixed amounts of *inherited* ability/intelligence would be undermined. Although the DIM thesis depends on IQ tests, not qualifications, it copes poorly with changes over time.

Alternatively, it is often alleged that A-levels and degrees have become easier. In DIM terms, getting a degree would now require less intelligence. Having been an undergraduate would still have a social effect in later life, in a more recent world of more graduates. The financial returns may be lower, with consequences for the resultant pattern of income inequality. In this case, statistical comparisons of the association between degree qualifications, employment and mobility are not using consistent measurements.

On the other hand, the SAD alternative can argue that there was an earlier pool of talented young people who were unfairly excluded from university, whereas now the abilities of more people are recognised. Government and academic conservatism's restrictions on degree courses had meant these people had to settle for some other route to employment; a route often leading to less attractive occupations. This kind of social engineering would also explain the earlier lack of education for women. Around 1960, only a quarter of university students were women (Dyhouse, 2007); in 2013, female students made up about 57% of the 'undergraduate' population (Coughlan, 2015b; HESA 2014). The HEIPR measurement reduces the gender gap by several percentage points.

But not all degrees have equal status. However unfairly, employers do devalue the 'post-1992' or 'modern' universities compared to the research-oriented Russell Group institutions. Subjects are evaluated and funded on the basis of traditional prejudices: supposedly vocational 'STEM' subjects are given preference over the social sciences and humanities, old vocational subjects like law or medicine far outrank the new (such as sports science, business studies or fashion design) and traditional disciplines (such as classics, maths or physics) are believed to be 'harder' than newer ones (such as cultural studies or criminology). Level of performance ('a good degree') is a further dimension in recruiters' selection of applicants.

Getting in, getting on

Chapter Three reported on the government documents and the recent forest of organisations concerned with 'fair access' to higher education that have sprung up. All have pointed to the importance of degree education as a means of social mobility. At the time of writing, the most recent example is the Conservatives' White Paper, *Success as a Knowledge Economy: Teaching Excellence, Social Mobility and Student Choice* (BIS 2016) – which despite its title makes fewer than 20 passing references to social mobility, each time assuming without any discussion that greater diversity in student entry will *automatically* raise upward mobility rates. Almost without exception, when these contributions lament the lack of diversity in the student population they refer to it not in terms of social class differences but other indirect indicators.

UCAS, for example, gave up collecting information on class backgrounds in 2008 (House of Commons 2010, 1), blaming incomplete data. While official agencies – SMCPC, Higher Education Funding Council for England (HEFCE), the Office For Fair Access (OFFA) and UCAS – have identified lack of diversity among undergraduates, they do not express this as a problem of social class. Instead, they have adopted indirect indicators such as lower incomes or homes in geographical areas with low rates of participation in higher education. The proportion of pupils receiving free school meals – about 20% – is used as a proxy for socioeconomic disadvantage at the school level (those eligible for but not taking FSM would add a few percentage points). The other 80% is treated as a single bloc, rather than further divided into, say, 'average' and 'advantaged' (for example, the 7% attending public schools).

A recent report from SMCPC (2015c) named and shamed Oxbridge colleges for choosing 41% of their intakes from independently schooled pupils (7% of their age group), noting that poor children with high academic attainment at the age of 11 are four times less likely to go on to an elite university than their high-attaining wealthier peers. The Sutton Trust (2010, 2) reported that independent school pupils are over 22 times more likely to be admitted to a highly selective 'high-entry tariff' university than state school children taking free school meals and 55 times more likely to gain an Oxbridge place. The social geography of origins also matters. In the period 2006 to 2015, English 18 year olds from the most advantaged areas were between 6.3 and 8.5 times more likely to enter higher tariff providers compared to the most disadvantaged areas (UCAS 2015).

Ethnicity is a further indicator of 'diversity'. Although candidates from Black and minority ethnic groups go to university in relatively good numbers, a Nuffield Foundation study reported that university applications by:

> candidates from Pakistani, Bangladeshi, Black African, Indian, Black Caribbean, Chinese and various 'other' groups were all found to be less likely to yield an offer than those made by white British candidates, ... ethnic and social class differences in offer rates could not be fully explained by differences in academic attainment or patterns of application. (Noden et al 2014, 7–8)

These differentials in university access are part of a long established pattern (Boliver 2011; Gorard et al 2007), although there is some debate about whether the problem lies in university entrance or in prior schooling (Chowdry et al 2010):

The evidence, as far as it goes, suggests that over the latter half of the 20th century there was little change in the proportion of university students from lower social classes. Their participation in higher education increased, but so did participation from all social classes and the gap that was apparent in the middle of the last century was broadly maintained to the end ... the coverage of the socio-economic data had been falling for some years. (House of Commons 2014,1; see also SMCPC 2014b)

As Coulson et al (2017) observe, the term 'class' is now seldom used by these public agencies and imprecise reference to '"background" and "disadvantage" do the discursive heavy lifting, without invoking structural inequalities or systemic failures'. The now-common university programs aimed at encouraging 'fair access', by use of 'contextual information' when deciding on applicants, show similar reluctance to consider class data directly. Admissions procedures that flag 'disadvantaged' schools have no matching flag for 'advantaged' public schools (Coulson et al 2017).

Defenders of current access arrangements rely ultimately, if often unconsciously, on the DIM thesis, with A-level performance standing as a direct indicator of ability and the consequent belief that applicants with the best A-levels *merit* places at elite universities. Excluding them to make way for disadvantaged students with lower A-level performance would therefore, it is argued, be unfair. High entry tariffs have elided into an explicit indicator of *institutional* high quality in the HE market place (in which one seldom encounters discussion of why the elite universities with the 'best' staff, facilities and largest budgets should teach the 'best' students, rather than teaching the supposedly less able students with lower A-level grades, who presumably would benefit more from such elite education environments). The lack of state-educated students at Oxbridge is attributed to their reluctance to apply, or – compared with their public school peers – a shortage of state pupils with the same ability level (that is, A-level scores and/or knowledge of how the recruitment system works), as demonstrated in college entrance interviews.

The fallacy in this version of the DIM explanation is that opportunities to obtain high A-level scores are not uniformly distributed; nor are A-level scores a precise guide to later academic performance. It must be acknowledged that fee-paying schools have the resources to provide superior education and obtain better A-level results, but on average their pupils subsequently cannot perform as well at university as similarly qualified students from state schools (HEFCE 2014). This cannot be a *direct* product of genetic superiority in IQ. If it were claimed that the parents' genetic superiority led to their greater wealth, and it is the wealth that buys the educational advantage, the argument regresses to *social advantage and disadvantage*. If possessing A-levels is a mark of ability, why do 60,000 18 year olds – who, at age 11, 14 or 16, have been among the top fifth of academic performers in English state schools – subsequently not enter HE each year (figures for 2004–5; Sutton Trust 2008, 2)?

But the DIM 'level playing field' model does not work even for those who do become undergraduates. Students from working-class families do not leave their backgrounds behind them when they enter the middle-class environment of Higher Education. 'Non-traditional' students come to university with dispositions, habits and preferences that leave them feeling that they do not fit in. A growing body of research influenced by Bourdieu's ideas of classed habitus and fields offers powerful accounts of how social, economic and cultural capitals shape choices, experiences and outcomes in HE (for example, Archer 2007; Archer et al 2003; Bathmaker et al 2013; Loveday 2015; Morrin 2013; Reay 2006; Reay et al 2001a; Reay et al 2009, 2010) – processes also, of course, present in connections between families and schooling (Reay 2000).

'First-generation' undergraduates are less well-informed about university culture, such as academic staff roles or the importance of active participation in seminars (Crozier et al 2008). They lack confidence and are self-conscious about their regional accents. Their financial circumstances mean they are more likely to take on paid employment during term, losing time for study and university social life. And they can encounter exclusion from friendships with other students who have been to fee-paying schools (Coulson et al 2017). The Paired Peers project has shown that otherwise matching students, but from different backgrounds, not only experience higher education in different ways but also whether they are attending an elite university or a less prestigious 'modern' university (for example, Bradley et al 2011; Bradley and Ingram 2013; Mellor et al 2012). It is hard to explain these distinctive experiences as outcomes of intelligence alone, as required by the DIM thesis.

Selection and selectivity

The differences between *types* of universities return us to institutional blockages in the education system. A degree from Oxbridge or an 'elite' university is a large factor in subsequent employment prospects; access to these higher education institutions (HEIs) can be seen as potentially connected to mobility, but the connection is a complicated one. Chapter Ten showed social inequalities cumulatively impeding progress through the educational system. Impediments operate through official and unofficial schooling policies, but also through subtle influences of social and cultural capital.

The latter influences leave the causal framework opaque because they do not show up well in standard statistical accounts. The tightening bond identified in quantitative analyses (often by researchers who have worked only inside academia) has underestimated both the complexity of the education system and the way recruitment uses other, non-educational requirements. In trying to cover a wider range of factors, Bond and Saunders' (1999) path model of occupational attainment is intellectually sophisticated but too complex to be very useful (Saunders 2010, 86). Analysis is hampered by a lack of data at a suitable level for reliable comparison, while education has changed over time in parallel to occupational transition.

We are left with a slightly confusing picture. There are considerable social inequalities, which – as SAD argues – constrain educational achievement. The cumulative evidence of these suggests that there is more to 'success' than the DIM thesis allows. But educational qualifications are unnecessary for many higher-class jobs. At the same time, absolute intergenerational mobility rates are high (it is worth noting that all mobility studies report high levels of short-range downward mobility from the advantaged Class 1 and 2 – contra DIM). The weakness in the tightening bond thus seems to be located both in strong educational inequalities and in the connection between education and career outcome. Qualifications may often be necessary but not sufficient. As we shall see in the final chapter, this is particularly true for both the elite and the most disadvantaged families. It may be unwelcome news to those who have achieved success as they see it on their own merits, but if possession of formal qualifications measures 'merit', Britain's selective education produces only a very partial meritocracy.

TWELVE

Moving on

The origins of this book lie in the increasing interest in social mobility that our politicians have shown in the last couple of decades. This interest is a good thing. However, they have misunderstood what mobility means, how much of it is happening, what produces mobility and what can be the consequences of mobility at both personal and national levels. Such misunderstandings are a bad thing. In place of this confused and misleading perspective, successive chapters have clarified definitions, offered an alternative explanation of the causes of mobility, described some features of current mobility patterns and argued that social mobility is better understood as a series of connected but separable issues than a single monolithic process (the latter being evident in, for example, the call for 'more mobility' or 'better schooling').

These arguments can be drawn together in two ways. On the one hand, mobility can be thought of as the product of interacting general forces and social processes. The groups that make up society are all subject to occupational transition, gender and ethnic differences and wider inequalities. On the other hand, the starting point for thinking through mobility can be the classes or groups themselves, each of which encounters (and generates) specific movements and displays distinctive mobility profiles.

This chapter starts with the second approach, because the disaggregation of mobility has been one of the book's underlying themes. Absolute mobility rates are generally high, albeit reflecting a different kind of mobility than most politicians want. However there are several pockets of immobility that need to be addressed before turning to some of the wider issues.

Four kinds of class mobility prospects: the upper reaches

The earlier discussion of education suggested that private schools and Russell Group universities combined with forms of familial cultural advantage offer a separate route to the best jobs, such as the old professions. But these are also the preferred – if not the only – entry routes for a smaller group of people who hold the very best rewarded and most influential positions in society, such as those portrayed in Table 12.1.

Table 12.1: British elites

Elite groups	% from private schools	% from 'elite' universities
Senior judges	71	75
Senior armed forces officers	62	15[1]
Conservative MPs	60	93
Civil service permanent secretaries	55	57
Diplomats	53	50
House of Lords	52	38
The Sunday Times rich list	44	12
Newspaper columnists	43	47
Labour MPs	17	65
British population	7	12

Note [1] Estimated from Stanworth 2013, 274.
Source: SMCPC 2014a, 9–15, 23.

Because this elite – or 'the establishment' (Harvey 2011; Hennessy 2014; Jones 2014; SMCPC 2014a; Stanworth 2013; Toynbee and Walker 2008) – is relatively small in number and consists of a number of sub-elites, its members have not normally been included in mobility studies as an identifiable group (there is no NS-SeC category for this elite). In addition, members of the elite tend to be reluctant to complete intrusive sociological surveys. Inconsistencies in definitions, data sources and time periods in elite research produce small variations in the size and social characteristics reported, but insofar as there is reliable evidence, the general picture is clear (*Sociological Review* 2015).

To the extent that elites share a privileged background, they consequently have less first-hand experience of going to ordinary state schools or the home life of other classes. This limits their personal knowledge and reduces their capacity to empathise with less fortunate people over and above their instinct to act in their own self-interest. The more they interact with each other (Bond 2012), the more inward-looking they become (Toynbee and Walker 2008). Their immobility at the top of society therefore raises issues of both fairness and effectiveness. Is it *fair* that so many of those with power come from a narrow, socially advantaged subset of British society and remain immobile at the top, generation after generation? Are their priorities and values *representative* of the population as a whole? Would upward mobility from a wider catchment improve the *effectiveness* of the elite and their capacity to govern *efficiently* in the interest of all? Are any particular groups (for example, women) *excluded*?

The evidence on the distribution of wealth over the last two decades indicates that material inequalities have changed in favour of the very rich under the policies implemented by the current elite. To illustrate, an Institute for Fiscal Studies (IFS) study in 2013 found the average annual *income* of the top 1% of earners was £368,940 (after tax), while the equivalent for the UK as a whole was £24,596 (Cribb et al 2013). 82% of British people think the income gap is too large (British Social Attitudes 2013, quoted in Dorling 2014, 2). The Gini coefficient (one of the standard measurements of inequality, in which 0 would be complete equality and 1.0 complete inequality) has risen from about 0.25 in the late 1970s to over 0.35 in the present decade; as such, 'the UK is now one of the most unequal societies in the developed world' (Equality Trust 2014). Britain is the only G7 country in which *wealth* inequality has grown since 2000 (Credit Suisse 2014; see also Piketty 2013).

Alongside between 7% and 17% of the population, some readers may think these inequalities are a moral and efficient way to run a society, or little to do with the backgrounds of those in power:

> Old Etonians do have a certain poise and an inbred air of self-confidence. To that extent I disagree with those who say that Cameron's background is immaterial. On the contrary, an Eton education goes some way to explaining why Cameron is as he is: debonair, unflappable, polite, gentlemanly, restrained and dutiful – a person of equable temperament. It is not, however, that Eton gives its pupils an air of superiority. Rather, it gives them the confidence to lead – along with the duties, demands and responsibilities implied. (Hershman 2010)

Nor should it be assumed that letting more people from outside into the elite would automatically change things; assimilation of able recruits from below can actually tighten the grip of the rulers.

However, as the elite increasingly shifted the burden of taxation onto poorer people and reduced public services for education, health and social care, inequalities increased, the gaps between social classes widened and the upward mobility prospects of more people began to be reduced. Every elite has to convince the masses that it is doing a good job. The disaffection of the Scottish and sections of the urban lower classes – partially due directly to blocked mobility and indirectly to our immobile elite's policy of increasing inequality – indicates that our current elite is not entirely successful. The elite may be small in number, but its control over society means its contribution to the 'mobility problem' is very large. This vulnerability is shared with the professionals and managers in Class 1. Neither group is going to give up its privileges without a fight.

Four kinds of class mobility prospects: the service class

The Class 1, service class, of senior managers and established professionals is as close to the elite as mainstream mobility analysis gets, so that it has to act as a proxy for the sorts of positions in Table 12.1. Researchers' concentration on Class 1 is partly due to it providing the sharpest contrast with Class 7, but it is also a result of the invisibility of the elite. Mobility into and immobility within Class 1 has been a major focus in research – indeed, to such an extent that other classes have been under researched. It is also the class to which mobility analysts belong, and we are all interested in our own destinies.

Chapter Nine showed how the world of professionals and managers is strongly self-recruiting, even if it does also draw on other classes. Some inhabitants of this world are exploiting privilege through the education system (chapters Ten and Eleven) while others – many managers – have relatively few qualifications. As part of the growing redistribution of inequalities, Class 1 has also lost out to the very rich – but not to the same extent as other classes. Nonetheless, the security of its children is threatened by rising costs of private education and housing.

The threat to their particular mobility situation (to some extent shared with Class 2) comes from three sources. Although occupational transition seems set to continue for the time being after its temporary glitch around the turn of the century, the 'bulge' of parents who became middle class during the initial expansion of the welfare state means there are more middle-class children today competing for middle-class jobs. Access for many is blocked by the social closure mechanisms of long training and high academic qualification levels, which hoard professional opportunities even from those who benefit from favourable cultural capital and educational advantage due to their family origins. Their daughters are doing better, but only insofar as obtaining the Class 2 occupations that women have traditionally filled, which is no help to the sons' expectations.

Because mainstream analysis has concentrated on rates of mobility, less work has been done to discover what people *feel* about their own mobility. It seems probable that their perspectives resemble the attitudes that Runciman (1966) identified towards material wellbeing: people compare themselves with those closest to themselves, rather than the whole social range (see Rose 2006, Wegener 1991). The upwardly mobile compare themselves to their origin circumstances, noting what has been achieved, as well as with others like themselves in the new class they have entered. Getting into Class 1 in particular is therefore initially self-satisfying – but the slow realisation that their upward mobility is actually limited and that they can go no further makes them distrust the elite. Worse, the potential or actual downward mobility of their offspring becomes all the more threatening.

Recent research also suggests that only one in three families retain Class 1 membership over three generations, with those who do having greater material assets and being more likely to buy private education (Boliver and Sullivan 2016). Parents who have been upwardly mobile are less secure about being able to pass on that advantage to the next generation. The call for 'more mobility' resonates with the anxieties of professional and managerial parents, for whom downward mobility of their *sons* is now shaming, even if it is only into Class 2 or Class 3. Even though opportunities for men in Class 2 show a small expansion, this offers a loss in status for those born in Class 1.

Four kinds of class mobility prospects: the middle of the pack

In Classes 2 and 3, gender intersects most obviously with class. Many women have to make do with upward mobility reaching these two classes at best – classes that largely consist of 'women's work'. By disaggregating mobility into class groupings it becomes obvious that women encounter different mobility prospects and experiences, and that 'mobility' itself does not mean the same for both genders or across all classes. The lack of attention to female social mobility in both the academic literature and public debate would seem remarkable were it not for British culture being so solidly patriarchal.

Women are also poorly represented in Class 4, the self-employed and small business class – a class whose rates of self-recruitment and upward mobility stand out from the other groups in the middle of the class hierarchy. The sphere of small businesses has a strong masculine culture (Giazitzoglu and Down 2015); it is a somewhat opaque sector, in which occupational class can be literally handed on from father to son. Although there have been studies of the petit bourgeoisie section of Class 4, the lower end of this class has not been well researched compared to other parts of the working class.

However, the bulk of this class has exchanged manual employment for manual self-employment, either as an aspirational career move or as a necessity following redundancy and unemployment – an increasingly common product of recent governments' long-term economic plans. Becoming self-employed (one of the two routes to upward *intra*generational mobility for the sorts of 'careers' that predominate in the lower classes) is possible in occupations in which there is little need for capital. This is evident for men in the construction trades, in which the skills required are skills that few women have had the opportunity to acquire. Class 5, the class of lower supervisors and technicians, is the least researched in mobility analysis – including here. Promotion to foreman or supervisor is the other *intra*generational route to upward mobility for employees who start work in Classes 6 and 7. While the lower technician grade can offer direct *inter*generational upward mobility from the latter classes, supervisory posts are not passed down from parents to their children. Class 5 is therefore relatively open to those born in the classes below it, and exchanges with other classes (except for Class 4) close to the proportions of its offspring that would occur if destinations were relatively independent of origins. In other words, it is the only class that could be said to require little policy intervention to improve its mobility rates.

Four kinds of class mobility prospects: the bottom of the heap

If only because of the utility of contrast with Class 1, the lowest class has featured more strongly in mobility analysis. Class 7 is a shrinking class, but families who remain in it for a second generation risk becoming detached from the rest of society. For example, the poor educational achievement of children who qualify for free school meals acts as a practical barrier to further necessary (but not sufficient) qualifications or professional employment. Parents with limited educational experience are in a poor place to assist with their children's schooling beyond general encouragement (Olantiti 2013). At the most extreme, not only do they experience the lowest chances of mobility and the least fair amount of disadvantage, but their very existence also fuels the underclass anxieties of governments.

The prospects for Classes 6 and 7 are indeed poor. These two classes have shrunk from 31.7% to 24.1% of the labour force since the late 1990s. If this trend continues and there is no upward mobility escape route, their children face unemployment as the likely alternative outcome. There may be fewer second-generation lower-class people, but they will become increasingly detached from the rest of the occupational order.

The prospects of changing this are poor. Social policies may be geared to assist the most disadvantaged, but they are usually framed in a way that also benefits others; for example, the Conservatives' Life Chances Strategy (Cameron 2016) or the recommendations of the Lib Dems' Commission (Narey 2009). Of course, other classes also need assistance, but Class 7 is the most pressing problem.

A more pessimistic view of mobility prospects

Suppose that we take the politicians' call for more (upward) mobility seriously. Their policies have largely concentrated on children and education, which means that we would have to wait another generation to see the benefits in higher mobility rates. However, for these benefits to spread across the whole of society, we would have to wait a further 40 years or so for the new patterns of added mobility to work their way throughout the whole of the labour force.

There are also grounds for pessimism about the potential of people in lower classes to be mobile, even if they benefit from these policies. The logic of the DIM explanation of mobility is that the inheritable abilities of those in the lower classes are weaker than those in the higher classes; even if the playing field were more level, they would still mainly turn out to be the losers. The alternative logic of the SAD thesis is that families have different social advantages: the offspring of those at the top are better able to maintain their positions. However, despite these birth advantages all surveys show considerable downward mobility from the class of senior managers and professionals – something in the order of one or more in every three. If this rate of 'failure' is occurring among the more advantaged, are we to believe that the more disadvantaged children of other classes are unlikely to show at least similar patterns of 'non-achievement'? From this perspective, only two in three (2,750,000) of the just over 4 million men currently in Class 7 would be likely to be upwardly mobile – even if new ameliorating policies were in place (male mobility is used here only to simplify the illustration).

If – with all the inherited advantages of family background, cultural capital and gender that all competent surveys show – Class 1 families are finding it hard to retain their status, what chance do members of Class 7 have of escape (even with policies of intervention), let alone make the leap to Class 1 in substantially increased numbers? If 'ability' is largely randomly distributed across classes (and all the more so if it is not), their scope for improved mobility is limited.

Applying real (albeit only ballpark) numbers to the politicians' rhetoric in this way is problematic but can be illuminating. How much 'more mobility' would be a 'success'? We could argue that, say, a 10% improvement in the upward mobility rate over the lifetime of four governments (two decades or one generation) would be a reasonable target. Where would this new mobility be located? Reductions in the number of second-generation denizens of Classes 6 and 7? Increased movements from Class 7 to Class 1? Or a scatter of movements from all lower classes to all higher classes? Whichever model is chosen, it would need about 2.1 million new jobs of a higher level to accommodate the 2.1 million men (and, of course, broadly similar numbers of women) required to make up that 10%.

Taking the simplest model, let us assume the extra mobility consisted of new moves from Class 7 to Class 1. We have seen that some 2,750,000 Class 7 males are notionally 'available' to be mobile, but Class 1 would have to expand its male employment from around 3.2 million to 5.3 million – that is, to grow by roughly two thirds – provided, of course, none of the new jobs were shared by Class 1 children who would otherwise have been downwardly mobile, or those who could now become upwardly mobile from other classes. Even in the unlikely event that the latter phenomenon did not happen, a 67% increase in the number of professionals and managers within 20 years seems unlikely, given that the 17-year period 1997 to 2014 (Table 8.3) saw an increase of about 21%. The alternative scenario is that the newcomers displace the children of Class 1 and force them to be downwardly mobile. Adding a further 2.1 million (5%) to the downward mobility rate is not the stated intention of the policy initiatives.

This is not the place to rehearse all of the permutations of alternative models that might offer the suggested 10% increase. We can note, however, that the expansion of Classes 1–4 amounted to just over 1.5 million men between 1997 and 2014. This may have *sustained* previous mobility patterns, but there is no sign yet of any substantial increase in the male upward mobility rate. Indeed, as the research of Bukodi et al (2015) suggests, it may be *downward* mobility rates that are increasing. The 10% goal is therefore unrealistic, but posing it as a straw figure helps to make the point that our political leaders have yet to set their own targets or to come to terms with the constraints that prohibit significant changes to the upward mobility rate. For the foreseeable future there are going to be substantial numbers of losers in the mobility competition, and yet they will be vilified for their lack of success. It follows that policies are needed to reduce their *unequal situation* rather than improve their *mobility*, because this group cannot avoid being second-generation Class 7. It seems the immobile, if not the poor, are always with us.

New Social *Mobilities?*

Although the discussion up to now has talked about a new social mobility in the singular, this mobility has in fact been constructed from several alternative new social *mobilities*. Its first and most obvious component was described as 'the politicians' view': the belief that mobility rates were low, declining and worse than other countries. This belief, as set out in the early chapters, is doubly incorrect. The 'evidence' on which it has been based is unreliable, chiefly because operational definitions of measurements like absolute mobility and relative mobility have not been properly understood or implemented. But this shoddy borrowing from what is actually an extensive research literature is only the *process* by which the politicians' beliefs were constructed. More fundamentally, their resulting *beliefs* are plain wrong. Mobility rates are high, they are not in decline nor is the UK noticeably a less mobile country than comparable European nations. As a consequence, assumptions that upward mobility rates can be easily improved by small-scale policy interventions to equalise *opportunity* are over-optimistic and misplaced.

This is not to say that our politicians are wrong in identifying mobility as a problem.

Middle-class families' fears of downward mobility, especially for their sons, are real. 'Underclass anxiety' is not completely unfounded. There *is* a current mobility problem, albeit not the one as understood by the politicians, nor one which in the short run is very amenable to change by the sorts of public policies that the elite and their middle class fellow travellers would tolerate. The silver bullet of social mobility will not kill social inequalities – even if there were a genuine desire to reduce such inequalities.

Although critical of the politicians' view, our new social mobility remains politically engaged. Despite differentiating between social mobility and other forms of social inequality, mobility has to be seen as working in concert with wider social trends. The disappointment of rising expectations in a Britain – in which real income levels have fallen for most people while public services are being privatised, reduced or abolished – links public perceptions of frustrated mobility to other sources of disillusionment. If people see meritocratic mobility as less likely, the continuity of social order and the security of the elite's rule are undermined.

As an alternative to the paradigm of low mobility, chapter Nine set out a description of contemporary mobility patterns, constituting a new mobility in terms of where we are in the first quarter of the 21st century. This showed in detail how four in every five adults were in a different class to the one in which they had grown up. We can note in passing that how this must weaken class-specific cultures, with a consequent disengagement in class identity and class action. This great stirring of the pot involves a large component of less welcome downward mobility and disguises considerable levels of class inheritance – particularly among professionals and managers and the self-employed (who are better able to hang on to their advantaged positions) and Class 7 (in which those with the lowest grade of employment are less able to escape the influences of birth).

In particular, this book has highlighted the social closure at the upper echelons of society and the isolation of those at the bottom as exceptions to otherwise high levels of mobility. In this respect, the Social Mobility and Child Poverty Commission (SMCPC), under the leadership of Alan Milburn, has been the most correct of the public bodies in recognising where the real 'problem of mobility' lies. However, its explanations of the causes and its policy solutions, like those of the Sutton Trust, still leave something to be desired. As the education chapters here showed, formal qualifications are important, but on their own they do not explain occupational outcomes (Bloodworth 2016). The discussion of qualifications and job recruitment not only cast doubt on a simple meritocratic model but also addressed this as a critique of individualistic explanations based on personal qualities and aspirations. This explicit critique of individualistic perspectives constitutes a third new view of mobility.

This is not to say that nothing should be done to improve access to schooling or diversity in higher education or that these are totally unrelated to mobility, let alone social inequality. The expansion of the middle classes increased mobility competition and a new line of class division – a new mobility regime – is emerging; one in which accumulated assets and graduation from a Russell Group university are becoming the new credentials for membership of the professions. The old working class may have disappeared, but class processes remain and new class formations are being produced. Education is a key element of this process, although it does not provide an adequate explanation of mobility.

Implicit in this comment is the idea that previous key studies have paid too much attention to education and thereby missed some of the other factors that determine mobility outcomes – not least gender and the labour market. By developing the idea of occupational transition, a fourth new mobility has outlined an alternative to more traditional approaches, with a renewed emphasis on absolute mobility and a concern for comparing chances of mobility in a way that takes direct account of available occupational structures and their gendered distribution. It also points to an alternative way of calculating relative chances of mobility, taking into account the changing sizes of the social classes. The fresh importance paid to labour markets shows how gender – previously largely neglected – is fundamental to the amount, type and therefore experience of mobility. The weight attached to the consequences of mobility adds to former work in which unfairness has been the dominant theme and in which data interpretation has sometime unwittingly been over-influenced by the political interests of the researchers.

An even newer social mobility

Looking forward, the implication of disaggregating mobility is that more detailed accounts are needed of the various forms this can take. In particular, there is a strong case for adding a more qualitative dimension to the quantitative paradigm typical of most mobility studies. Movement (or lack thereof) involves issues of personal experience, feelings, relationships and meanings; we need to know more about the small-scale dynamics of mobility, following the lead of Lawler (1999), Miles et al (2011), Giazitzoglu (2014) and Friedman (2015).

Futurology is best left to futurologists, but readers are entitled to ask where all this leaves us. What does the future hold for the mobility of our children and us? One thing is certain: mobility rates have not changed very much or very rapidly since the establishing of the welfare state and there is no reason to expect substantial and rapid change in coming years. Well-intentioned social policies take at least a generation to bear fruit. Nor will there be uniform effects; there will be different mobility prospects for various groups and some trends will counterbalance others. The mobility outcome will depend on the balance of competing trends and forces. On the whole, it seems probable that upward mobility will not increase. The most likely kind of 'more mobility' is downward mobility – not because ameliorative policies must fail, but because stronger social forces are in operation.

Against this negative expectation, it is unlikely that the occupational transition effect – which has sustained mobility and arguably increased rates – will disappear overnight; the data indicate that these changes are still happening, most notably for women. However, this effect cannot be relied upon to continue indefinitely. Even if it does continue at the same level, so that mobility rates are likely to be increased by the overall drift of occupational transition, this will not provide rapid change in mobility.

We cannot all be middle class, and there can no continuous increase in the room at the top. Gordon Brown's vision of a high-tech, high-skill economy would expand this room, but British industry remains reluctant to invest in training its own workforce – or to pay its share of the costs of state education, health and so on, through fair taxation, to produce high quality workers. The dreams of a disappearing unskilled working class are dependent on technological fantasies. At a national level, the slow gains of women in better jobs are largely netted out by the loss of status of men from middle-class families, but these gender differences have been largely ignored in public debate.

In addition, mobility is likely to be *reduced* by the growing bulge of parents who are now more middle class, which produces more competition for a limited supply of middle-class occupations. It is also likely to be reduced by the Conservative government's policies of shrinking public services and welfare support, which will add to social inequality and isolate those near the bottom of the social hierarchy. The further the British economy moves to a low-wage, low-skill economy, the more people will be dependent on insecure work contracts in 'burger-flipping' industries.

Much depends on the balance of types of employment in the emerging labour force. Opportunities may slowly grow for Classes 1 and 2, although the increasing requirement for specialist technical expertise among managers will require more education and will therefore close some avenues to management for uneducated working-class recruits. The financial services on which Britain depends for employment and earnings will continue to dominate and London and the South East of England will therefore become further differentiated from the rest of the nation. However, a parallel development is that already over 60% of the carers in London have come from abroad to look after an aging population, which will require more carers. When the Brexiters achieve their 'control of immigration' the impact will be both swift and sharp. These novel occupational transitional effects work more quickly than current social policies designed to intervene in mobility processes.

This is not to say that policy interventions are bound to fail. Rather, wider social changes operate in more immediate and powerful way. The problem is that the policies that would work quickly and powerfully are politically unpalatable. Resistance to reforms aiming to improve gender equality in pay and employment, especially in the higher reaches of companies, provides a solid example of how this works. Abolition of public and selective schools; imposition of class intake quotas on Russell Group universities; progressive taxation (on inheritance, property values and very high incomes), regional redistribution of expenditure and specific benefits for those in poverty and poor-quality jobs would shake up British mobility. Such policies may be those most often embraced by the Left, but the fundamental truth that needs to be faced is that those with advantages must give up some of them to make space for those who start off with disadvantages. If we really want more mobility, improving equality of *opportunity* is a red herring – what matters is improving equality of *outcome*. Improving mobility rates will do little to reduce social inequality, but reducing social inequality is the sure way to achieving greater social mobility.

Appendix

The mobility table

The core of mobility analysis has been the 'mobility table': a cross-tabulation of origins and destinations. Conventionally, origins are shown in the rows across the table and destinations down the columns, with the row and column totals on the right and bottom margins of the table respectively. These totals are often referred to as 'the marginals' or the 'marginal distributions'.

The categories of origins and destinations are ranked from highest to lowest on their social advantages and entered into the table, starting at the top left-hand corner. An example is given in Table A.1, which for simplicity shows three social classes.

Table A.1: An illustrative mobility table

		Destinations			
		1 & 2	3, 4 & 5	6 & 7	Totals
Origins	1 & 2	3,081	1,156	578	4,815 (30.0%)
	3, 4 & 5	2,702	2,190	1,277	6,169 (38.5%)
	6 & 7	1,688	1,724	1,642	5,054 (31.5%)
	Totals	7,471 (46.6%)	5,070 (31.6%)	3,497 (21.5%)	16,038 (100%)

Table A.1 contains the data from Table 9.1 for seven NS-SeC classes of men (to simplify the example), regrouped into three classes, for example this creates a new class 'Class 1& 2' from SeC Class 1 and SeC Class 2. The logic of a 3 × 3 mobility table with nine cells applies to any table with a higher number of categories. Because of the ordering of the categories, the cells that form a diagonal from the top left to the bottom right of the table contain those who are immobile or 'self-recruited'. The cells below and to the left of this 'main diagonal' show upward mobility, while those above and to the right show downward mobility. Thus in Table A.1, adding the numbers in the cells in each of these zones shows that 43.1% (3,081 + 2,190 + 1,642) are immobile, 38.1% (2,702 + 1,688 + 1,724) are upwardly mobile and 18.8% (1,156 + 578 + 1,277) are downwardly mobile. These figures are calculated by adding together the relevant cells and expressing them as a percentage of the overall total of 16,038. Had we used more categories (as in Table 9.1), the mobility rates would have been higher.

Mobility can also be calculated as movements out of origins or inflow into destinations. Here, the outflow from Class 6 & 7 is (1,688 + 1,724) ÷ 5,054, or 67.5%. The inflow to Class 1 & 2 is 58.8% ((2,702 + 1,688) ÷ 7,471). Outflow mobility is more often used when researchers are most concerned with unfairness in chances of mobility. Inflow mobility is mainly used in discussions of the consequences of mobility for new social formations.

Absolute and relative mobility

Mobility tables from different countries or time periods can have very different marginal distributions, which makes comparison of their mobility rates difficult: are measured rates due to the sizes of the categories, or to greater or lesser equality in their social mobility processes? More recent analysis has distinguished between absolute mobility (the people actually being mobile) and relative mobility; that is, the *chances* of moving between origins and destinations. These chances have been measured in two main ways: disparity ratios and odds ratios.

The disparity ratio compares the proportion of people from one origin who reached a specified destination with the proportion of people from another origin who reached the same destination. In Table A.1 (top row), 3,081 out of 4,815 who started in Class 1 & 2 ended up in Class 1 & 2, compared with (bottom row) 1,688 out of 5,054 who started in Class 6 & 7. Those from Class 1 & 2 were twice as likely to become members of Class 1 & 2 themselves, as were those from Class 6 & 7. The 2:1 ratio compares the 'successful' movers with the marginal total of all those from their origin.

The odds ratio is somewhat less intuitive. First, it compares the proportion of 'successes' (those who meet our specified condition) with the proportion of 'failures', rather than the proportion of successes with the total. In mathematical terms, this removes the size of the category from the calculation.

Second, rather than comparing two origins and *one* destination it combines two origins and *two* destinations. For instance, we can compare the chances for those starting in Class 1 & 2 with starters from Class 6 & 7, of having reached the destination of Class 1 & 2 rather than the destination of Class 6 & 7. In Table A.1, 3,081 of those from Class 1 & 2 were 'successes' in reaching the destination of Class 1 & 2, which 1,734 'failed' to achieve. Meanwhile, 578 'succeeded' in moving to Class 6 and 7 and 4,237 'failed' to do so. The equivalents for those originating from Class 6 & 7 were 1,688 and 3,348, and 1,642 and 3,412, respectively. When these ratios are combined and standardised to show the Class 6 & 7 chance as 1.0, this indicates that those from Class 1 & 2 are 12.6 times more likely, than those from Class 6 & 7 origins, to end up in Class 1 & 2 rather than Class 6 & 7. Further examples of calculations can be found in Goldthorpe (1987, 81–5) and Breen and Rottman (1995, 105-9).

While this method can be used for further statistical analysis, the odds ratio is less straightforward than the disparity ratio. The odds ratio also treats upward and downward mobility as directly equivalent. As noted in the text, the conditional disparity ratio, although producing apparently lower comparison scores, takes explicit account of the marginal distributions.

A further attraction of odds ratios is that the method of calculation means that if there were complete equality of chances, the values of all the intergroup odds ratios would be 1.0. This provides a fixed point against which all actually observed odds ratios/mobility can be measured. It shows how far mobility falls short of perfect equality. Goldthorpe's insistence on the lack of change in 'social fluidity' rates is dependent on the use of odds ratios in this way. However, some critics (Noble 1995; Saunders 2010) have argued that this is an unrealistic test.

Odds rations have the effect of emphasising the limitations of mobility in Britain instead of recognising the relatively high degree of openness. This is not only because they produce larger numbers (18:1 vs 6 or 3 to 1) but also because relative mobility rates show less change than absolute mobility rates. For academics wedded to theories of a rigid class society and politicians pushing an ideological line, odds ratios were therefore welcomed because low or no relative mobility could be opposed to the claim from absolute mobility that Britain was an 'open' society with high rates of mobility. In the process, the specific technicalities of the calculations and what they actually measured were largely ignored in public commentaries.

Odds ratios can also be incorporated in other analytical techniques, in particular log liner modelling. In a highly influential pair of articles in 1975, Hauser and colleagues used this method to enable them to specify the effect of the changing origin and destination distributions in the USA and to test the strengths of other factors – such as changes in the rate of mobility remaining, after allowing for changes in the shape of origins and destinations (Hauser et al 1975a; 1975b). By comparing the extent to which alternative models consisting of different combinations of variables predict the actual distributions (and thereby estimating the significance of each variable), their results suggested that social mobility was not changing over time – once overall structural features of the available occupations had been taken into account. Similar results were reported from the Nuffield Mobility Study of England and Wales. Later studies took up the modelling technique to test which causal factors most influenced mobility rates by testing models with various combinations of variables. However, this approach is still dependent on odds ratios and the question remains whether seeing mobility as chances *net* of structural changes is the most fruitful way forward.

Despite this sceptical view of odds ratios, relative mobility is centrally important, bearing on moral fairness and the efficient mobilisation of all the talents of all the people. The argument here is not that relative mobility is unimportant, but rather that its value has been overestimated because there is little advantage to be gained by treating mobility as independent of actual labour market conditions . The simple disparity ratio does not facilitate statistical modelling, but it does say something valuable and in straightforward terms. *The New Social Mobility* therefore seeks to restore both disparity ratios and absolute mobility rates to more prominent positions in the contemporary mobility debate – among mobility analysts, politicians and the chattering classes.

Classes and categories

The Office for National Statistics Socio-Economic Classification (ONS 2010) allocates those in employment or temporary unemployment to sets of categories distinguished by the terms of their employment. In mobility analysis, the most commonly used number of categories is seven (in fact, eight – the extra category consisting of those who have never worked and the long-term unemployed – but these have usually been excluded from the mobility analysis). The categories do not constitute a strict hierarchy, but they are normally treated as if they did.

The categorisation is based on social relationships in the workplace; that is, by how employees are regulated by employers through employment contracts. There are two main types of contract:

- *the service contract*, in which employees provide a service to their employers in return for immediate rewards (such as salary) and long-term benefits (such as job security and career opportunities);
- *the labour contract*, in which employees gives discrete amounts of labour for wages based on the work done or time worked.

A third type is a mixture of the above two contracts. Those in the higher categories are employed under service contract terms, with greater autonomy at work and better employment benefits (time off, pensions, promotion prospects and so on; see Rose and O'Reilly 1997; 1998). The lower categories have decreasing degrees of discretion over how their work tasks are completed and are less likely to be part of a progressive career structure as shown in Table A.2 (see ONS 2010, section 6 for further details). Although labour contracts are associated with lower levels of occupational skills, the defining principle is the contract, not the skills involved.

Table A.2: ONS-SeC analytical categories

Higher managerial and professional occupations People who employ others (and so assume some degree of control over them) in enterprises that employ 25 or more people or that involve general planning and supervision of operations on behalf of the employer, and all types of higher professional work.	1
Lower managerial and professional occupations Lower professional and higher technical occupations, who generally plan and supervise operations on behalf of the employer under the direction of senior managers, or involve formal and immediate supervision of others engaged in the intermediate occupations.	2
Intermediate occupations Clerical, sales, service, engineering, intermediate technical and auxiliary occupations that do not involve general planning or supervisory powers and are subject to quite detailed bureaucratic regulation and standardized procedures where discretion is minimal.	3
Small employers and own account workers Non-higher or lower professionals, who carry out all or most entrepreneurial and managerial functions and assume some degree of control over fewer than 25 employees. Self-employed non-professionals in trade, personal service, or semi-routine, routine or other occupation with no employees other than family workers.	4
Lower supervisory and technical occupations Positions that involve formal and immediate supervision of others engaged in lower technical craft, technical process and related occupations. Positions with a modified labour contract, in which are engaged in lower technical and related occupations.	5
Semi-routine occupations Semi-routine sales, service, technical, clerical or childcare occupations where the work involved requires at least some element of employee discretion.	6
Routine occupations These positions have the least need for employee discretion and employees are regulated by a basic labour contract.	7

Despite some limitations regarding part-time employment and the classification of those who are retired, the ONS-SeC is the conventional framework for analysing mobility.

Operational difficulties in comparisons

It would be nice if all mobility studies used the same definitions and procedures, but sadly this is not the case. It is hard to estimate how much difference in calculated mobility rates is introduced by varying how the basic concepts are implemented, but the range of choices is extensive. Table A.3 gives the main permutations.

Table A.3: Operational definitions in British mobility studies

Item defined	Alternative ways of definition
Age at origin (gives year of origin)	Minimum school leaving age: 14; 15; 16; 18
Origin parent(s) (gives origin 'class')	Father; 'dominance' (parent with highest class)
Age at first destination (start of adult career)	20; 23; 25
Upper age range	38; 59; 62; 69
Gender data	Male only; male and female pooled; male and female
Area covered	England; Wales; Scotland; England and Wales; UK
Area indicator	Place of residence; place of birth
Seven-class schema	Goldthorpe; truncated Goldthorpe; NS-SeC; truncated NS-SeC
Unit of analysis	Full sample; pseudo cohorts; cohorts
Unemployed	Treated as 'last job'; shown separately

Mobility rates change slowly and in small increments. This is because innovations in recruitment, education and types of employment have the greatest impact on younger people, who are less embedded in established careers. It takes some time for such changes to work throughout the labour force as these young people grow older. Given that rate changes are small, the variations in operational definitions is important; however, devoting effort to bringing them into better comparability is unlikely to be productive and making detailed comparisons across studies is not the most promising way forward. It should be noted, though, that mobility estimates from broadly similar studies fall into a small ballpark zone and offer grounds for claiming reproducibility of the findings.

The 'Social Mobility Identification Kit'

Rather than taking statements about social mobility at face value, readers are advised to consider how the mobility has been measured, whether the rates quoted include upward and downward mobility and immobility, and what are the origins and destinations being talked about. This involves a series of questions, as set out in the Social Mobility Identification Kit in Table A.4.

Table A.4: The Social Mobility Identification Kit

When people talk of 'social mobility', do they mean movements ...

1.	Of individuals, social groups or 'society as a whole'?
2.	Measured in absolute simple numbers or relative chances of achieving destinations?
3.	Between classes, or occupations (particularly professions) or incomes, or some other characteristic or social position?
4.	In an upward, downward or sideways direction?
5.	Across generations or within careers?
6.	As proportions (net or gross) of inflow to new destinations or outflow from origins?
7.	Of sons compared with their fathers, or all children compared with both their parents?
8.	Over what length of time, and at which point in history?
9.	As age groups in a single study or a comparison between multiple studies?
10.	Calculated with which statistical techniques to generate the results?

Inconvenient though it may be, the various ways of measuring mobility cannot sensibly be ignored. However, the terminology in the ten questions of the Social Mobility Identification Kit – such as 'absolute' and 'relative' mobility, 'inflow' and 'outflow' – is not merely technical definitions that require explanation, but rather frameworks for conceptualising mobility itself. The terms shape the way mobility is thought about and discussed: the 'thing' takes its form as part of its measurement. The choice of answers to the ten questions will not only determine how much mobility is perceived but also influence how desirable that level of mobility is felt to be. Having a more precise view of mobility makes it possible both to explain how it comes about and to explore potential policies for changing it. In other words, we can shift from arguments about current *outcomes* or levels to investigation of the *social processes* that *generate* mobility, and their consequences.

Alternative ways of seeing mobility: mobility between incomes

The main alternative to using occupations and social class, as used in this book, has been income. Although deployed only relatively recently (and much less frequently than class), income mobility research has had a profound effect on how mobility is perceived. One reason for this is that income has an intuitive, common-sense appeal: there is little problem accepting that there are rich and poor, with gradations of material wellbeing in between. It offers us a dimension in which movements can be said to be clearly 'upward' when they obviously bring more advantaged material circumstances, and 'downward' when they bring about a reduction in purchasing power.

In addition, we can *count* money and conduct direct mathematical operations with it. Because it is a continuous scale of uniform £1 (or even smaller) increments and has a genuine zero point of no income, it qualifies as a 'ratio' level of measurement. Thus the scale can be sliced up into any subsets required; for example, allowing discussion of 'the top 10%' or 'the top quarter of earners'. This facilitates analysis of inequalities; for example, how those in the top 1% of incomes pass on that advantage to their offspring (Dorling 2014). The relatively higher degree of mathematical flexibility and precision of income are valuable features – not only for interpreting the evidence in a straightforward way, but also for applying some of the more sophisticated statistical techniques from economics (for example, Blanden et al 2004; Ermisch and Nicoletti 2005). Commentators in public life have been quick to adopt the essence (if not the detail) of those income mobility findings but slow to consider the actual technical methods that generated these research conclusions.

This has largely ignored the vigorous debate in academic circles over the use of income to measure mobility. The main battle lines have been between sociologists (advocating measurement of mobility in terms of occupations and classes) and economists (advocating the use of income), although there are a number of different positions in each camp (for example, Goldthorpe 2012; Gorard 2008; Portes 2011; Saunders 2010). The reluctance of sociologists to treat mobility as income stretches back more than half a century and is partly a consequence of sociology's traditional reliance on social class as an explanatory mechanism. Indeed, Peter Saunders (2010, 3) has alleged that 'academic sociology in Britain was (and still is) heavily dominated by a left-leaning ideology ... Left-wing academics like to believe that Britain is a class-ridden, unfair society'.

However, the reluctance to use income as the key independent variable also reflects doubts about the quality of income data as an indicator. As with class, defining and measuring income results in problems caused by the unreliability of data (in particular on the incomes of the self-employed); the way benefits and taxation have impacts on earnings; regional variations in purchasing power and housing costs; the different financial requirements of large and small households, the way household incomes are subject to rapid changes – for example, being poor is not simply a persistent phenomenon ('Almost a third (33%) of the UK population experienced poverty in at least one year between 2010 and 2013, equivalent to approximately 19.3 million people', ONS 2015) and social implications of income for lifestyle (our real interest in discussing mobility), which evolve over time (Joseph Rowntree Foundation 2014; ONS 2015a; Parker 2000; Platt 2013; Ringen 1988; Townsend 1979).

The tension between sociologists and economists is not only about technical issues, but also due to differences in interpreting what mobility has taken place. The work of economists Blanden and Machin has been taken to show that mobility has sharply declined in the last 50 years, whereas most sociological evidence points towards either a basic constancy, minor trendless fluctuations or a small increase in mobility over much of this period – certainly until the last decade. The main indicators adopted in the rest of this book have been occupations and classes, in keeping with a sociological, rather than economic, approach.

References

Abbott, P. (1990) 'A re-examination of "Three Theses Re-examined"' in Payne, G. and Abbott, P. (eds.) (1990) *The Social Mobility of Women: Beyond Male Mobility Models.* Basingstoke: Falmer Press.

Abbott, P. (2013) 'Gender' in Payne, G. (ed.) *Social Divisions* (3rd edn). Basingstoke: Palgrave Macmillan.

Abbott, P. and Sapsford, R. (1987) *Women and Social Class.* London: Tavistock.

Academy of Medical Sciences (2015) *Reproducibility and Reliability of Biomedical Research: Improving Research Practice.* Symposium Report. www.acmedsci.ac.uk/policy/policy-projects/reproducibility-and-reliability-of-biomedical-research/.

Adonis, A. (2006) quoted in *The Guardian*, 22 March, 8.

Adonis, A. (2008) 'Academies and social mobility'. Speech to the National Academies Conference, London, 7 February. www.standards.dfes.gov.uk/academies/software/Andrew_Adonis_Speech_feb08.doc?version=1.

Afriyie, A. (2013) 'Social mobility is in our own hands'. *The Voice*, 1 July. www.voice-online.co.uk/article/social-mobility-our-own-hands.

Alcock, P. (1997) *Understanding Poverty*. Basingstoke: Palgrave Macmillan.

Aldridge, S. (2001) *Social Mobility: a discussion paper.* London: Cabinet Office Performance and Innovation Unit.

Aldridge, S. (2004) *Life Chances and Social Mobility.* London: Cabinet Office Strategy Unit. www.swslim.org.uk/documents/themes/lt10_lifechances_socialmobility.pdf.

Allen, B. and Bytheway, B. (1973) 'The effects of differential fertility on sampling in studies of intergenerational social mobility', *Sociology*, 7(2): 273–6.

All-Party Parliamentary Group (APPG) on Social Mobility (2012) *Interim Report: 7 Truths About Social Mobility.* www.raeng.org.uk/publications/other/7-key-truths-about-social-mobility.

All-Party Parliamentary Group (APPG) on Social Mobility (2013) *Character and Resilience Manifesto.* www.centreforum.org/assets/pubs/character-and-resilience.pdf.

Anderson, P. (2012) 'Ghandi centre stage', *London Review of Books*, 34(13): 3–11.

Archer, L. (2007) 'Diversity, equality and higher education: a critical reflection on the ab/uses of equity discourse within widening participation', *Teaching in Higher Education*, 12 (5–6): 635–53.

Archer, L., Hutchings, M. and Ross, A. (2003) *Higher Education and Social Class: Issues of Inclusion and Exclusion*. London: Routledge.

Aron, R, (1967) *18 Lectures on Industrial Society*. London: Weidenfeld and Nicolson.

Atherton, G. (2015) *The Success Paradox*. Bristol: Policy Press.

Attwood, A. (2008) 'Elite institutions' class bias simply reflects "meritocracy": Higher IQs mean upper-class domination is "natural", academic says'. *Times Higher Education Supplement*, 22 May. www.timeshighereducation.com/comment/columnists/elite-institutions-class-bias-simply-reflects-meritocracy/401980.article.

Baker, D., Eslinger, P., Benavides, M., Peters, E., Dieckmann, N. and Leon, J. (2015) 'The cognitive impact of the education revolution: a possible cause of the Flynn Effect on population IQ', *Intelligence*, 49 (March–April): 144–58.

Ball, C. (2013) 'Most people in the UK do not go to university – and maybe never will'. *The Guardian*, 4 June. www.theguardian.com/higher-education-network/blog/2013/jun/04/higher-education-participation-data-analysis.

Ball, S. (2013) *The Education Debate*. Bristol: Policy Press.

Bamfield, L. and Horton, T. (2009) *Understanding Attitudes to Tackling Economic Inequality*. York: Joseph Rowntree Foundation. www.jrf.org.uk/publications/attitudes-economic-inequality.

Barford, V. (2014) 'Should 16-year-olds get the vote following referendum?' *BBC News*, 23 September. www.bbc.co.uk/news/uk-29327912.

Basit, T. and Tomlinson, S. (2014) *Social Inclusion and Higher Education*. Bristol: Policy Press.

Bathmaker, A-M., Ingram, N. and Waller, R. (2013) 'Higher education, social class and the mobilisation of capitals: recognising and playing the game', *British Journal of Sociology of Education,* 34 (5–6): 723–43.

Bauer, P. and Yamey, B. (1951) 'Economic progress and occupational distribution', *The Economic Journal*, 61 (December): 741–55.

Bauman, Z. (1972) *Between Class and Elite*. Manchester: Manchester University Press.

Baumberg, B. (2014) 'Perceived social mobility: do we think that money buys success?' *Inequalities*, 15 May. http://inequalitiesblog.wordpress.com/2014/05/15/perceived-social-mobility-do-we-think-that-money-buys-success/.

BBC (2008) *Report of PM's Speech to the Scottish Labour Conference*, Aviemore, 28 March. http://news.bbc.co.uk/1/hi/scotland/7319082.stm.

BBC (2014) 'Scotland decides'. *BBC News*. www.bbc.co.uk/news/events/scotland-decides/results.

BBC Radio 4 (2008) 'Social inequality and the proposed new inequality law'. *Call You and Yours*, 22 July. www.bbc.co.uk/radio4/youandyours/.

Bell, C. (1968) *Middle Class Families*. London: Routledge and Kegan Paul.

Bell, D. (1973) *The Coming of Post-Industrial Society.* New York: Basic Books.

Bell, D. (1975) *Crime as an American way of life.* Bobbs-Merrill: Indianapolis.

Benjamin, B. (1958) 'Inter-generational differences in occupational mobility', *Population Studies*, 11 (3): 262–8.

Benn, M. and Downes, J. (2015) *The Truth About Our Schools: Exposing the Myths, Exploring the Evidence.* Abingdon: Routlege.

Benyon, J. and Solomos, J. (eds.) (1987) *The Roots of Urban Unrest.* New York: Pergamon.

Bibby, J, (1975) 'Methods of measuring mobility', *Quality and Quantity*, 9 (2): 107–36.

BIS (Department for Business Innovation and Skills) (2011a) *Supporting Analysis for the Higher Education White Paper.* BIS Economics Paper No. 14. www.gov.uk/government/publications/supporting-evidence-for-the-higher-education-white-paper-2011.

BIS (Department for Business Innovation and Skills) (2011b) *Higher Education: Students at the Heart of the System.* www.gov.uk/government/uploads/system/uploads/attachment_data/file/32409/11-944-higher-education-students-at-heart-of-system.pdf.

BIS (Department for Business, Innovation and Skills) (2014) *National Strategy for Access and Student Success in Higher Education.* www.gov.uk/government/uploads/system/uploads/attachment_data/file/299689/bis-14-516-national-strategy-for-access-and-student-success.pdf.

BIS (Department for Business, Innovation and Skills) (2015) *Fulfilling Our Potential: Teaching Excellence, Social Mobility and Student Choice.* BIS/15/623, London: HMSO.

BIS (Department for Business, Innovation and Skills) (2016) *Success as a Knowledge Economy: Teaching Excellence, Social Mobility and Student Choice.* BIS/16/265, London: HMSO. www.gov.uk/government/uploads/system/uploads/attachment_data/file/523396/bis-16-265-success-as-a-knowledge-economy.pdf.

Blair, T. (1996) Leader's speech at Labour Party Conference, Blackpool. www.britishpoliticalspeech.org/speech-archive.htm?speech=202.

Blair, T. (1997) Launch of Education Manifesto for 1997 General Election, London. www.youtube.com/watch?v=kz2ENxjJxFw.

Blair, T (2001a) *The Government's Agenda for the Future,* Enfield, 8 February. http://www.lgcplus.com/the-governments-agenda-for-the-future-blairs-speech/1352530.article.

Blair, T. (2001b) Full text of Tony Blair's speech on education. *The Guardian,* 23 May. www.theguardian.com/politics/2001/may/23/labour.tonyblair.

Blair, T. (2004) quoted in *The Guardian,* 12 October.

Blair, T. (2005) quoted in *Mail Online,* 'Blair harks back to education, education, education'. 10 April. www.dailymail.co.uk/news/article-344376/Blair-harks-education-education-education.html.

Blair, T. (2015) 'Labour must be the party of ambition as well as compassion'. *The Guardian,* 9 May. www.theguardian.com/commentisfree/2015/may/09/tony-blair-what-labour-must-do-next-election-ed-miliband.

Black, A. (2011) 'SNP Conference: Salmond in free education pledge'. *BBC Scotland News,* 12 March. www.bbc.co.uk/news/uk-scotland-12711509.

Blanden, J., Goodman, A., Gregg, P. and Machin, S. (2001) *Changes in Intergenerational Mobility in Britain.* CMPO Working Paper 01/43. London: Centre for Economic Performance.

Blanden, J., Goodman, A., Gregg, P. and Machin, S. (2004) 'Changes in Intergenerational Mobility in Britain' in Corak, M. (ed.) *Generational Income Mobility in North America and Europe.* Cambridge: Cambridge University Press.

Blanden, J., Gregg, P. and Machin, S. (2005) *Intergenerational Mobility in Europe and North America: A Report Supported by the Sutton Trust.* London: Sutton Trust/Centre for Economic Performance. http://cep.lse.ac.uk/about/news/IntergenerationalMobility.pdf.

Blau, P and Duncan, O. (1967) *The American Occupational Structure.* New York: John Wiley and Sons.

Block, F. (1990) *Postindustrial Possibilities.* Berkeley: University of California Press.

Bloodworth, J. (2016) *The Myth of Meritocracy.* London: Biteback Publishing.

Blunkett, D. (2008) *The Inclusive Society?* London: Progress.

Board of Education (1943) *White Paper: Educational Reconstruction.* Cmd. 6458. London: HMSO.

Boliver, V. (2011) 'Expansion, differentiation and the persistence of social class inequalities in UK higher education', *Higher Education*, 61(3): 229–42.

Boliver, V. and Sullivan, A. (2016) 'Getting up and staying up: understanding social mobility over three generations in Britain'. Paper presented to the *Every One a Winner?* Conference, York: University of York.

Boliver, V. & Swift, A. (2011) 'Do comprehensive schools reduce social mobility?', *British Journal of Sociology*, 62(1): 89–110.

Bond, M. (2012). 'The bases of elite social behaviour: patterns of club affiliation among Members of the House of Lords', *Sociology*, 46(4): 613–32.

Bond, R. and Saunders, P. (1999) 'Routes to success: influences on the occupational attainment of young British males', *British Journal of Sociology*, 50(2): 217–49.

Bottero, W. (2005) *Stratification: Social Division and Inequality*. Abingdon: Routledge.

Bottomore, T. (1965) *Classes in Modern Society*. London: Allen and Unwin.

Bourdieu, P. (1984) *Distinction* (trans. R. Nice). Boston: Harvard University Press.

Bradley, H. and Ingram, N. (2013) 'Banking on the Future: Choices, Aspirations and Economic Hardship in Working-Class Student Experience' in Atkinson, W., Roberts, S. and Savage, M. (eds.) *Class Inequality in Austerity Britain*. Basingstoke: Palgrave Macmillan.

Bradley, H., Ingram, N. and Abrahams, J. (2011) 'Gateways to success? The influence of class on transitions into higher education', British Education Research Association Conference. London: Institute of Education.

Braverman, H. (1974) *Labor and Monopoly Capital*. New York: Monthly Review.

Breen, R. (2000) 'Class inequality and social mobility in Northern Ireland, 1973-1996', *American Sociological Review*, 65(3): 392–406.

Breen, R. and Goldthorpe, J. (1999), 'Class inequality and *meritocracy*: a critique of Saunders and an alternative analysis', *British Journal of Sociology*, 50(1): 1–27.

Breen, R. and Goldthorpe, J. (2001) 'Class, mobility and merit: the experience of two birth cohorts', *European Sociological Review*, 17(2): 81–101.

Breen, R. and Goldthorpe, J. (2002) 'Merit, mobility and method: another reply to Saunders', *British Journal of Sociology*, 53(4): 575–82.

Breen, R. and Rottman, D. (1995) *Class Stratification*. London: Harvester-Wheatsheaf.

Breiger, R. (1990) *Social Mobility and Social Structure*. Cambridge: Cambridge University Press.

Bremen J. (2013) 'A bogus concept?' *New Left Review*, 84 (November–December): 130–8.

British Social Attitudes Survey (2013) *30th Report*. http://bsa-30.natcen.ac.uk/read-the-report/social-class/introduction.aspx.

Brown, G. (2004) *Joseph Rowntree Centenary Lecture*, London. www.theguardian.com/society/2004/jul/08/socialexclusion.speeches1, and www.theguardian.com/society/2004/jul/08/socialexclusion.speeches.

Brown, G. (2008) 'Education and social mobility.' Speech to the Specialist Schools and Academies Trust, 12th Annual Lecture, 23 June. London: Specialist Schools and Academies Trust.

Brown, M. (2014) *Higher Education as a Tool of Social Mobility*. London: CentreForum.

Browning, H. and Singelmann, J. (1975) *The Emergence of a Service Society,* Springfield: National Technical Information Service.

Browning, H. and Singelmann, J. (1978) 'The transformation of the US labour force', *Politics and Society*, 8(3–4): 481–509.

Bukodi, E., Goldthorpe, J., Waller, L. and Kuha, J. (2015) 'The mobility problem in Britain', *British Journal of Sociology*, 66(1): 93–117.

Buscha, F. and Sturgis, P. (2014) 'Increasing inter-generational social mobility: is educational expansion the answer?' Paper presented at National Centre for Research Methods Conference, 'Social Mobility Grinding to a Halt?', London, British Academy.

Bush, J. (2015) 'Mitt Romney has been a leader in our party for many years…' (Facebook), 31 January. www.facebook.com/jebbush/posts/644638242331889.

Byers, S. (2006) quoted in *The Guardian*, 27 March.

Cabinet Office Strategy Unit (SU) (2008b) *Life chances: supporting people to get on in the labour market*. www.cabinetoffice.gov.uk/media/cabinetoffice/strategy/assets/life_chances_180308.pdf.*ASSM* www.gov.uk/government/uploads/system/uploads/attachment_data/file/61964/opening-doors-breaking-barriers.pdf.

Cameron, D. (2005) 'Full text: David Cameron's speech to the Conservative Conference 2005'. *The Guardian*, 4 October. http://www.theguardian.com/politics/2005/oct/04/conservatives2005.conservatives3.

Cameron, D. (2008) Speech to the House of Commons on the Government's draft legislative programme, *Hansard*, col. 1390, 14 May.

Cameron, D. (2015) 'Tory Party Conference 2015: David Cameron's speech in full'. *The Independent*, 7 October. www.independent.co.uk/news/uk/politics/tory-party-conference-2015-david-camerons-speech-in-full-a6684656.html.

Cameron, D. (2016) 'David Cameron: Parents should be taught how to control children'. *The Guardian*, 10 January. www.theguardian.com/politics/2016/jan/10/david-cameron-parents-children-lessons.

Cannadine, D. (1998) *Class in Britain,* New Haven: Yale University Press.

Caradog Jones, D. (ed.) (1934) *The Social Survey of Merseyside. Vol. 2.* Liverpool: University of Liverpool Press.

Carpenter, J. and Plewis, I. (2011) 'Analysing Longitudinal Studies with Non-Reponse: Issues and Statistical Methods' in Williams, M. and Vogt, P. (eds.) *The Sage Handbook of Methodological Innovation.* London: Sage.

Carr-Saunders, A. and Wilson, P. (1933) *The Professions.* Oxford: Clarendon Press.

Carvel, J. (1999). 'Grammar schools "no escape route for poorer children"'. *The Guardian,* 29 May. www.theguardian.com/education/1999/may/29/grammarschools.secondaryschools.

Cassen, R. and Kingdon, G. (2007) *Tackling Low Educational Achievement.* York: Joseph Rowntree Foundation. www.jrf.org.uk/sites/default/files/jrf/migrated/files/2063-education-schools-achievement.pdf.

Cayton, H. and Drake, S. (1954) *Black Metropolis.* New York: Harcourt, Brace.

CEBR (Centre for Economics and Business Research) (2015) *Professionals Risk Being Priced Out of Private Schools, as Fees Continue to Rise.* London: CEBR. www.cebr.com/reports/professionals-risk-being-priced-out-of-private-schools-as-fees-continue-to-rise/.

CentreForum (2013) *Character and Resilience Manifesto.* www.centreforum.org/assets/pubs/character-and-resilience.pdf.

Champion, T. (2013) 'The "escalator region" hypothesis two decades on: a review and critique'. Paper presented at Centre for Population Change, Southampton. www.southampton.ac.uk/demography/news/seminars/2013/05/02_the_escalator_region_hypothesis_two_decades_on.page.

Champion, T., Coombes, M. and Gordon, I. (2013) *Urban Escalators and Inter-Regional Elevators: The Difference that Location, Mobility and Sectoral Specialisation Make to Occupational Progression'.* Spatial Economics Research Centre (SERC), Discussion Paper No. 139. http://ssrn.com/abstract=2342282.

Chapman, S. and Abbott, W. (1913) 'The tendency of children to enter their father's trades', *Journal of the Royal Statistical Society*, 76(6): 599–604.

Chapman, S. J. and Marquis, F. (1912) 'The recruiting of the employing classes from the ranks of the wage earners in the cotton industry', *Journal of the Royal Statistical Society*, 75(3): 293–306.

Chapman, T. (1990a) 'The Mobility of Women and Men', in Payne, G. and Abbott, P. (eds.) *The Social Mobility of Women*. Basingstoke: Falmer Press.

Chapman, T. (1990b) 'The Career Mobility of Women and Men', in Payne, G. and Abbott, P. (eds.) *The Social Mobility of Women*, Basingstoke: Falmer Press.

Chowdry, H., Crawford, C., Dearden, L., Goodman, A. and Vignoles, A. (2010) *Widening Participation in Higher Education: Analysis Using Linked Administrative Data*. IFS Working Paper W10/04. London: Institute for Fiscal Studies. www.ifs.org.uk/publications/4951

ChronicleLive (2015) *Newcastle City Council budget: How will the cuts affect you?* http://www.chroniclelive.co.uk/news/north-east-news/newcastle-city-council-budget-how-8767460.

Clark, C. (1940) *The Conditions of Economic Progress*. London, Macmillan.

Clark, T. (2010) 'Is social mobility dead?' *The Guardian*, 10 March. www.theguardian.com/society/2010/mar/10/is-social-mobility-dead.

Cleary, H. and Reeves, R. (2009) *The 'Culture of Churn' for UK Ministers and the Price We All Pay*. Demos Research Briefing. www.demos.co.uk/files/Ministerial_Churn.pdf.

Clegg, N. (2007) Liberal Democrats leadership acceptance speech, London, 18 December. http://garstonld.org.uk/news/000463/nick_clegg_acceptance_speech.html.

Clegg, N. (2008a) 'Nick Clegg on social mobility and education.' YouTube. www.youtube.com/watch?v=nzVSKsvyNGM.

Clegg, N. (2008b) 'Education and social mobility: challenges and opportunities'. Speech to IPPR, London, 5 June. http://lindyloosmuze.blogspot.co.uk/2008/06/nick-clegg-on-education-you-heard-it.html.

Clegg, N. (2008d) 'A home for progressives'. *The Guardian*, 1 July. www.theguardian.com/commentisfree/2008/jul/01/henley.liberaldemocrats.

Clegg, N. (2014) Parliamentary answer in House of Commons debate. *Hansard*, col. 155, 7 January.

Cohen, D. (2013) 'The new boom in home tuition – if you can pay £40 an hour'. *The Guardian*, 25 October. www.theguardian.com/education/2013/oct/25/new-boom-home-tuition.

Cohen, S. and Zysmen, J. (1987) *Manufacturing Matters*. New York: Basic Books.

Coleman, A. (2014) 'Social mobility: a leg up', *Economia Magazine*, 3(12). http://economia.icaew.com/business/april-2014/a-leg-up.

Collins, M. (2004) *The Likes of Us: A Biography of the White Working Class*. London: Granta Books.

Conservative Party (1959) 'The Next Five Years: Conservative Manifesto 1959'. http://www.conservativemanifesto.com/1959/1959-conservative-manifesto.shtml.

Conservative Party (1964) *General Election Manifesto: Prosperity With A Purpose*. www.conservativemanifesto.com/1964/1964-conservative-manifesto.shtml.

Conservative Party (2008a) *Building Skills, Transforming Lives*. Policy Green Paper No. 7. London: The Conservative Party.

Conservative Party (2008b) *Through the Glass Ceiling: A Conservative Agenda for Social Mobility*. London: The Conservative Party. www.conservatives.com/~/media/Files/Downloadable%20Files/SocialMobilityPaper.ashx?dl=true.

Cooke, G. and Lawton, K. (2008) *Working Out of Poverty: a Study of the Low Paid and the 'Working Poor'*. London: IPPR.

Cooper, C. (2012). 'Understanding the English "riots" of 2011: "mindless criminality" or youth "Mekin Histri" in austerity Britain?', *Youth & Policy*, 109. www.youthandpolicy.org/wp-content/uploads/2013/04/cooper_riots_2011.pdf.

Coughlan, S. (2015a) 'The persistent appeal of grammar schools'. *BBC News*, 15 October. www.bbc.co.uk/news/education-30483031

Coughlan, S. (2015b). 'Women further ahead in university places'. *BBC News*, 18 August. www.bbc.co.uk/news/education-33975930

Coulson, S., Garforth, L., Payne, G. and Wastell, E. (2017, in press) 'Admissions, Adaptations and Anxieties: Social Class Inside and Outside the Elite University', in Waller, R. (ed.) *Higher Education and Social Inequalities: Getting in, Getting on and Getting out*. Abingdon: Routledge.

Cox, P., and Hobbly, A. (2014) *Shopgirls: True Stories of Friendship, Hardship and Triumph From Behind the Counter*. London: Hutchinson.

Crawford, C., Johnson, P., Machin, S. and Vignoles, A. (2011) *Social Mobility: A Literature Review*. London: Department of Business, Innovation and Skills. www.gov.uk/government/uploads/system/uploads/attachment_data/file/32111/11-750-social-mobility-literature-review.pdf.

Credit Suisse (2014) *Global Wealth Report 2014*. Zurich: Credit Suisse Research Institute.

Cribb, J., Hood, A., Joyce, R. and Phillips, D. (2013) *Living Standard, Poverty and Inequality in the UK 2013*. IFS Report R81. London: Institute of Fiscal Studies.

Crompton, R. (2008) *Class and Stratification* (3rd edn). Cambridge: Polity Press.

Crosland, A. (1956) *The Future of Socialism*. London: Jonathan Cape.

Crozier, G., Reay, D., Clayton, J., Colliander, L. and Grinstead, J. (2008) 'Different strokes for different folks: diverse students in diverse institutions – experiences of higher education', *Research Papers in Education*, 23(2): 167–77.

Curtice, J. (2014) 'So who voted yes and who voted no?' *What Scotland Thinks*, 26 September. http://blog.whatscotlandthinks.org/2014/09/voted-yes-voted/.

D'Ancona, M. (2011) 'Nick Clegg is ready to use shock and awe to force social change'. *Daily Telegraph*. 2 April. http://www.telegraph.co.uk/comment/columnists/matthewd_ancona/8423508/Nick-Clegg-is-ready-to-use-shock-and-awe-to-force-social-change.html.

Davidson, N. (2014) 'A Scottish watershed', *New Left Review*, 89. http://newleftreview.org/II/89/neil-davidson-a-scottish-watershed.

DCSF (Department for Children, Schools and Families) (2006) *Social Class Educational Attainment Gaps Supporting Materials*. www.dcsf.gov.uk/rsgateway/DB/STA/t000657/SocialMobility26Apr06.pdf.

Dench, G. (2006) *The Rise and Rise of Meritocracy*. Oxford: Wiley-Blackwell.

Dent, S. (2011) 'The word of the year? "Squeezed middle" says Oxford Dictionary'. *The Independent*, 23 November. www.independent.co.uk/news/uk/this-britain/the-word-of-the-year-squeezed-middle-says-oxford-dictionary-6266506.html.

Deputy Prime Minister's Office (2014) *Research and Analysis: Social Mobility Indicators*. London: Government Digital Service. www.gov.uk/government/publications/social-mobility-indicators/social-mobility-indicators.

de Piero, G. (2014) Speech to Labour Party Conference, Manchester, September. http://press.labour.org.uk/post/98058070059/speech-by-gloria-de-piero-mp-to-labour-party-conference.

Devine, F. (2004) *Class Practices: How Parents Help Their Children Get Good Jobs.* Cambridge: Cambridge University Press.

DfE (Department for Education) (2012) *Schools, Pupils and their Characteristics.* SFR 10/2012. www.gov.uk/government/uploads/system/uploads/attachment_data/file/219260/sfr10-2012.pdf.

DfE (Department for Education) (2014) *Measuring Disadvantaged Pupils' Attainment Gaps Over Time (Updated).* SFR 40/2014. http://dera.ioe.ac.uk/21974/1/SFR_40_2014_Measuring_disadvantaged_pupils_attainment_gaps_over_time__updated_.pdf.

Domenico, D. and Jones, K. (2006) 'Career aspirations of women in the 20th century', *Journal of Career and Technical Education*, 22(2): 1–7.

Dorling, D. (2014) *Inequality and the 1%.* London: Verso.

Drake, S and Cayton, H. (1945) *Black Metropolis: A Study of Negro Life in a Northern City.* Harcourt, Brace: New York.

Duncan, O. (1966) 'Methodological Issues in the Analysis of Social Mobility' in Smelser, N. and Lipset, S. (eds.) *Social Structure and Social Mobility in Economic Development.* London: RKP.

Duncan Smith, I. (2006) 'BBC Today', BBC Radio 4, 17 April.

DWP (Department for Work and Pensions) (2007) *Factors Influencing Social Mobility.* Research Report No 450. http://webarchive.nationalarchives.gov.uk/20130128102031/http://research.dwp.gov.uk/asd/asd5/rports2007-2008/rrep450.pdf.

Dyhouse, C. (2007) 'Going to university: funding, costs, benefits'. *History & Policy.* www.historyandpolicy.org/policy-papers/papers/going-to-university-funding-costs-benefits.

Elgot, J. and Mason, R. (2016) 'Theresa May launches Tory leadership bid with pledge to unite country'. *The Guardian,* 30 June. www.theguardian.com/politics/2016/jun/30/theresa-may-launches-tory-leadership-bid-with-pledge-to-unite-country.

Ellen. B. (2006) 'Nepotism, talent, good looks…'. *The Observer*, 7 August.

Engels, F. (1887) *The Condition of the Working Class in England.* New York: J.W. Lovell Co.

Erikson, R. and Goldthorpe, J. (1992) *The Constant Flux.* Oxford: Clarendon Press.

Erikson, R. and Goldthorpe, J. (2010) 'Has social mobility in Britain decreased? Reconciling divergent findings on income and class mobility', *British Journal of Sociology*, 61(2): 211–30.

Ermisch, J, and Nicoletti, C. (2005) *Intergenerational earnings mobility: Changes across cohorts in Britain,* Institute for Social and Economic Research Working Paper 2005-19. Colchester: University of Essex.

Esping-Andersen, G. (ed.) (1993) *Changing Classes.* London: Sage.

Feldman, A. (1960) 'The nature of industrial societies', *World Politics*, 12(4): 614–20.

Felstead, A, Gallie, D, Green, F. and Inanc, H. (2013) *Skills At Work In Britain: First Findings from the Skills and Employment Survey 2012*, London: Centre for Learning and Life Chances in Knowledge Economies and Societies, Institute of Education.

Field, F. (2016) Letter to *The Guardian*, 4 January.

Fielding, A. (1992) 'Migration and social mobility: south east England as an escalator region', *Regional Studies*, 26(1): 1–15.

Finegold, D. (2006) *The Roles of Higher Education in a Knowledge Economy*. Paper presented as Seminar One, Seminar Series on Mass Education in UK and International Contexts, Ottershaw. 9 November. http://www.heart-resources.org/wp-content/uploads/2015/10/The-Roles-of-Higher-Education-in-a-Knowledge-Economy.pdf

Fisher, A. (1935) *The Clash of Progress and Security*. London: Macmillan.

Fisk, R. (2016) 'Warriors for the dispossessed: Michael Gove promising to make Britain the best place in the world for everyone if he becomes the next PM'. *The Sun*, 6 July. www.thesun.co.uk/news/1397262/michael-gove-promising-to-make-britain-the-best-place-in-the-world-for-everyone-if-he-becomes-the-next-pm/.

Foote, N. and Hatt, P. (1953) 'Social mobility and economic advancement', *American Economic Review*, 18(2): 364–78.

Ford, R. and Goodwin, M. (2014a) 'Why UKIP and the radical right matter for progressives'. *Policy Network*, 10 April. www.policy-network.net/pno_detail.aspx?ID=4620&title=Why-UKIP-and-the-radical-right-matter-for-progressives.

Ford, R. and Goodwin, M. (2014b) *Revolt on the Right: Explaining Support for the Radical Right in Britain*. Abingdon: Routledge.

Ford, R., Goodwin, M. and Cutts, D. (2011) 'Strategic Eurosceptics and polite xenophobes: support for the UK Independence Party (UKIP) in the 2009 European Parliament Elections', *European Journal of Political Research*, 51(2): 204–34.

Fox, L. (2016) 'Liam Fox's launch statement: full text'. *ConservativeHome*, 30 June. www.conservativehome.com/parliament/2016/06/liam-foxs-launch-statement-full-text.html.

Franklin, P. (2015) 'How can we stop house prices from strangling social mobility?' *ConservativeHome*, 24 February. www.conservativehome.com/the-deep-end/2015/02/how-can-we-stop-house-prices-from-strangling-social-mobility.html.

Friedman, S. (2014) 'The price of the ticket: rethinking the experience of social mobility', *Sociology*, 48(2): 352–68.

Friedman, S. (2015) 'Habitus Clivé and the emotional imprint of social mobility', *Sociological Review,* 64(1): 129–47.

Fuchs, V. (1968) *The Service Economy.* New York: California University Press.

Gans, H. (1990) 'Deconstructing the Underclass', *Journal of the American Planning,* 56(3): 271–277.

Gallie, D. (1994) 'Are the unemployed an underclass?' *Sociology,* 28(3): 737–57.

Gayle, V. and Lambert, P. (2011) *An Analysis of Detailed Parental Occupational Differences and Their Effects on Children's School Attainment in Britain.* Paper presented to the ISA Research Committee 28th Spring meeting, University of Essex.

Gershuny, J. (1978) *After Industrial Society?* London: Macmillan.

Gershuny, J. (1983) *The New Service Economy.* New York: Praeger.

Giazitzoglu, A. and Down, S. (2015) 'Performing entrepreneurial masculinity: an ethnographic account', *International Small Business Journal,* published online before print, 19 August.

Gibb, N. (2016) 'Schools as the engines of social mobility'. Speech to Sutton Trust Conference, 'Best in Class Summit', 9 March. London: Sutton Trust.

Giddens, A. (1973) *The Class Structure of the Advanced Societies.* London: Hutchinson.

Ginsberg, M. (1929) 'Interchange between social classes', *Economic Journal,* 29(December): 555–65.

Glass, D. (1954) (ed.) *Social Mobility in Britain.* London: RKP.

Glass, D. and Hall, J. (1954) 'A Description of a Sample Inquiry into Social Mobility in Great Britain', in Glass, D. (ed.) *Social Mobility in Britain.* London: RKP.

Goldthorpe, J. (1987) *Social Mobility and Class Structure in Modern Britain.* Oxford: Clarendon Press.

Goldthorpe, J. (1983) 'Women and class analysis: in defence of the conventional view', *Sociology,* 17(4): 465–88.

Goldthorpe, J. (1984) 'Women and class analysis: a reply to the replies', *Sociology,* 18(4): 491–9.

Goldthorpe, J. (2012) *Understanding – and Misunderstanding – Social Mobility in Britain.* Barnett Papers in Social Research 2/2012. Oxford: Department of Social Policy and Intervention, Oxford University.

Goldthorpe, J. and Hope, K. (1974) *The Social Grading of Occupations.* Oxford: Clarendon Press.

Goldthorpe, J. and Jackson, M. (2007) 'Intergenerational class mobility in contemporary Britain: political concerns and empirical findings', *British Journal of Sociology,* 58(4): 525–46.

Goldthorpe, J. and Mills, C. (2008) 'Trends in intergenerational class mobility in modern Britain', *National Institute Economic Review,* 205(1): 83–100.

Goldthorpe, J. and Payne, C. (1986) 'On the class mobility of women', *Sociology,* 20(4): 531–55.

Gorard, S. (2008) 'A re-consideration of rates of "social mobility" in Britain', *British Journal of Sociology of Education,* 29(3): 317–24

Gorard, S. with Adnett, N., May, H., Slack, K., Smith, E. and Thomas, L. (2007) *Overcoming the Barriers to Higher Education.* Stoke-on-Trent: Trentham.

Gorringe, H. and Rosie, M. (2011) 'King Mob: perceptions, prescriptions and presumptions about the policing of England's riots', *Sociological Research Online,* 16(4): 17. www.socresonline.org. uk/16/4/17.html> 10.5153/sro.2521.

Gove, M. (2008) Speech to Centre Forum, London, 25 March.

Gove, M. (2013) 'I refuse to surrender to Marxist teachers hell-bent on destroying our schools'. *Mail Online,* 23 March. www.dailymail. co.uk/debate/article-2298146/I-refuse-surrender-Marxist-teachers-hell-bent-destroying-schools-Education-Secretary-berates-new-enemies-promise-opposing-plans.html.

Gove, M. (2014) Interview in the *Financial Times, FT Magazine,* 14 March. http://www.ft.com/cms/s/2/ebe8018c-aa45-11e3-8497-00144feab7de.html#axzz2w1tfjVmh.

Gove, M. (2016) 'Michael Gove promising to make Britain the best place in the world for everyone if he becomes the next PM', *The Sun,* 6 July. https://www.thesun.co.uk/news/1397262/michael-gove-promising-to-make-britain-the-best-place-in-the-world-for-everyone-if-he-becomes-the-next-pm/.

Green Party (2005) *Real Progress: The Green Party General Election Manifesto.* London: Green Party of England and Wales.

Green Party (2010a) *Fair is Worth Fighting For: The Green Party General Election Manifesto.* London: Green Party of England and Wales.

Green Party (2010b) 'Greens offer free membership to students and young people'. Green Party website, 11 December. www.greenparty. org.uk/news/2010-12-09-free-membership.html.

Green Party (2013) 'High wage differentials damage us all: vote Green for a better deal for everyone'. Green Party website, 25 November. http://greenparty.org.uk/deputy-leaders-blog/2013/11/25/a-decent-wage-for-all/.

Grover, C. (2011) 'Social Protest in 2011: material and cultural aspects of economic inequalities', *Sociological Research Online,* 16(4): 18. www.socresonline.org.uk/16/4/18.html>10.5153/sro.2538.

Grusky, D. (2015) *Poverty, Mobility and the Commodification of Everything.* Paper presented to the CRESC Rethinking Social Mobility Conference, Manchester.

Guardian, The and LSE (2011) *Reading the Riots.* London: The Guardian.

Gurney-Dixon Report (1954) *Early Leaving: Report of the Central Advisory Council for Education (England).* London: HMSO.

Hain, P. (2007) *Statement to Parliament.* House of Commons Hansard, cols 104W-107W, 16 July. www.publications.parliament.uk/pa/cm200607/cmhansrd/cm070716/text/70716w0022.htm.

Hall, T. (2003) *Better Times than This: Youth Homelessness in Britain.* London: Pluto Press.

Halsey, A., Heath, A. and Ridge, J. (1980) *Origins and Destinations.* Oxford: Clarendon Press.

Hampshire, A., Highfield, R., Parkin, B. and Owen, A. (2012) 'Fractionating human intelligence', *Neuron*, 76(60): 1225–37.

Hansard (2014) *Oral Questions to the Deputy Prime Minister*, 14 October, cols 140–2. www.publications.parliament.uk/pa/cm201415/cmhansrd/cm141014/debtext/141014-0001.htm.

Harris, A. (1939) 'Pure capitalism and the disappearance of the middle class', *Journal of Political Economy*, 47(3): 328–56.

Hart, R., Mioro, M. and Roberts, E. (2012) *Date of Birth, Family Background, and The 11 Plus Exam: Short- and Long-Term Consequences of the 1944 Secondary Education Reforms In England and Wales.* Stirling Economics Discussion Paper 2012–10. Stirling: University of Stirling.

Harvey, W. (2011) 'Strategies for conducting elite interviews.' *Qualitative Research* 11(4): 431–441.

Hauser, R., Koffel, J., Travis, H. and Dickinson, P. (1975a) 'Temporal change in occupational mobility', *American Sociological Review*, 40(2): 79–97.

Hauser, R., Dickinson, P., Travis, H. and Koffel, J. (1975b) 'Structural change in occupational mobility among men in the US', *American Sociological Review*, 40(4): 585–98.

Heath, A. (1981) *Social Mobility.* London: Fontana.

Heath, A. (1992) 'The attitudes of the underclass' in *Understanding the Underclass.* London: Policy Studies Institute. www.psi.org.uk/site/publication_detail/1623/.

Heath, A. F and McMahon, D. (2005) 'Social Mobility of Ethnic Minorities' in Loury, G., Modood, T. and Teles, S. (eds.) *Social Mobility and Public Policy: Comparing the US and the UK.* Cambridge: Cambridge University Press.

Heath, A. and Payne, C. (1999) *Twentieth Century Trends in Social Mobility*. Working Paper No. 70. Oxford: Centre for Research into Elections and Social Trends.

Heath, A. and Payne, C. (2000) 'Social Mobility', in Halsey, A. and Webb, J. (eds.) *Twentieth-Century British Social Trends*. Basingstoke: Macmillan.

HEFCE (Higher Education Funding Council for England) (2014) *Differences in Degree Outcomes: Key Findings*. Bristol: HEFCE. www.hefce.ac.uk/pubs/year/2014/201403/#d.en.86821.

Hennessy, P. (2014) *Establishment and Meritocracy*. London: Haus Publishing.

Hernon, I. (2006) *Riot!: Civil Insurrection From Peterloo to the Present Day*. London: Pluto Press.

Herrnstein, R. and Murray, C. (1994) *The Bell Curve: Reshaping of American Life by Differences in Intelligence*. New York: Simon and Schuster.

Hershman, G. (2010) 'Old school tie: David Cameron and Nick Clegg'. *The Sofia Echo*, 13 May. http://sofiaecho.com/2010/05/13/900233_old-school-tie-david-cameron-and-nick-clegg.

HESA (Higher Education Statistics Agency) (2014) *Student Introduction 2012/13*. www.hesa.ac.uk/intros/stuintro1213.

Hibbert, C. (2004) *King Mob: Story of Lord George Gordon and the Riots of 1780*. Stroud: Sutton.

Hill, J. et al (2010) *An anatomy of economic inequality in the UK*. London: Centre for Analysis of Social Exclusion, London School of Economics and Political Science.

Hinchcliffe, J. (2006) 'Chairman's address'. *Tottenham Conservatives*, May. www.tottenhamconservative.com/news.

Hinds, D. (2012) 'The seven key truths about social mobility'. *ConservativeHome*, 2 May. www.conservativehome.com/platform/2012/05/damian-hinds.html.

Hinsliff, G. (2015) 'Grammar schools are not the answer: the road to a better life starts at birth, not at 11'. *The Guardian*, 15 October. www.theguardian.com/commentisfree/2015/oct/15/grammar-schools-social-mobility.

Hobcraft, J. (2001) 'Intergenerational transmission of inequality in a British birth cohort'. Paper presented at the Population Association of America Annual Meeting, Washington DC.

Holmwood, J. and Scott, J. (eds.) (2014) The *Palgrave Handbook of Sociology in Britain*. Basingstoke: Palgrave.

Hope, C. (2013) 'Truly shocking that the private-school educated and affluent middle class still run Britain, says Sir John Major'. *The Daily Telegraph*, 10 November. www.telegraph.co.uk/news/politics/conservative/10439303/Truly-shocking-that-the-private-school-educated-and-affluent-middle-class-still-run-Britain-says-Sir-John-Major.html.

Hope, K. (1975) 'Trends in the Openness of British Society in the Present Century'. Paper circulated at the SSRC International Seminar on Social Mobility, University of Aberdeen, September.

Hoselitz, B. and Moore, W. (eds.) (1963) *Industrialization and Society*. The Hague: UNESCO–Mouton.

House of Commons (2010) *Higher Education and Social Class*. SN/SG/620. London: House of Commons Library.

House of Commons (2014) *Oxbridge Elitism*. SN/SG/616. London: House of Commons Library.

Hunt, T. (2014) Speech to Labour Party Conference 2014, Manchester. http://press.labour.org.uk/post/98055389239/speech-by-tristram-hunt-mp-to-labour-party-conference.

Hurst, G. (2013) 'Teachers outnumbered by rise of the home tutor'. *Times Education Supplement*, 8 October. www.thetimes.co.uk/tto/education/article3889395.ece.

Hutton, J. (2006) 'What will it take to end child poverty?' Speech to the Joseph Rowntree Foundation, 6 July. Ministers Speeches: Ref Number 80069, library.archive@dwp.gsi.gov.uk.

Hutton, J. (2007) Speech to the Welfare to Work Convention, Birmingham. Ministers Speeches: Ref Number 80143' library. archive@dwp.gsi.gov.uk.

Iannelli, C. and Paterson, L. (2006) 'Social mobility in Scotland since the middle of the twentieth century', *Sociological Review*, 54(3): 520–45.

Iannelli, C. and Paterson, L. (2007) 'Education and social mobility in Scotland', *Research in Stratification and Mobility*, 25(3): 219–32.

IEA (Institute of Economic Affairs) (2015) 'Social mobility in the UK: New IEA briefing explains why the Prime Minister is wrong on social mobility', 10 October. www.iea.org.uk/publications/research/social-mobility-in-the-uk. er,–imeg,–

Iganski, P., Street, D. and Payne, G. (*1994)* 'Discordant racism: "race", IQ and "The Bell Curve"', *Public Policy Review*, 2(3): 41–5.

IPPR (Institute for Public Policy Review) (2008) *Social Mobility: A Background Review*. London: IPPR.

Jackson, M. (2001) 'Non-meritocratic job requirements and the reproduction of class inequality: an investigation', *Work, Employment and Society*, 15(3): 619–30.

Johnson, A. (2007) 'Improving social mobility: the next ten years'. Speech at Institute for Public Policy Research, London, 17 May.

Johnson, B. (2011) 'Deriving trends in life expectancy by the national statistics socio-economic classification using the ONS longitudinal study', *Health Statistics Quarterly*, 49(Spring):1–39.

Johnson, B. (2013) 'What would Maggie do today?' Annual Margaret Thatcher Lecture. Centre for Policy Studies, London, 27 November. www.cps.org.uk/events/q/date/2013/11/27/the-2013-margaret-thatcher-lecture-boris-johnson/.

Johnson, B. (2016) 'Tory leadership ruling out statement: full text'. *The Independent*, 30 June. www.independent.co.uk/news/uk/politics/boris-johnsons-tory-leadership-ruling-out-statement-full-text-a7111056.html.

Jones, O. (2014) *The Establishment*. London: Allen Lane.

JRF (Joseph Rowntree Foundation) (2006) 'The persistence of poverty across the generations', *Findings*, April. York: JRF.

JRF (Joseph Rowntree Foundation) (2007) 'Experience of poverty and educational disadvantage', *Round-Up*, September. York: JRF.

JRF (Joseph Rowntree Foundation) (2014) *A Minimum Income Standard for the UK in 2014*. www.jrf.org.uk/publications/minimum-income-standard-2014.

Kaelble, H. (1985) *Social mobility in the 19th and 20th centuries : Europe and America in comparative perspective*. Leamington Spa: Berg.

Katwala, S. (2007) *Diverse Britain 2007*. Lecture to *The Guardian* and Equality and Human Rights Commission Conference, London, December. http://fabians.org.uk/events/transcripts/breaking-cycle-disadvantage-full.

Kaufman, J. (ed.) (2009) *Intelligent Testing*. Cambridge: Cambridge University Press.

Keegan, V. (1998) 'The new economy'. *The Guardian*, 19 June.

Kellner, P. (2013) 'How UKIP voters compare'. *YouGov UK*. yougov.co.uk/news/2013/03/05/analysis-ukip-voters/.

Kellner, P. (2014) 'Where UKIP gets its support'. *YouGov UK*. yougov.co.uk/news/2014/02/24/where-ukip-gets-its-support/.

Kelly, R. (2005) 'Education and social progress'. Speech at Institute for Public Policy Research, London, 26 April.

Kelly, R. (2006a) Speech at the North of England Conference, Newcastle, 6 January.

Kelly, R. (2006b) 'Social mobility: narrowing educational social class attainment gaps'. Speech at Institute for Public Policy Research, London, 26 April. www.dfes.gov.uk/rsgateway/DB/STA?t000657/index.shtml.

Kelly, R. (2007) 'Speech to the Fabian Society'. *The Times*, 13 February. www.timesonline.co.uk/tol/news/politics/article1379447.ece.

Kendler, K., Turkheimer, K., Ohlsson, H., Sundquist, J. and Sundquist, K. (2015) 'Family environment and the malleability of cognitive ability: a Swedish national home-reared and adopted-away cosibling control study', *Proceedings of the National Academy of Sciences of the United States of America*, 112: 4612–17.

Kerr, C., Dunlop, J., Harbison F. and Myers, C. A. (1960) *Industrialism and Industrial Man*. Boston: Harvard University Press.

Killik (2014) *Killik Private Education Index*. London: Killik and Co. www.killik.com/documents/private-education-report/.

Kuznets, S. (1958) 'Quantitative aspects of the economic growth of nations, III: Industrial distribution of income and labour force by states, US 1919–21 to 1955', *Economic Development and Cultural Change,* July, 6(4): 1–128.

Labour Government (2009) *New Opportunities: Fair Chances for the Future.* www.gov.uk/government/uploads/system/uploads/attachment_data/file/228532/7533.pdf.

Labour Party (1997) *The Labour Party Manifesto.* http://www.politicsresources.net/area/uk/man/lab97.htm.

Labour Party (2001) *The Labour Party Manifesto.* http://www.politicsresources.net/area/uk/e01/man/lab/lab01.htm.

Labour Party (2005) *The Labour Party Manifesto.*http://news.bbc.co.uk/1/shared/bsp/hi/pdfs/13_04_05_labour_manifesto.pdf.

Labour Party (2015) *The Labour Party Manifesto.* www.labour.org.uk/blog/entry/the-labour-party-manifesto-2015.

Lambert, P. and Prandy, K. (2012) 'CAMSIS: Social Interaction and Stratification Scale'. CAMSIS website. www.camsis.stir.ac.uk/.

Lambert, P., Prandy, K. and Bottero, W. (2007) 'By slow degrees: two centuries of social reproduction and mobility in Britain', *Sociological Research Online*, 12(1). www.socresonline.org.uk/12/1/prandy.html.

Lammy, D. (2007) 'New employability skills programme'. DWP press release. www.gnn.gov.uk/Content/Detail.asp?ReleaseID=304329&NewsAreaID=2.

Lansley, S. (2013) 'The "squeezed middle" and the "poor". *Poverty and Social Exclusion.*www.poverty.ac.uk/articles-inequality-income-distribution-economic-policy-living-standards/%E2%80%98squeezed-middle%E2%80%99-and-%E2%80%98poor.

Lareau, A. (2003) *Unequal Childhoods*. Los Angeles: University of California Press.

Laughland-Booÿ, J., Mayall, M. and Skrbiš, Z. (2015) 'Whose choice? Young people, career choices and reflexivity re-examined', *Current Sociology*, 63(4): 586–603.

Laurison, D. and Friedman, S. (2015) *Introducing the Class Ceiling: Social Mobility into Britain's Elite Occupations*. London: LSE Sociology Department Working Paper. www.lse.ac.uk/sociology/pdf/Working-Paper_Introducing-the-Class-Ceiling.pdf.

Lawler, S. (1999) 'Getting out and getting away: Women's narratives of class mobility', *Feminist Review* 63(3): 3–24.

Lawler, S. and Payne, G. (eds.) (2017, forthcoming). *A Social Mobility for the 21st Century: Every One a Winner?* Abingdon: Routledge.

Learner, S. (2012) 'Why send your child to independent school?' *The Daily Telegraph*, 28 September. www.telegraph.co.uk/education/9565079/Why-send-your-child-to-independent-school.html.

Lee, D. and Turner, B. (eds.) (1996) *Conflicts About Class: Debating Inequality in Late Industrialism*. London: Longman.

Leitch, Lord S. (2006) *Review of Skills Final Report*. Norwich: HMSO.

Lerner, D. (1958) *The Passing of Traditional Society*. New York: Free Press.

Levy, M. (1966) *Modernization and the Structure of Societies* (2 vols). Princeton: Princeton University Press.

Lewis, R. and Maude, A (1949) *The English Middle Classes*. London: Phoenix House.

LexisNexis Academic Butterworth Archive (2014) *LexisNexis Academic Newspapers and Wires*. www.lexisnexis.com/ap/academic/form_news_wires.asp.

LFS (Labour Force Survey) (2011) *Labour Force Survey 1990 and 1991*. Office of Population Censuses and Surveys, LFS Series No. 9. London: HMSO.

Li, Y. and Devine, F. (2011) 'Is Social Mobility Really Declining?' *Sociological Research Online*, 16(3): 4. www.socresonline.org.uk/16/3/4.html10.5153/sro.2424.

Liberal Democrats (2008) 'Nick Clegg establishes social mobility commission'. Liberal Democrats website. http://www.smf.co.uk/nick-cleggs-speech-to-launch-the-commission-on-inequality-in-education/.

Liberal Democrats (2015) *Opportunity for All: Liberal Democrats Manifesto*. www.libdems.org.uk/read-the-full-manifesto.

Lipsett, A. (2008) 'Clegg: We will stop academic selection in schools', *The Guardian*. 29 January. /www.theguardian.com/education/2008/jan/29/schools.uk3.

Lipset, S. (1959) 'Some social requisites of democracy: economic development and political legitimacy', *American Political Science Review*, 53(1): 69–105.

Lipset, S and Bendix, R. (1959) *Social Mobility in Industrial Society*. London: Heinemann.

Lister, R. (1996) 'In Search of the 'Underclass' in Lister, R. (ed.) *Charles Murray and the Underclass: The Developing Debate,* Choice in Welfare No.33. London: IEA Health and Welfare Unit.

Lloyds Bank (2012) 'Private school fees rise nearly twice as fast as inflation in the past decade'. Press release, 27 August. www.lloydsbankinggroup.com/globalassets/documents/media/press-releases/lloyds-bank/2012/2708privateschool.pdf.

Lockwood, D. (1989) *The Black-Coated Worker* (2nd, rev. edn). London: Allen & Unwin; Oxford: Clarendon Press.

Loveday, V. (2014) 'Working-class participation, middle-class aspiration?', *Sociological Review*, 63(3): 570–88.

Loveday. V. (2015) 'Embodying deficiency through 'affective practice': shame, relationality, and the lived experience of social class and gender in higher education', *Sociology*, published online before print, 30 June. http://soc.sagepub.com/content/early/2015/06/30/0038038515589301.full.

LSE Press and Information Office (2008) www.lse.ac.uk/collections/pressAnd InformationOffice/newsAndEvents/archives/2005/LSE SuttonTrust report.htm.

Lynn, R. and Irwing, P. (2005a) 'Sex differences in means and variability on the Progressive Matrices in university students: a meta-analysis', *British Journal of Psychology*, 96(4): 505–24.

Lynn, R. and Vanhanen, T. (2005b) 'The Role of Human Capital and Intelligence in the Economic Development of the Asian Economies' in Kidd, J. and Richter, F.-J. (eds.) *Infrastructure and Productivity in Asia*. Basingstoke: Palgrave Macmillan.

MacDonald, R. (1997) *Youth, the 'Underclass' and Social Exclusion*. Abingdon: Psychology Press.

Mansell, W (2015) 'The 60% extra funds enjoyed by England's free school pupils'. *The Guardian*, 25 August. www.theguardian.com/education/2015/aug/25/extra-funds-free-schools-warwick-mansell.

Marshall, T. (1965) *Class, Citizenship and Social Development*. New York: Doubleday.

Marshall, G. and Swift, A. (1996) 'Merit and mobility: a reply to Peter Saunders', *Sociology*, 30(2): 375–86.

Mason, D. (2006) 'Ethnicity', in Payne, G. (ed.) *Social Divisions* (2nd edn). Basingstoke: Palgrave Macmillan.

May, T. (2016) *Statement from the new Prime Minister Theresa May.* www. gov.uk/government/speeches/statement-from-the-new-prime-minister-theresa-may.

Mehta, J. (2004) 'Changing agrarian structure in the Indian economy', *Revolutionary Democracy*, 10(1). www.revolutionarydemocracy.org/rdv10n1/agrarian.htm.

Mellor, J., Waller, R. and Hoare, A. (2012) 'UK university students and paid employment'. Paper presented to the BSA Annual Conference, Leeds.

Michels, R. (1911) *Political Parties*. New York: Free Press.

Migration Observatory (2015) 'Migrants in the UK: an overview'. www.migrationobservatory.ox.ac.uk/briefings/migrants-uk-labour-market-overview.

Milburn, A. (2004) 'Inequality, Mobility and Opportunity'. Speech given to IPPR, London. 9 November. House of Commons Library Deposited Papers, Dep. 04/2036: 22 December, Cabinet Office.

Milburn, A. (2006) quoted in *The Guardian*, 'No, a return to grammar schools would not increase social mobility', 26 January.

Milburn, A. (2015) Interview on *Daily Politics*, BBC TV, 12 May.

Miles, A. (1999) *Social Mobility in Nineteenth and Early Twentieth Century England.* Basingstoke: Macmillan.

Miles, A., & Vincent, D. (ed.) (1993) *Building European Society: Occupational and Social Mobility in Europe, 1840–1940.* Manchester: Manchester University Press.

Miles, A., Savage, M. and Bühlmann, F. (2011) 'Telling a modest story: accounts of men's upward mobility from the National Child Development Study', *British Journal of Sociology*, 62(3): 418–41.

Miliband, E. (2008) 'Fighting Poverty and Inequality in an Age of Affluence.' Fabian Society Research Project Launch Lecture. London. http://fabians.org.uk/events/speeches/ed-miliband-speech.

Miliband, E. (2010) 'These education proposals risk setting back social mobility for a generation'. *The Guardian*, 4 December. www.guardian.co.uk/commentisfree/2010/dec/04/ed-miliband-tuition-fees1.

Miliband. R. (1969) *The State in Capitalist Society*. London: Weidenfeld and Nicholson.

Miller, R. and Hayes, B. (1990) 'Gender and Intergenerational Mobility' in Payne, G. and Abbott, P. (eds.) (1990) *The Social Mobility of Women: Beyond Male Mobility Models.* Basingstoke: Falmer Press.

Miller S. (1960) 'Comparative Social Mobility', *Current Sociology*, 9(1): 1–89.

Milne, S. (2012) *The Revenge of History: The Battle for the 21st Century*. London: Verso.

Mitchell, B. (1988) *British Historical Statistics*. Cambridge: Cambridge University Press.

Monaghan, A. (2014) 'Self-employment in UK at highest level since records began.' *The Guardian*, 20 August. www.theguardian.com/uk-news/2014/aug/20/self-employment-uk-highest-level.

Moore, R. (1993) 'Citizenship and the Underclass' in Coenen, H. and Leisink, P. (eds.) *Work and Citizenship in the New Europe*. Aldershot: Edward Elgar.

Moore, S. (2011) 'Speak to us peasants, posh boys, for we know all about social mobility.' *The Guardian*. 9 April. www.theguardian.com/commentisfree/2011/apr/09/social-mobility-suzanne-moore.

Morrin, K. (2013) 'The end of the road? Attitudes, aspirations and educational attainment in a north west town'. Paper presented at the BSA Annual Conference, London.

Morris, L. (1994) *Dangerous Classes: The Underclass and Social Citizenship*. London: Routledge.

Mosca, G. (ed.) (1896) *Elementi di Scienza Politica*. Trans. and reprinted as Mosca, G. (ed. A. Livingston) (1939) *The Ruling Class*. New York: McGraw Hill.

Moser, C. and Hall, J. (1954) 'The Social Grading of Occupations' in Glass, D. (ed.) *Social Mobility in Britain*. London: RKP.

Mumsnet (2012) 'Why did you choose private school?' Forum discussion, *Mumsnet*. www.mumsnet.com/Talk/education/1382701-why-did-you-choose-private-school-at-reception.

Murji, K. and Neal, S. (2011) 'Riot: Race and Politics in the 2011 Disorders', *Sociological Research Online*, 16(4): 24. www.socresonline.org.uk/16/4/24.html> 10.5153/sro.2557.

Murdoch, S. (2007) *A Smart History of a Failed Idea*. Hoboken, NJ: John Wiley and Sons.

Narey, M. (2009) *Report of the Liberal Democrats Independent Commission on Social Mobility*. www.mnarey.co.uk/resources/Social%20Mobility%20%28Narey%20Report%29%20Final.pdf.

National Statistics (2012) *Scottish Index of Multiple Deprivation 2012*. Scottish Government. http://simd.scotland.gov.uk/publication-2012/simd-2012-results/domain-results/education-skills-and-training-domain/.

Noble, T. (1972) 'Social mobility and class relations in Britain', *British Journal of Sociology*, 23(4): 422–36.

Noble, T. (1995) 'Occupational mobility and social change in Britain', *Hitotsubashi Journal of Social Studies*, 27(1): 65–90.

Noble, T. (2000) 'The mobility transition', *Sociology*, 34(1): 35–51.

Noden, P., Shiner, M. and Modood, T. (2014) *Black and Minority Ethnic Access to Higher Education: A Reassessment*. London: LSE Department of Social Policy.

Nuttall, P. (2014) 'Selection by ability is key to social mobility'. Press release, 10 October. www.paulnuttallmep.com/?p=3551.

O'Hara, M. and Shepherd, J. (2011) 'Ministers cut millions from evaluation budgets.' *The Guardian*. 26 February. www.guardian.co.uk/politics/2011/feb/25/government-research-evaluation-budgets-cuts?INTCMP.

O'Kane, J. (1992) *The Crooked Ladder: Gangsters, Ethnicity and the American Dream*. New Brunswick: Transactions.

Olantiti, A. (2013) *Students' Perceptions of Parental Involvement in Education*. Paper presented at the BSA Annual Conference, London.

ONS (Office for National Statistics) (2010) *Standard Occupational Classification 2010 Volume 3: The National Statistics Socio-economic Classification (Rebased on the SOC2010 User Manual)*. Basingstoke: Palgrave.

ONS (Office for National Statistics) (2011a) *Frequently Asked Questions: Births & Fertility*. faqsbirthfertility_tcm77-22930-pdf.

ONS (Office for National Statistics) (2011b) *Employment by Status, Occupation and Sex*, Table EMP16. www.ons.gov.uk/employmentandlabourmarket/peopleinwork/employmentandemployeetypes/datasets/employmentbyoccupationemp04.

ONS (Office for National Statistics) (2013) *Graduates in the UK Labour Market: 2013*. http://www.ons.gov.uk/employmentandlabourmarket/peopleinwork/employmentandemployeetypes/articles/graduatesintheuklabourmarket/2013-11-19.

ONS (Office for National Statistics) (2014) *Self-Employed Workers in the UK: 2014*. www.ons.gov.uk/ons/rel/lmac/self-employed-workers-in-the-uk/2014/rep-self-employed-workers-in-the-uk-2014.html.

ONS (Office for National Statistics) (2015) *Persistent Poverty in the UK and EU, 2008–2013*. www.ons.gov.uk/ons/rel/household-income/persistent-poverty-in-the-uk-and-eu/2008-2013/persistent-poverty-in-the-uk-and-eu--2008-2013.html.

Osborne, G. (2008) 'A blueprint for fairness'. *The Guardian*, 20 August, 28.

Osborne, G. (2014a) 'The Andrew Marr Show Interview: George Osborne MP Chancellor of the Exchequer', BBC One TV, 14 March.

Osborne, G. (2014b) *Autumn Statement*. London: HM Treasury. www.gov.uk/government/uploads/system/uploads/attachment_data/file/382327/44695_Accessible.pdf.

Oshima, H. (1971) 'Labour-force 'explosion' and the labour-intensive sector in Asian growth', *Economic Development and Cultural Change*, 19(January): 161–83.

Owen, G. (2012) *The Cabinet Rich List*. This is Money.co.uk. www.thisismoney.co.uk/money/news/article-1694722/The-Cabinet-rich-list.html.

Panel on Fair Access to the Professions (2009) *Unleashing Aspiration: The Final Report of the Panel on Fair Access to the Professions*. London: Cabinet Office. http://webarchive.nationalarchives.gov.uk/+/http://www.cabinetoffice.gov.uk/media/227102/fair-access.pdf.

Panel on Fair Access to the Professions (2010) *Unleashing Aspiration: The Government Response to the Final Report of the Panel on Fair Access to the Professions*. webarchive.nationalarchives.gov.uk/20100407162311/http://interactive.bis.gov.uk/unleashingaspiration.

Pareto, V. (1902) *Les Systems Socialistes* (Socialist Systems). Paris: Giard et Briere.

Parker, H. (ed.) (2000) *Low Cost and Acceptable Incomes for Older People*. Bristol: Policy Press.

Parker, G. and Warrell, H. (2014) 'How far will Michael Gove go?' *Financial Times,* 14 March. www.ft.com/cms/s/2/ebe8018c-aa45-11e3-8497-00144feab7de.html#axzz2w1tfjVmh.

Parkin, F. (1971) *Class Inequality and Political Order*. London: Tavistock.

Parliamentary Briefing (2015) 'Participation in higher education'. Briefing paper SN/SG/2630. www.parliament.uk/briefing-papers/sn02630.pdf.

Parsons, T. (1951) *The Social System*. New York: Free Press.

Paterson, L. and Ianelli, C. (2007) 'Patterns of absolute and relative social mobility: a comparative study of England, Wales and Scotland', *Sociological Research Online*, 12(6): 15. www.socresonline.org.uk/12/6/15.html.

Paton, G. (2013) 'Ofsted chief: grammar schools "stuffed full" of rich pupils'. *The Daily Telegraph*, 15 December. www.telegraph.co.uk/education/educationnews/10518893/Ofsted-chief-grammar-schools-stuffed-full-of-rich-pupils.html.

Payne, G. (1973) 'Middle class mobility typologies', *Sociology,* 7(3): 417–28.

Payne, G. (1987a) *Mobility and Change in Modern Society*. Basingstoke: Macmillan.

Payne, G. (1987b) *Employment and Opportunity*. Basingstoke: Macmillan.

Payne, G. (1999) 'Does economic development modify social mobility?' Paper presented at British Sociological Association Annual Conference, Glasgow.

Payne, G. (2003) 'Size doesn't matter: the fallacy of class-differential fertility in social mobility analysis', *International Journal of Social Research Methodology*, 6(2): 141–57.

Payne, G. (2005) 'Onwards and Upwards: assumptions about social mobility and intergenerational life courses'. Paper presented to British Sociological Association Annual Conference.

Payne, G. (2007) 'Social divisions, social mobilities and social research: methodological issues after 40 Years', *Sociology*, 41(5): 901–15.

Payne, G. (2011) 'Mapping the Academic Landscape of Quantitative Methods' in Payne, G. and Williams, M. (eds.) *Teaching Quantitative Methods: Getting the Basics Right*. London: Sage.

Payne, G. (2012a) 'A New Social Mobility? The political redefinition of a sociological problem.' *Contemporary Social Science*, 7, 1: 55–71.

Payne G. (2012b) 'Labouring Under a Misapprehension: Politicians' Perceptions and the Realities of Structural Social Mobility in Britain, 1995–2010' in Lambert, P., Connelly, R., Blackburn, R. and Gayle, V. (eds.) *Social Stratification: Trends and Processes*. Farnham: Ashgate.

Payne, G. (2014) 'Research Methodology in Sociology' in Holmwood, J. and Scott, J. (eds.) *The Palgrave Handbook of Sociology in Britain*. Basingstoke: Palgrave.

Payne, G. and Abbott, P. (eds.) (1990) *The Social Mobility of Women: Beyond Male Mobility Models*. Basingstoke: Falmer Press.

Payne, G. and Grew, C. (2005) Unpacking 'class ambivalence': some conceptual and methodological issues in accessing class cultures', *Sociology*, 39(5): 893–910.

Payne, G. and Roberts, J. (2002) 'Opening and closing the gates: recent developments in British male social mobility', *Sociological Research Online*, 6(4).

Piketty, T. (2013) *Capital in the Twenty-First Century*. Cambridge, MA: Harvard University Press.

Plaid Cymru (2013) 'From the Senedd: Party of Wales reaction to PISA results'. *The Slate Blog*, 3 December. www.partyofwales.org/the-slate/2013/12/03/from-the-senedd-party-of-wales-reaction-to-pisa-results/?force=1.

Platt, L. (2005) *Migration and Social Mobility: the Life Chances of Britain's Minority Ethnic Communities*. Bristol: Policy Press.

Platt, L. (2013) 'Poverty' in Payne, G. (ed.) *Social Divisions* (3rd edn). Basingstoke: Palgrave Macmillan.

Policy Exchange (2011) YouGov Poll. d25d2506sfb94s.cloudfront.net/today_uk_import/yg-archives-fairness-policyexchange260411.pdf.

Portes, J. (2011) 'Poverty and inequality: introduction', *National Institute Economic Review*, 218: 1–6.

Prandy, K. and Bottero, W. (1998) 'The use of marriage data to measure the social order in nineteenth-century Britain', *Sociological Research Online*, 3(1).

Prandy, K. and Bottero, W. (2000a) 'Social reproduction and mobility in Britain and Ireland in the nineteenth and early twentieth centuries', *Sociology*, 34(2): 265–81.

Prandy, K. and Bottero, W. (2000b) 'Reproduction within and between generations: the example of nineteenth-century Britain', *Historical Methods*, 33(1): 4–15.

Proctor, K. (2015) 'Newcastle City Council budget: how will the cuts affect you?' *ChronicleLive*, 4 March. www.chroniclelive.co.uk/news/north-east-news/newcastle-city-council-budget-how-8767460.

PSE (Poverty and Social Exclusion) (2014) 'Social mobility'. PSE Website. www.poverty.ac.uk/tags/social-mobility.

Purnell, J. (2007) 'The aspiration society.' Lecture to the Fabian Society, London. http://fabians.org.uk/events/speeches/-unrelenting-focus-on-education-the-key-to-improving-life-chances-says-purnell.

Purnell, J. (2008) 'Progressive manifesto.' Lecture to the Fabian Society, London. http://fabians.org.uk/events/speeches/purnell-progressive-speech-text.

Queiro, A & Eardley, N. (2014) 'Where now for independence supporters?', *BBC Scotland News*, 19 October. www.bbc.co.uk/news/uk-scotland-29630077.

Raab, D. (2015) 'Let's not throw away this chance to build an Opportunity Society'. *ConservativeHome*, 6 May. www.conservativehome.com/platform/2015/05/dominic-raab-mp-the-best-reason-to-vote-conservative-tomorrow-the-progress-weve-made-towards-an-opportunity-society.html.

Rallings, C. and Thrasher M. *The 2010 General Election: Aspects of Participation and Administration*. Plymouth: LGC Elections Centre, University of Plymouth. www.electoralcommission.org.uk/_data/assets/pdf_file/0011/105896/Plymouth-GE2010-report-web.pdf.

Rammell, B. (2006), 'Courageous reform', *The Guardian*, 27 March. www.theguardian.com/education/2006/mar/27/furthereducation.uk1.

Random House Dictionary (2011) 'Social mobility'. *Dictionary.com*. http://dictionary.reference.com/browse/social mobility.

RCVP (Riots Communities and Victims Panel) (2012) *After the Riots: The Final Report of the Riots Communities and Victims Panel.* London: RCVP.

Reay, D (1998) *Class Work: Mothers involvement in their primary schooling.* London: University College Press.

Reay, D. (2000) 'A useful extension of Bourdieu's conceptual framework: emotional capital as a way of understanding mothers' involvement in children's education?', *Sociological Review*, 48(4): 568–85.

Reay, D. (2006) 'The zombie stalking English schools: social class and educational inequality', *British Journal of Educational Studies,* 54(3): 288–307.

Reay, D., David, M. and Ball, S. (2001a) 'Making a difference?: Institutional habituses and higher education choice', *Sociological Research Online*, 5(4). www.socresonline.org.uk/5/4/reay.html.

Reay, D., Davies, J., David, M. and Ball, S. (2001b) 'Choices of degree or degrees of choice?' *Sociology,* 35(4): 855–74.

Redwood, J. (2011) 'How do you promote social mobility?' John Redwood website, 6 April. http://johnredwoodsdiary.com/2011/04/06/how-do-you-promote-social-mobility/.

Richardson, H. (2015). 'Grammar schools: what are they and why are they controversial?' *BBC News*, 15 October. www.bbc.co.uk/news/education-34538222.

Ridge, J. and MacDonald, K. (1972) 'Social Mobility' in Halsey, A. (ed.) *Trends in British Society Since 1900.* London: Macmillan.

Ringen, S. (1988) 'Direct and indirect measure of poverty', *Journal of Social Policy,* 17(3): 351–65.

Robbins, L. (1963) *The Robbins Report: Higher education: report of the Committee on Higher Education (23 September 1963),* Cmnd. 2154, London: HMSO.

Roberts, D. (ed.) (2011) *Reading the Riots: Investigating England's summer of disorder.* London: Guardian Books.

Rose, D. (2006) 'Social comparisons and social order: issues relating to a possible re-study of W. G. Runciman's relative deprivation and social justice'. ISER Working Paper 2006–48. Colchester: University of Essex.

Rose, D. and O'Reilly, K. (1997) *Constructing Classes: Towards a New Social Classification for the UK.* Swindon: ERSC/ONS.

Rose, D. and O'Reilly, K. (1998) *The ESRC Review of Government Social Classifications.* Swindon: ESRC/ONS.

Rose, D. and Pevalin, D. with O'Reilly, K. (2005) *The National Statistics Socio-economic Classification: Origins, Development and Use.* Basingstoke: Palgrave.

Rostow, W. (1960) *The Stages of Economic Growth: A Non-Communist Manifesto*, Cambridge: Cambridge University Press.

Routh, G. (1987) *Occupations of the People of Great Britain 1801–1981.* Basingstoke: Macmillan.

Rubinstein, D. and Simon, B. (1969) *The Evolution of the Comprehensive School, 1926–1966.* London: Routledge and Kegan Paul.

Runciman, G. (1966) *Relative Deprivation and Social Justice.* London: Routledge Kegan Paul.

Russell, J. (2008) 'The mirage of meritocracy has sold our children short'. *The Guardian*, 5 June. www.theguardian.com/commentisfree/2008/jun/05/education.labour.

Saunders, C. (1931) 'A study of occupational mobility', *Economic Journal*, 162 (June): 227–40.

Saunders, P. (1989) 'Left write in sociology', *Network*, 44. Durham: BSA.

Saunders, P. (1995) 'Might Britain be a meritocracy?', *Sociology*, 29(1): 23–41.

Saunders, P. (1996) *Unequal But Fair?* London: IEA.

Saunders, P. (1997) 'Social mobility in Britain: an empirical evaluation of two competing explanations', *Sociology*, 31(2): 261–88.

Saunders, P. (2002) 'Reflections on the meritocracy debate in Britain', *British Journal of Sociology*, 53(4): 559–74.

Saunders, P. (2010) *Social Mobility Myths.* London: Civitas.

Saunders, P. (2012) *Social Mobility Delusions.* London: Civitas.

Savage, M. (1988) 'The missing link? The relationship between spatial mobility and social mobility', *British Journal of Sociology*, 39(4): 554–77.

Savage, M. (2010) *Identities and Social Change in Britain since 1940: the politics of method.* Oxford: Oxford University Press.

Savage, M. (2013) 'Concerned about the BBC's Class Calculator? Let me explain'. *The Guardian,* 10 April. www.theguardian.com/commentisfree/2013/apr/10/bbc-class-calculator.

Savage, M., Bagnall, G. and Longhurst, B. (2001) 'Ordinary, ambivalent and defensive: class identities in the northwest of England', *Sociology*, 35(4): 875–92.

Savage, M., Cunningham, N., Devine, F., Friedman, S., Laurison, D., McKenzie, Miles, A., Snee, H. and Wakeling, P. (2015) *Social Class in the 21st Century.* London: Penguin Random House.

Scase, R. (1976) 'Review of "Class in a Capitalist Society"', *Sociology,* 10(3): 548–9.

Scase, R. (1992) *Class*. Buckingham: Open University Press.

ScotlandGov (The Scottish Government) (2014) 'Summary: demographics'. www.scotland.gov.uk/Topics/People/Equality/Equalities/PopulationMigration.

Scott, J. (2013) 'Class and Stratification', in Payne, G. (ed.) *Social Divisions* (3rd edn). Basingstoke: Palgrave Macmillan.

Seymour, R. (2012) We are all precarious: on the concept of the 'precariat' and its misuses. *New Left Project*, 10 February. www.newleftproject.org/index.php/site/article_comments/we_are_all_precarious_on_the_concept_of_the_precariat_and_its_misuses.

Shapps, G. (2013) 'Grant Shapps says small firms are the key to social mobility'. *The Observer*, 29 December. www.theguardian.com/politics/2013/dec/29/grant-shapps-small-business-social-mobility.

Shelp, R. (1981) *Beyond Industrialization*. New York: Praeger.

Singelmann, J. (1978) 'The sectoral transformation of the labour force in seven industrialized countries, 1920–1979', *American Journal of Sociology*, 38(5): 1224–34.

Skipp, A., Vignoles, A., Jesson, D., Sadro, F., Cribb, J. and Sibieta, L. (2013) *Poor Grammar: Entry Into Grammar Schools Disadvantaged Pupils In England*. Centre for Market and Public Organisation, University of Bristol: Sutton Trust. www.suttontrust.com/researcharchive/poor-grammar-entry-grammar-schools-disadvantaged-pupils-england/.

SMCPC (Social Mobility and Child Poverty Commission) (2012) *Fair Access to Professional Careers: A Progress Report by the Independent Reviewer on Social Mobility and Child Poverty*. London: SMCPC. www.gov.uk/government/uploads/system/uploads/attachment_data/file/61090/IR_FairAccess_acc2.pdf.

SMCPC (Social Mobility and Child Poverty Commission) (2014a) *Elitist Britain?* London: www.gov.uk/government/uploads/system/uploads/attachment_data/file/347915/Elitist_Britain_-_Final.pdf.

SMCPC (Social Mobility and Child Poverty Commission) (2014b) *State of the Nation 2014: Social Mobility and Child Poverty in Great Britain*. 2nd Annual Report of the SMCPC. London: HMSO. www.gov.uk/government/publications/state-of-the-nation-2014-report.

SMCPC (Social Mobility and Child Poverty Commission) (2015a) *A Qualitative Evaluation of Non-Educational Barriers to the Elite Professions*. London: SMCPC.

SMCPC (Social Mobility and Child Poverty Commission) (2015b) *Downward Mobility, Opportunity Hoarding and the 'Glass Floor'*. London: SMCPC.

SMCPC (Social Mobility and Child Poverty Commission) (2015c) *State of the Nation 2015: Social Mobility and Child Poverty in Great Britain.* 3rd Annual Report of the SMCPC, London: The Stationery Office. www.gov.uk/government/publications/state-of-the-nation-2015.

SNP (Scottish Nationalist Party) (2007) *Manifesto: It's time.* www.politicsresources.net/area/uk/ass07/man/scot/snp.pdf.

Sociological Review (2015) 'Sociologies of class: elites (GBCS) and critiques', *Sociological Review*, Special Issue, 63(2): 205–549.

Solomos, J. *(2003) Race and Racism in Britain* (3rd edn). Basingstoke: Palgrave Macmillan.

Solomos, J. (2011) 'Race, Rumours and Riots: Past, Present and Future.' *Sociological Research Online*, 16(4): 20. www.socresonline.org.uk/16/4/20.html> 10.5153/sro.2547.

Sorokin, P. (1927) *Social Mobility.* New York: Harper.

Standing G (2011) *The Precariat: The New Dangerous Class.* London: Bloomsbury Academic.

Stanworth, P. (2013) 'Elites' in G. Payne (ed.) *Social Divisions.* (3rd edition). Basingstoke: Palgrave Macmillan.

Stewart, H. (2015) 'The Case for Comprehensive Schools' in de Waal, A. (ed.) *The Ins and Outs of Selective Secondary Schools: A Debate.* London: Civitas.

Stratton, A. (2011) 'Playing the long game: Miliband shuns quick fixes in first 100 days'. *The Guardian*, 4 January. www.guardian.co.uk/politics/2011/jan/03/ed-miliband-first-100-days?INTCMP=SRCH.

Stratton, A and Mulholland, H. (2011) 'Clegg announces child poverty and social mobility commission'. *The Guardian,* 5 April. www.theguardian.com/society/2011/apr/05/nick-clegg-child-poverty-social-mobility.

Stuart, G. (2007) House of Commons Debates: School reform, Hansard, col. 1241, 21 November.

Sullivan, A., Parsons, S., Wiggins, R., Heath, A. and Green, F. (2014) 'Social origins, school type and higher education destinations', *Oxford Review of Education*, 40(6): 739–76.

Sutton Trust (2008) *Wasted talent? Attrition rates of high-achieving pupils between school and university.* London: Sutton Trust. www.suttontrust.com/researcharchive/wasted-talent-attrition-rates-high-achieving-pupils-school-university/.

Sutton Trust (2010) *Responding to the new landscape for university access.* London: Sutton Trust. www.suttontrust.com/researcharchive/responding-new-landscape-university-access/.

Sutton Trust (2014) 'Richest parents four times more likely than poorest to pay for extra classes for their children'. Press release, 4 September. www.suttontrust.com/newsarchive/richest-parents-four-times-more-likely-than-poorest-to-pay-for-extra-classes-for-their-children/.

Sutton Trust (2015a) *Evaluating access.* Sutton Trust Research Brief 9. London: Sutton Trust. www.suttontrust.com/wp-content/uploads/2015/12/Evaluating-Access_December-2015.pdf.

Sutton Trust (2015b) 'Half of new cabinet was privately educated'. Press release, 11 May. www.suttontrust.com/newsarchive/half-of-new-cabinet-was-privately-educated/.

Swinford, S. (2014) 'Nigel Farage says Ukip will cut taxes for rich and poor'. *Daily Telegraph,* 1 July. www.telegraph.co.uk/news/politics/nigel farage/10868079/Nigel-Farage-says-Ukip-will-cut-taxes-for-rich-and-poor.html.

Theobald, R. (1995) *Understanding Industrial Society.* London: Macmillan.

Tilly, C. (1998) *Durable Inequality.* Oakland, CA: University of California Press.

Timms, S. (2008) Speech to the Association of Learning Providers, Nottingham, 6 May. http://webarchive.nationalarchives.gov.uk/20100208082644/http://dwp.gov.uk/newsroom/ministers-speeches/2008/06-05-08.shtml.

Totaljobs.com (2014) '40% of graduates still out of work six months on', Research report, 18 February. http://press.totaljobs.com/release/40-of-graduates-still-out-of-work-six-months-on/

Townsend, P. (1979) *Poverty in the United Kingdom.* Harmondsworth: Penguin.

Touraine, A. (1974) *The Post Industrial Society.* New York: Random House.

Toynbee, P. (2005) 'Don't shrug off low pay'. *The Guardian,* 26 August. www.theguardian.com/money/2005/aug/26/pay.britishairwaysbusin.

Toynbee, P. (2008) 'The education boom has proved a curse for the poor'. *The Guardian,* 5 July. www.theguardian.com/commentisfree/2008/jul/05/education.communities.

Toynbee, P. and Walker, D. (2005) *Better or Worse: Has Labour Delivered?* London: Bloomsbury.

Toynbee, P. and Walker, D. (2008) *Unjust Rewards: Exposing Greed and Inequality in Britain Today.* London: Granta Books.

Toynbee, P. and Walker, D. (2011) *The Verdict.* London: Granta Books.

Triantes, S. (1953) 'Economic progress, occupational redistribution, and international terms of trade', *Economic Journal*, 63(September): 627–37.

TUC (Trades Union Congress) (2010) *Social Mobility*. London: TUC.

TUC (Trades Union Congress) (2014) *Dismantling the Barriers to Social Mobility*. London: Touchstone Extra.

UCAS (Universities and Colleges Application System) (2015) *Record numbers of students accepted to UK universities and colleges this year, UCAS report shows*. www.ucas.com/corporate/news-and-key-documents/news/record-numbers-students-accepted-uk-universities-and-colleges.

Universities UK (2014) *Patterns and Trends in Higher Education 2014*. London: Universities UK.

US Congress (1985) *Annual Report of the President of the United States on the Trade Agreements Program*. Washington DC: Office of the US Trade Representative.

Vaizey, E. (2006) www.edvaizey.mpblogs.com/2006/11/.

Wallop, H. (2013) 'I've called in a private tutor to give my child a chance in the academic arms race'. *The Daily Telegraph*, 8 October. www.telegraph.co.uk/education/secondaryeducation/10364395/Ive-called-in-a-private-tutor-to-give-my-child-a-chance-in-the-academic-arms-race.html.

Watson, W. (1964) 'Social Mobility and Social Class in Industrial Communities' in Gluckman, M. (ed.) *Closed Systems and Open Minds*. London: Aldine.

Weber, M. (1920/1968) 'Status Groups and Classes' in Roth, G. and Wittich, C. (eds.) *Economy and Society*. New York: Bedminster Press.

Weedon, K. and Grusky, D. (2005) 'The case for a new class map', *American Journal of Sociology*, 111(1): 141–212.

Weedon, K. and Grusky, D. (2012) 'The three worlds of inequality', *American Journal of Sociology*, 117(6): 1723–85.

Welshman, J. (2007) *From Transmitted Deprivation to Social Exclusion*. Bristol: Policy Press.

Westergaard, J. and Resler, R. (1975) *Class in a Capitalist Society*. New London: Heinemann.

White, M. (2011) 'Social mobility: remember, it can go downwards too'. *The Guardian*, 5 April. www.theguardian.com/politics/blog/2011/apr/05/social-mobility-remember-downwards-too.

Wicherts, J., Borsboom, D. and Dolan, C. (2010a) 'Why national IQs do not support evolutionary theories of intelligence', *Personality and Individual Differences*, 48(2): 91–6.

Wicherts, J., Dolan, C. and van der Maas, H. (2010b) 'The dangers of unsystematic selection methods and the representativeness of 46 samples of African test-takers', *Intelligence*, 38(1): 30–7.

Wikipedia (2016) *Social mobility.* en.wikipedia.org/wiki/Social_mobility.

Wilby, P. (2008) 'When there's no more room at the top'. *New Statesman*, 10 January. www.newstatesman.com/society/2008/01/social-mobility-blunkett.

Williams, Z. (2012) 'What's the point of social mobility? It still leaves some in the gutter'. *The Guardian*, 23 May. www.theguardian.com/commentisfree/2012/may/23/social-mobility-nick-clegg.

Willetts, D. (2011) 'David Willetts blames feminism over lack of jobs for working men'. *The Guardian*, 1 April. www.theguardian.com/politics/2011/apr/01/david-willetts-feminism-lack-of-jobs.

Wilson, W. (1987) *The Truly Disadvantaged: The Inner City, the Underclass, and Public Policy.* Chicago, IL: University of Chicago Press.

Wintour, P. (2015a) 'Tristram Hunt: Labour must regain trust of working class'. *The Guardian*, 11 May. www.theguardian.com/politics/2015/may/11/tristram-hunt-labour-must-regain-trust-working-class.

Wintour, P. (2015b) 'Labour's soul-searching begins as modernisers attack Miliband "mistakes"'. *The Guardian*, 10 May. www.theguardian.com/politics/2015/may/10/labour-soul-searching-modernisers-attack-miliband-mistakes.

Worsley, P., Fitzhenry, R., Mitchell, G., Morgan, D., Pons, V., Roberts, B., Sharrock, W. and Ward, R. (1977) *Introducing Sociology* (2nd edn). Harmondsworth: Penquin.

Worsthorne, P. (2010) 'Cleared on all counts'. *The Spectator*, 16 October. www.spectator.co.uk/2010/10/cleared-on-all-counts/.

Wucherpfennig, J. and Deutsch, F. (2009) 'Modernization and democracy: theories and evidence revisited', *Living Reviews in Democracy*, 1. www.lrd.ethz.ch/index.php/lrd.

Yandell, J. (2009) *Lighthouses or follies? Academies and New Labour's version of history.* http://eprints.ioe.ac.uk/1582/1/Yandell2009Lighthouses125.pdf.

Young, M. (1958) *The Rise of the Meritocracy.* London: Thames and Hudson.

Young, M. (2001) 'Down with meritocracy'. *The Guardian*, 29 June. http://www.theguardian.com/politics/2001/jun/29/comment.

Zhang, M. (2015) 'Social mobility over three generations in Britain'. Paper presented at British Sociological Association Annual Conference, 'Societies in Transition'. Glasgow: BSA.

Index

A

A-levels 141, 146, 157–8
  ease of 154–5
Abbott, P. 118, 129–30, 153
Abbott, W. 90
'absolute' social mobility 7–8, 13, 57, 59,
  176–8
  definitions 176–7
  'mis-definitions' of 65–7, 69–70
  political interpretations 57, 59
  uses for 96, 176–8
  and gendered rates of occupational
    change 129–34
  and 'inter-generational upward social
    mobility' 65–6
academy schools 33–4, 141, 147
Adonis, Lord Andrew 33
Afriyie, Adam 36
age and occupational categorisation
  97–100, 180
Age Participation Index (API) 154
Alcock, P. 80
Aldridge, S. 57, 64, 68–70
All-Party Parliamentary Group on Social
  Mobility (APPG) 48–9
Allen, B. 93
Anderson, P. 26, 56
Archer, L. 158
Aron, R. 24
'aspiration'
  under Conservative party (2015-) 37–8
  under New Labour 32, 36
Atherton, G. 139
austerity policies 6–7, 121
automated technologies 112–13, 172

B

Baccalaureate qualification 58
Baker, D. 142
Ball, S. 140, 153–4
Bamfield, L. and Horton, T. 8–9
Bangladeshi women 105–6
Banks, Professor Joe 93–4
Barford, V. 84
Basit, T. 140

Bathmaker, A-M. 158
Bauer, P. 111
Bauman, Z. 90
Baumberg, B. 8–9
BBC Radio-4, *Today* programme 44–5,
  146
The Bell Curve (Herrnstein and Murray)
  80, 143
Bell, C. 105
Bell, Daniel 12, 111, 113
Bendix, R. 25
Benjamin, B. 90
Benn, M. 146
Benyon, J. 83
Bibby, J. 109
BIS (Dept. for Business, Innovation and
  Skills) 48, 56, 57– 60
Blair, Tony 32–3, 74–5
Blanden, J. 57, 69, 89, 100–4, 125, 136,
  182–3
Blau, P. 22, 27
Bloodworth, J. 170
Blunkett, David 34–6, 79, 81
Blytheway, B. 93
Boliver, V. 165
Bond, M. 162
Bond, R. 141, 159
Booth, Charles 110
Bottero, W. 113
Bottomore, T. 91–2
Bourdieu, P. 18, 158
Bradley, H. 158
Braverman, H. 112–13
Breen, R. 137, 141, 177
Breiger, R. 107
Bremen, J. 78
Brexit, support for 79, 85–6, 87
Bridge Group 40
British Cohort Study (1970–) 4, 99,
  101–2, 145
British Election Study 77–8, 99, 122,
  136–7
British Household Panel Surveys 3, 6
British Social Attitudes Survey (2013) 9,
  142, 163

Brown, Gordon 34, 75–6, 172
Browning, H. 23–4, 111
Bühlmann, P. 100
Building Skills, Transforming Lives
(Conservative Party 2008a) 48, 53–4
Bukodi, E. 4, 99, 129, 135, 137, 168
Buscha, F. 6
Bush, Jeb 71–2

C

Cabinet Office 48, 64, 65–8, 69–70,
145–6
on social mobility definitions 65–7
Cable, Vince 57–8
Cambridge Social Grading Scale
(CAMSIS) 6
Cameron, David 12, 14, 31, 36–8, 101,
163, 167
campaigns and charities 40–1
Cannadine, D. 109
Capital (Marx 1894) 25–6
Caradog Jones, D. 90
Caribbean peoples 105–6
Carpenter, J. 102
Carr-Saunders, A. 90
Carvel, J. 146
caste systems 19–20
Census Data 110–11, 117, 119
Champion, T. 105, 129
'chance' *see* life chances; mobility chances
Chapman, S. 90
Chapman, T. 117
'character' and mobility 48–9
Civitas 40–1
Clark, C. 23
Clark, T. 47
classes *see* occupational classes; social class;
named classes
Cleary,H. 73
Clegg, Nick 38–9, 55
on low mobility 73, 76
media reports 43–4
clerical work, occupational categorisation
179
Coalition government
austerity policies 6–7, 121
on education 55–6, 57–60
on social mobility 14, 36–7
policy document analysis 48–9, 54–7,
57–61
usefulness of 'low mobility' discourses
76–7
Cohen, D. 147
Cohen, S. 111–12
Collins, M. 82
The Coming of Post-Industrial Society
(Bell 1973) 113
communism 24

competition, impact on professions
149–50
The Condition of the Working Class in
England (Engels 1887) 26
'conditional disparity ratios' 135–6
Conservative government policies 6–7
and class divisions 7
on 'equality of opportunity' 12–13
and education 31
perspectives on social mobility 14, 30–1
document analysis 48, 53–4, 60–1
early concerns 30–1
rediscovery of 36–8
political usefulness of 'low mobility'
76–7
Conservative party demographics 76
ConservativeHome blog 121
Corbyn, Jeremy 35
Coughlan, S. 146, 155
Coulson, S. 59, 157–8
Cox, P. 117–18
Crawford, C. 57
Cribb, J. 163
Crime as an American Way of Life (Bell)
12
Crosland, A. 30
Crozier, G. 158
cultural indicators of social class 13
curry houses 110
'cycles of transmitted deprivation' (Joseph)
31

D

d'Ancona, Matthew 43
de Piero, Gloria 33
'de-skilling' of the workforce 112–13
degree status 155
democratic pluralism 24
Demos Centre for London 41
Dench, G. 34, 140
Denmark, income mobility studies 03
Dent, S. 78
Department for Business, Innovation and
Skills (BIS) 48, 56, 57–60, 155
Department for Education 146–7
deprivation indices 85
development (economic/social) discourses
23–4
Deutsch, F. 22
Devine, F. 3–4, 123–4, 129–30, 132, 147
difference ratios *see* disparity (difference)
ratios
digital technologies 112–13, 172
DIM (Due to Innate Merit) thesis
(Saunders) 143, 154–5, 157–9, 167
disparity (difference) ratios 50–1, 57,
134–5, 176, 178
definitions 176

in gender difference studies 134–6
uses 178
Domenico, D. 130
dominance method of occupational
    change analysis 129, 180
Dorling, D. 163, 182
Douglas-Home, Alec 31
Down, S. 76, 165
Downes, J. 146
downward social mobility 4, 50–1,
    57, 67–8, 126, 133–9, 150–1, 159,
    165–71, 175–7, 182
Duncan Smith, Ian 36
Duncan, O. 22, 27, 93
Dyhouse, C. 155

E

Eardley, N. 84
economic development and mobility 23–4
education 139–48, 170
    'as' social mobility 70–1
    measurement of differences 141, 145–8
    and meritocracy 139–48
    and the 'new social mobility' 170–1
    and opportunity 31
        Coalition policy analysis 55–6, 57–60,
            65
        and the Conservatives 36
        and New Labour 32–3, 77
    teacher training 149–50
educational qualifications 146–59, 170
    A-levels 141, 146, 154–5, 157–8
    and access to the professions 149–59
    and earnings 152
    and employability 146–8
    GCSE's 145–6
    graduate degrees 58–9, 153–9
    vs. 'person specifications' 151–3
    postgraduate degrees 149
Egerton, M. 69
'elites' 18–19, 58–9, 70, 158–9,
    annual incomes 163
    occupational profiles 162
    mobility prospects 161–4
    and private education 162
    and social fluidity 66–8
    university access 58–9, 70, 158–9, 164
employment categorisations see
    occupational classes
employment opportunities see job
    opportunities
End Child Poverty Coalition 38
Engels, F. 26
England riots-2011 81–3
'equality of opportunity' 173
    in contemporary discourses 11–12,
        172–3
    historical political perspectives 24–8

under Conservative and Coalition
    governments 37–8
Equality Trust 163
Erikson, R. 100
Ermisch, J. 182
Esping-Andersen, G. 111
ethnicity
    migration and mobility studies 105–6
    and university access 156
    US IQ studies 80
Eton 163
Europe
    far-Right radicalisation 86–7
    income mobility studies 103

F

'fairer chances' 66–7
    see also life chances; mobility chances
'fairness' and social mobility 35–6
    and 'ability' 143–5
    in education 55–6, 57–61, 77
faith schools 147
far-Right parties 86–7
Farage, Nigel 39
Fascism 18
fathers
    mobility data 121–2, 124–5, 180
    occupational codings for 93–4
    parent—child differentials 121–5
    sons cf. daughters mobility prospects
        121, 122–3, 126, 137, 164–5
Feinstein, L. 145
Felsted, A. 153–4
fertility and social class 92–3
Field, Frank 33
Fielding, A. 104–5
Finegold, D. 154
Fisher-Clark thesis 23, 111, 112
Fisher, A. 23
Follett, Barbara 44–5
Foote, N. 21, 113
Ford, R. 86–7
Franklin, P. 121
'free schools' 147
Friedman, Sam 4, 13, 138, 171
Fulfilling our Potential: Teaching
    Excellence, Social Mobility and
    Student Choice (BIS 2015) 38
Further Education (FE) 33
    see also Higher Education (HE)
Future First 40
The Future of Socialism (Crosland 1956)
    30

G

Gallie, D. 80
Gandhi, Mahatma 19–20
Gans, H. 80

GCSE's 145–6
gender and employment 128–38, 165–6, 170–1, 180
  and occupational change 117–20, 172–3
  rates of absolute mobility 129–34
  sons cf. daughters mobility prospects 121, 122–3, 126, 137, 164–5
gender and university access 155
General Election (UK) 77–8, 84
General Household Surveys (GHS) 3
geographical variations in occupations 104–6, 127
Gershuny, J. 111
Getting On, Getting Ahead (Cabinet Office 2008a) 48, 64, 65–8
  on 'absolute' vs. 'relative' mobility 65–7
  sources of 'mis-definitions' in 64, 69
Giazitzoglu, A. 13, 76, 165, 171
Gibb, Nick 33
Giddens, A. 75, 91
Ginsberg, M. 90
Glass, David 15, 18, 30, 89, 90–5, 139
Glass, Ruth 94
globalisation 105–6
Goldthorpe Class Schema 123
Goldthorpe, John 3, 3–4, 27, 29, 49, 51, 53, 66–8, 95–100, 100–1, 128–9, 141, 177, 180, 182
Goodman, A. 100–4
Goodwin, M. 86
Gorard, S. 69, 101–3, 156, 182
Gorringe, H. 82
Gove, Michael 36–7, 150
graduates 58–9, 153–9
  job prospects 121, 164
  measurement of 153
grammar schools 146–7
Great British Class Survey (2013) 9, 13, 107
Green Party 40
Green, Kate 33
Gregg, P. 69, 89, 100–4
Grover, C. 82
Grusky, D. 6, 7, 64
The Guardian newspaper 33, 41–3, 47, 82–3, 106
Gurney-Dixon Report (1954) 146

H

Hall, J. 30
Hall, T. 80
Hall-Jones occupational classification scheme 93–4
Halsey, A. 95, 139
Hampshire, A. 144
"hard working families" and New Labour 32
Harris, A. 26

Hart, R. 146
Harvey, W. 162
Hatt, P. 21, 113
Hauser, R. 96, 177–8
Hayes, B. 129
Heath, A. 6, 68, 99, 105, 128, 137
Heath, Edward 31
HEIPR (Higher Education Initial Participation Rate) 153–5
Hennessy, P. 139, 162
Hernon, I. 82
Herrnstein, R. 80, 143
Hershman, G. 163
Hibbert, C. 82
Higher Education: Students at the Heart of the System (BIS 2011b) 48, 56, 57–60
Higher Education (HE) 33
  access and selection practices 155–9
  and selectivity 158–9
  and downward mobility 70
  and higher occupations 153–5
  policy documents analysis 48, 57–60
  widening participation 38, 70
Hill, J. 14, 63
Hinchcliffe, J. 36
Hinds, Damian 36
Hinduism 19–20
Hinsliff, G. 146
historical perspectives on social mobility 18–28
  early political philosophies 18–19
  early 20th Century concerns 30–1
  international perspectives and traditional societies 19–22
  multistage economic developments and modernisation 23–4
  myth of 'opportunity' 24–8
  as a 'safety valve' 25–7
  see also social mobility studies
Hobcraft, J. 102
Holmwood, J. 95
Honley, A. 117–18
Hope, C. 37
Hope, K. 95
Hope-Goldthorpe occupational classification scale 95–6
hospitality industries 110–11
housing markets 121, 164
Humphreys, John 146
Hunt, Tristram 32–3
Hutton, John 34

I

Iannelli, C. 5–6, 63–4, 141
Iganski, P. 80, 105
immigration and mobility studies 105–6
The Inclusive Society? (Blunkett 2008) 35

'income classes', as new mobility indicator 182–3
'income gap' 163
income inequalities 163
income mobility 8, 100–4, 182–3
  cf. social class mobility 100
  international comparisons 102–3
  key early studies 100–4
  see also social mobility
'Independent Commission on Social Mobility' (Narey 2009) 14, 48, 51–3, 55
The Independent newspaper 43
independent schools 147–8
  Oxbridge admissions 156
India
  caste system 19–20
  imperial rule of 25, 26
  perceptions of opportunities 25, 26
individualism, and mobility 27
industrial sectors 110–13
industrialisation trends 23–4
  sector changes 110–13
infancy and pre-school 145
Ingram, N. 158
inheritance of capital 91–2, 167
Institute of Economic Affairs (IEA) 101
  and Civitas 40–1
Institute for Fiscal Studies (IFS) 163
intelligence
  and genetic inheritance 143
  measures 143
  and 'merit' 143–5
  and poverty 80
'intergenerational' mobility 7–8, 55–7, 65–7, 100
  vs. income differences between generations 101–2
'intergenerational income mobility' 100–4
Intergenerational Mobility in Europe and North America (Blanden et al 2005) 100–4
Interim Report: 7 Key Truths About Social Mobility (APPG 2012) 48–9
international comparisons, income mobility studies 103
'intragenerational mobility' 98, 103, 166
IPPR (Institute for Public Policy Review) 64, 70
IQ levels 80, 143

J

Jackson, M. 3–4, 29–30, 99, 152
job categories *see* occupational classes
job opportunities
  availability of 121–6
  changing nature of 110–26
  competition for 164–5

and downward mobility 67–8, 70, 167–8, 169–70
  qualification requirements of 152–3, 153–5
  recruitment practices 151–3, 170
  and social mobility measures 65–7
job recruitment practices 151–3, 170
job security 78, 120–1
  middle class anxieties 78, 120–1, 148, 164–5, 169
Johnson, Alan 33
Johnson, B. 115–16
Johnson, Boris 82–3, 139
Jones, Graham 33
Jones, K. 130
Jones, O. 162
Joseph Rowntree Foundation 183
Joseph, Sir Keith 31

K

Kaelble, H. 113
Katwala, S. 75
Kaufman, J. 144
Keegan, V. 110
Kellner, P. 86
Kelly, Ruth 33
Kendler, K. 142
Kuznets, S. 23

L

'labour contract' 178–9
Labour Force Survey (LFS) data 4, 115–20, 127, 129–34, 134– 5, 137–8
labour markets 110–26, 170–1
  see also job opportunities; occupational transitions
Labour Party
  rediscovering social mobility 32–6
  see also New Labour
Labour Party's 'White Paper' *see New Opportunities: Fair Chances for the Future* (Labour Party/TSO 2009)
labour sectors 109–10, 110–13
Lambert, P. 6, 68, 113
Lammy, David 33–4
Lareau, A. 140
Laughland-Booy, J. 130
Laurison, Daniel 4, 138
Lawler, S. 171
legal profession 149
Leitch, Lord S. 153
Lewis, R. 90
LFS *see* Labour Force Survey (LFS) data
Liberal Democrats
  'Orange Book' faction 76–7
  perspectives on social mobility 14, 38–9
  policy document analysis 51–3

usefulness of 'low mobility' discourses 76–7
librarians 149–50
life chances,
cf. 'social mobility' 69–70
see also mobility chances
Life Chances and Social Mobility (Cabinet Office Strategy Unit 2004/2008) 64, 69–70
Lipset, S. 25, 27
Lister, R. 80
lived experiences of mobility studies 13, 171
Li, Y. 3–4, 123–4, 129–30, 132
local authority funding 7
Lockwood, D. 117–18
log linear modelling 177–8
London
2011-riots 81–3
in-migration 106
longitudinal studies
challenges of 102
see also named studies; social mobility studies
Longitudinal Study Census 6
Loveday, V. 41, 158
lower management, occupational classifications 179
lower occupational classes (ONS-SeC 6 and 7) 179
mobility prospects 166–8
LSE (London School of Economics and Political Science)
Centre for Analysis of Social Exclusion 14, 63
study on Social Mobility in Britain (1954) 18, 67, 89, 90–5
Sutton Trust research 43–4
Lynn, R. 143

M

Macaulay, Lord Thomas 26
MacDonald, K. 93
MacDonald, R. 80
Machin, S. 52–3, 69, 89, 100–4, 125, 136, 183
McMahon, D. 105
Major, John 31, 37
'malleable intelligence' (Kendler et al.) 142
managers
occupational classes 179
qualification levels of 152–3
senior 164–5
Mansell, W. 141
manual work, occupational classifications 179
manufacturing sector 110–12
Marquis, F. 90

Marshall, G. 141
Marshall, T.H. 145
Marxist perspectives
on class 9, 10
on social mobility 25–7, 96
Mason, D. 106
Maude, A 90
media perspectives on social mobility 14–15, 41–5
medical profession 149
Mehta, J. 111
Mellor, J. 158
men's mobility prospects 122–5, 137–8
see also gender and employment; gender and university access
meritocracy 11–12, 139
and schooling 139–48
under New Labour 34–5
and university access 157–9
Michels, R. 18, 27
middle classes
competing for jobs 164–5
expansion of 109
occupational classifications for 179
'opportunity hoarding' and 'social closure' 149–59, 164
Scotland 84
and social fluidity 66–8
social and job anxieties 78, 120–1, 148, 164–5, 169
sons cf. daughters mobility prospects 121, 122–3, 126, 137, 164–5
mid-range occupational classes (ONS-SeC 2 to5) 179
gendered bias 165
mobility prospects 165–6
migration and mobility studies 105–6
Migration Observatory 106
Milburn, Alan 34, 60, 79, 81, 121, 150, 170
Miles, A. 13, 113, 171
Miliband, David 34–6
Miliband, Ed 75, 78
Miliband, R. 91–2
Miller, R. 129
Miller, S. 91, 93
'million+' 40
Mills, C. 49, 51, 68, 99
Milne, S. 82
Mitchell, B. 143
mobility chances 15, 50–1, 56–61, 66–70, 97–100
and gender difference 134–6
see also social mobility
'mobility industry' 41
mobility studies see social mobility studies
mobility tables 5–6, 175–6
modernisation trends and mobility 23–4

Monaghan, A. 130
Moore, Suzanne 43
Morrin, K. 158
Morris, L. 80
Mosca, G. 18, 25
mothers
  occupation and class 129
  see also gender and employment
Mulholland, Helene 43
multinationals 106
multiple deprivation indexes 85
Mumsnet 148
Murdoch, S. 144
Murray, C. 80, 143
Muslim communities 78

N

Narey, Martin 14, 38, 48, 51–3, 55, 167
National Child Development Study
  (NCDS 1958–) 4, 99, 101–2
National Equality Panel 14
  on economic inequalities 63–4
nationalism 86–7
'nature vs nurture' debate 144
New Labour
  perspectives on social mobility 32–6
  policy document analysis 47–8, 49–51
  political usefulness of 'low mobility'
    74–6, 77
New Opportunities: Fair Chances for the
  Future (Labour Party/TSO 2009) 14,
  34, 48, 49–51
'New Social Mobility' 13, 48, 169–71
  and disparity ratios 178
  future prospects 171–3
  impact of gender differences 127–38
  and income mobility 182–3
  and new socio-economic environments
    109–26
New Statesman 43
newspaper coverage of social mobility
  41–5
Nicoletti, C. 182
Noble, T. 93, 138, 177
Noden, P. 156
Non-professional classes (NS-SeC) 152–3
Northern Ireland 137
Norway, income mobility studies 103
Nuffield Mobility Study (1972/1987) 3,
  66–7, 69, 89, 95– 100, 128, 152–3,
  178
  on changing rates of mobility 97–100
  political and ideological orientations
    95–6
Nuttall, Paul 39

O

occupational classes 9–10, 114–15,
  116–20, 122–5, 178–80
  coding difficulties 93–4
  descriptions of 178–9
  future prospects for 161–9
  gendered differences 117–20, 127–38
  geographical mobility and local labour
    markets 104–6
  history of sector and class transitions
    110–15
  impact of migration 105–6
  impact of participant age 97–100
  and intergenerational inheritance 91–2,
    165, 167
  as mobility indicator 13
  and 'obstructive mobility thresholds'
    (Westergaard and Riesler) 92
  ONS-SeC categories 179–80
  parent—child differentials 121–5
  profiles over time 100
  and recruitment practices 151–3
  use of 'desirability' factors 95
  see also 'elites'; occupational transitions;
    social class; 'underclasses'
'occupational inheritance' 149–53
occupational transitions 92–3, 110–26,
  164, 171–2
  difficulties ascertaining 94
  gendered differences 117–20, 129–34,
    171–2
  history of sectoral changes 110–13
    and occupational class changes 113–15
  'mobility table' 175–6
  'origins' and 'destinations' analysis
    122–6, 129–34, 169–78
  in recent times 116–21
odds ratios 51, 57, 67, 97, 99–100, 135–6,
  176–8, 200
  definitions 176–7
  emphasising limitations of mobility 177
  and gender difference 135–6
  uses 176–8
OECD 68
Office for Fair Access 58–9
Office for National Statistics (ONS) 121,
  130,
  occupational classifications 178–80
office work
  classification of 179
  gender differences 117–18
O'Hara M. 43
Olantiti, A. 166
ONS-SeC analytic categories 178–80
Opening Doors, Breaking Barriers (Cabinet
  Office 2011) 14, 48, 54–7
  origins of 65, 68

'opportunity'
  'hoarding' 149–59, 164
  myths of 24–8
  see also Higher Education (HE); job
    opportunities
Osborne, George 31, 36–7
Oshima, H. 111
Owen, G. 1
Oxbridge 156, 158–9

P

Paired Peers project 158
Pakistani women 105–6
Panel on Fair Access to the Professions
  60, 150
Pareto, V. 18
Parker, G. 37
Parker, H. 183
Parkin, F. 91–2, 150–1
Paterson, L. 5–6, 63–4, 141
Paton, G. 146–7
Payne, C. 6, 68, 99
Payne, G. 2, 6, 14–15, 24, 27, 29, 90,
    93, 104–5, 114, 117– 19, 121, 123–4,
    128–30, 137
personal failings and mobility 48–9
Pevalin, D. 115–17, 119
Platt, L. 105, 183
Plewis, I. 102
Policy Exchange 142
political philosophy and social mobility
    18–19
politics and social mobility, contemporary
    'rediscovering of' 13–16, 29–45, 101
Portes, J. 182
poverty
  deprivation indices 85
  and IQ studies 80
  see also 'underclasses'
Powel, Lucy 33
Prandy, K. 6, 113
'precariat' (Standing) 78–9
  see also 'underclasses'
pressure groups 40–1
private schools 147–8, 162–3
  costs of 164
  and the 'elite' 162–3
  Oxbridge admissions 156
  subsequent performance at university
    157–8
private tuition 147
professions
  access to 60–1, 149–59, 164, 170
  occupational classes of 179
  recruitment practices 151–3
Professions For Good 40
Progression Trust 40
'pseudo-cohorts' in samples 97–100, 180

public perceptions, shaping of 11–12
public sector 110–11, 121
'pupil premium' 145–6
Purnell, James 34, 75

Q

qualifications *see* educational qualifications
'qualitative' mobility studies 171
Queiro, A. 84

R

Raab, Dominic 37
Rallings, C. 84
Rammell, B. 33
Reay, D. 13, 158
recruitment practices 151–3, 170
  social and cultural capital requirements
    151–2
Redwood, John 36
Reeves, R. 73
relative 'intergenerational' social mobility
    55–7
relative social mobility 176–8
  definitions and explanations 8, 50–1,
    66–7, 96, 176–8
  'mis-definitions' of 65–7, 69–70
  and mobility rate changes 97–100
  policy document interpretations of
    49–51, 56–7, 59
  uses and mis-uses of 96–7, 97–100
Rentoul, John 43
Report of the Liberal Democrats
  Independent Commission on Social
  Mobility (Narey 2009) 14, 48, 51–3,
  55
research studies *see* social mobility studies
retail work, gender differences 117–18
Richardson, H. 146
Ridge, J. 93
Riesler, R. 91–2
Right radicalisation 86–7
religion and social hierarchies 20
Ringen, S. 183
riots-2011 (UK) 81–3
The Rise of Meritocracy (Young 2001)
  25
Robbins Report (1963) 58
Roberts, J. 6, 121, 123, 137
Robinson, Winifred 44–5
Romney, Mitt 71–2
Rose, D. 115–17, 119, 165
Rosie, M. 82
Rottman, D. 177
Routh, G. 110, 114–15
Runciman, G. 164–5
Russell Group universities 58–60, 155,
    158–9, 161–2, 170

S

SAD (Social Advantages and Disadvantages) thesis (Saunders) 143, 155, 159, 167
'safety valve' mobility (Engels) 26
Salmond, Alex 39, 74
Sapsford, R. 129
Saunders, C. 90
Saunders, Peter 31, 41, 44, 94, 97–8, 141–4, 154, 159, 177, 182
Savage, M. 69, 104, 107, 115
Scandinavian countries, income mobility studies 103
Scase, R. 91–2
school academies 33–4, 141, 147
schools
  differential performance in 145–8
  as 'engines for social mobility' 36, 58
  measurement of differences 141
  and meritocracy 139–48
  selectivity for 146–8
  see also education; private schools
Scotland
  rise of separatism 83–6
  SNP on mobility 39
  support for Brexit 79
Scott, J. 95
selectivity
  and school education 146–8
  and university access 158–9
self-employment 130–2, 165–6, 179, 183
self-recruitment 133, 164
senior managers 164–5
service contract 178–9
service classes (ONS-SeC 1 and 2) 179
  mobility prospects 164–5
service sectors 111–12
Seymour, R. 78
Shapps, Grant 36–7
Shelp, R. 111–12
Shepherd, J. 43
Singlemann, J. 23–4, 111
Skipp, A. 146
SMCPC see Social Mobility and Child Poverty Commission (SMCPC)
Smith, Adam 23
social class 2–3, 8
  cultural significance 8–9
  early models of 92
  and females 128–9
  fertility differences 92–3
  history 19–22
  immobility of 19–22
  as mobility indicator 8–10
  and social fluidity 66–8
  and university access 59–60
  see also occupational classes; social mobility
social class categories see occupational classes
'social closure' 149–51
social exclusion 79
  anxieties about 79–81
  and riots 81–3
'social fluidity' (Goldthorpe) 67, 177
'social inequality' 9
  impact of meritocracy 11–12
  see also income inequalities; social mobility
Social Mobility: a Background Review (IPPR 2008) 64, 70
social mobility
  'absolute' vs 'relative' 7–8, 50–1, 56–7, 176–8
  'mis-definitions' of 65–8, 69
  and class hierarchies 7–10
  consequences of 11–13
  downward 4, 50–1, 57, 67–8, 126, 133–9, 151, 159, 165–71, 175–7, 182
  extent and rates 14–15, 68
  current situation (overview) 3–5
  future patterns 137–8
  historical perspectives 18–28
  income cf. class mobility 100
  and 'intragenerational mobility' 98, 103, 166
  key early studies of 90–5, 95–100
  life 'chances' of 15, 50–1, 56–61, 66–70, 97–100
  and gender difference 134–6
  media portrayals 14–15, 41–5
  as movements out of origins 176
  as movements within classes 7–10
  myths surrounding 24–8
  paradigms of 15–16
  perceived 'lack of' 29–45
  policy document analysis 47–61
  political nature of 23–4, 25–8
    as solution to new anxieties 77–87
    usefulness of 'low mobility' 73–7
  political philosophies 18–19
  political rediscovery of 13–16, 29–45
  portrayed as moral issue 34
  pressure groups 40–1
  rates 14–15, 97–100
  as 'safety valve' 25–7
  scale of 'reform' activities 40–1
  schooling 148
  as 'social efficiency' 34
  and social processes 3, 11, 22, 124, 134, 161, 181
  sons of the middle classes 121, 122–3, 126, 137, 164–5,
  trends 68

unevenness of distribution 127, 136–8
within classes 7–10
see also occupational transitions; social mobility studies
Social Mobility in Britain (Glass 1954) 18, 89, 90–5
  concerns about findings 90–3
  explanations for discrepancies 93–5
Social Mobility and Child Poverty Commission (SMCPC) 14, 39, 48, 60–1, 90, 139, 150–4, 162, 170
Social Mobility Delusions (Saunders 2012) 1
Social Mobility Foundation 40
Social Mobility Identification Kit 181
social mobility studies 3–4, 13, 63–4
  cf. public and political perceptions 14–16
  as 'complex' and 'contradictory' 56
  concepts and terminology challenges 180
  early sociological research findings 89–107
    on changing rates of mobility 97–100
    economist's perspectives 100–4
    limitations on conventional analysis 104–7
    LSE *Social Mobility in Britain* (1954) 18, 67, 89, 90–5
    Nuffield study (1980/1987) 95–100
  future directions for 171–3
  impact of interconnected processes 127
    gendered difference 117–20, 128–37
    geographical factors 104–6
    migration 105–6
  limitations of analysis 104–7
    toolkit for identifying 181
  and lived experiences 13, 171
  and occupational groupings 13, 15
  occupational transition effect 121–6
  operational difficulties 180
  qualitative approaches 171
  as source of 'mis-definitions' 63–72
  see also social mobility
social mobility tables 5–6, 175–6
social processes generating mobility 3, 11, 22, 124, 134, 161, 181
social work profession 149–50
socio-economic changes 109–26
  development discourses 23–4
socio-political challenges 77–87
  'dangerous underclasses' 79–81, 81–3
  rise of UKIP and radical Right 86–7
  Scottish separatism 83–6
  urban unrest 78–9, 81–3
Solomos, J. 82–3
Sombart, Werner 27

sons of the middle classes 121, 122–3, 126, 137, 164–5,
Sorokin, P. 12, 26
specialisation trends 112
'squeezed middle' 30, 78, 121
'stages of development' and mobility 23–4
Standing, G. 78
Stanworth, P. 162
status attainment 27
'status groups' 9–10
Stewart, H. 146
Stratton, Allegra 35, 43
Stuart, Graham 36
Sturgis, P. 6
Success as a Knowledge Economy (BIS 2016) 155
'success' and upward mobility 11–12
Sullivan, A. 147, 165
supervisory roles, occupational classifications 179
Sure Start centres 7
Sutton Trust 40, 43–4, 101, 139, 146–7, 156, 158, 170
Sweden, income mobility studies 103
Swift, A. 141, 147
Swinford, S. 39

T

Tawney, R. 27
taxation regimes 163, 173
teacher training 149–50
teaching profession 149–50
technology sector 21, 112–13, 172
The Telegraph 41, 43
Thatcher, Margaret 31
Theobald, R. 111
think tanks 40–1
Thrasher, M. 84
Through the Glass Ceiling (Conservative Party 2008b) 48, 53–4
Tilly, C. 20, 149
Times Educational Supplement 147
Timms, Stephen 34
Tomlinson, S. 140
Tottenham riots (2011) 81–3
Touraine, A. 111
Townsend, P. 183
Toynbee, Polly 42, 47, 162
Trade Union Congress (TUC) 40
traditional societies
  cf. 'modern societies' 19–22
  stages of development 24
Triantes, S. 111

U

UCAS 155–8
UKIP (United Kingdom Independence Party) 39, 80, 83–4, 86–7

'underclass anxiety' 45, 79, 83, 87, 169
'underclasses' 30, 78–81
  exclusion and riots 81–3
  immobility of 55–6, 79–81
  poverty and IQ studies 80
unemployment, graduates 121
Unequal But Fair? (Saunders 1996) 143–4
United States
  industrialisation trends 24
  legitimising mobility analysis 27–8
  opportunity and ethnicity 28
  perspectives on mobility
    historical 23–5, 26–8
    current 71–2
  on poverty and IQ 80
university access 58–61, 70, 161–2, 170
  and class mix 59–60, 156–8
  diversity concerns 155–7
  and gender 155
  'modern' vs 'elite' 158–9
  selection practices 155–9
University Alliance 40
Unleashing Aspiration (Panel on Fair Access
  to the Professions 2009) 60, 150
'Untouchables' 19–20
upper-range classes (no-ONS-Sec) 179
  mobility prospects 161–4
  see also 'elites'
urban unrest 78–83

V

Vaizey, Ed 36
Vincent, D. 113

W

Wales, Plaid Cymru on mobility 39
Walker, D. 47, 162
Warrell, H. 37
Watson, W. 105
wealth inequalities 163
Weber, Max 10
Weedon, K. 6
Westergaard, J. 91–2
White, Michael 43
Wicherts, J. 143
Wilby, Peter 43
Willetts, David 57–8, 120
Wilshaw, Sir Michael 146–7
Wilson, P. 90
Winnick, David 33
Wintour, P. 32
women
  comparative mobility chances 134–6
  and ethnicity 105–6
  mobility rate change studies 99–100
  and paid work 128–38
    and class 128–9

gendered occupational change 117–20,
  129–34, 165–6, 171–2
  percentage in 129
  university access 155
work
  better jobs and mobility 65–7
  changing nature of 109–26
  fairer chances and mobility 66–7
  gendered differences 127–38
  see also job opportunities; occupational
    transitions
working classes
  and fertility 92–3
  loss of leadership 25–6
  mobility prospects for 165–6
  occupational classifications of 179
  and social fluidity 66–8
  university access and experiences 158
Worsley, P. 91
Worsthorne, P. 31
Wucherpfennig, J. 22

Y

Yamey, B. 111
Yandell, J. 34
Yorke, Peter 42–3
YouGov survey data 8–9, 142
young people
  access to higher education 153–9
  discontent amongst 77–8, 81–3
Young, Michael 11–12, 25, 144

Z

zero-hours contracts 121
Zhang, M. 6
Zysmen, J. 111–12

the progress of women / those with a disability / from BAME communities

Ability to be mobile through work?

Another level on social mobility + the protected characteristics?

Equalities Act - did it remove practice of discrim and create more opportunity for access + promotion?
→ quotas?
→ did it just mean visible diversity whilst relative SM stunted?

- professionalisation of work — ↑ SM

- did ↑ in HE mean ↑ entry quals + less opportunity

Like top jobs with FTSE 100 - shd only
Which ones have increased × jobs
what happened
in the ones that
given the most?
because we need more
jobs offering long range + progression
to have opportunities
→ demand??
can only be mobile if norms of x car
put educational achievement us
in some outcomes in working
lives.

SM [labour market]
as a recognised lever
+ essential
joined up
Govt —

-it's about
fair chances
+ structural change